Discretionary, Systematic, AI, ESG and Quantamental

QUANTITATIVE HEDGE FUNDS

Discretionary, Systematic, AI, ESG and Quantamental

Richard D Bateson

World Scientific

NEW JERSEY · LONDON · SINGAPORE · BEIJING · SHANGHAI · HONG KONG · TAIPEI · CHENNAI · TOKYO

Published by

World Scientific Publishing Europe Ltd.

57 Shelton Street, Covent Garden, London WC2H 9HE

Head office: 5 Toh Tuck Link, Singapore 596224

USA office: 27 Warren Street, Suite 401-402, Hackensack, NJ 07601

Library of Congress Cataloging-in-Publication Data

Names: Bateson, Richard D., author.

Title: Quantitative hedge funds : discretionary, systematic, AI, ESG and quantamental /
   Richard D. Bateson.

Description: New Jersey : World Scientific, [2023] | Includes bibliographical references.

Identifiers: LCCN 2022019482 | ISBN 9781800612167 (hardcover) |
   ISBN 9781800612372 (paperback) | ISBN 9781800612174 (ebook) |
   ISBN 9781800612181 (ebook other)

Subjects: LCSH: Hedge funds.

Classification: LCC HG4530 .B347 2023 | DDC 332.64/524--dc23/eng/20220420

LC record available at https://lccn.loc.gov/2022019482

British Library Cataloguing-in-Publication Data

A catalogue record for this book is available from the British Library.

For any available supplementary material, please visit
https://www.worldscientific.com/worldscibooks/10.1142/Q0358#t=suppl

Desk Editors: Balasubramanian Shanmugam/Adam Binnie/Shi Ying Koe

Typeset by Stallion Press
Email: enquiries@stallionpress.com

Printed in Singapore

Preface

This is a book for those with a financially inquisitive mind wishing to discover more about the hidden and often secretive world of quantitative hedge funds. The topics covered range from discretionary management and computer-driven strategies to perspectives on AI-based and quantamental investing.

Some people will be perhaps excited to read this book with the expectation of a formal textbook on quantitative hedge fund techniques. A book jammed full of equations about trading strategies and portfolio and risk management techniques. Luckily for you, this book is something far more useful. Rather than a classic textbook, it is a short compendium of my odd experiences and reckless opinions derived from almost three decades working as a quant, trader and portfolio manager for leading banks and hedge funds. Hopefully, you may learn a few useful insights that may stick in your mind, and if you are super keen, I have relegated all the mainly superfluous mathematical details to the appendices.

The book focuses on discretionary corporate trading involving equities and credit, followed by systematic macro and equity methodologies. These disciplines cover the majority of modern hedge fund strategies. I have somewhat neglected contemporary discretionary macro trading, but this is arguably and essentially a medley of discretionary techniques and systematic fundamental indicators combined with a touch of nowcasting and alternative data.

The origins of the chapters are based on several lectures, talks and articles I have written over the years.

As a starting point, Chapter 1 *Efficient Markets* outlines where I started my financial career in the then rapidly evolving derivatives market. The almost quasi-religious ideology at the time was the efficient market hypothesis (EMH). Any of the well-fed, old-school bond traders I worked with at the time would have told you this dogma was total nonsense. However, efficient markets along with the Black–Scholes equation and Mr Ito's lemma formed the bedrock of the derivatives revolution. Questioning the doctrine of random walks, continuous hedging and most of the other core assumptions in most investment banks was almost enough to get you lynched. As time wore on, I experienced the development and evolution of interest rate, equity and credit derivatives on the front line. Gradually, I realised that real markets are not efficient, derivatives busting crises seemed to occur virtually every other year, and trading opportunities abound, if only you know where to look.

Chapter 2 *Real Markets* provides a historical background of how real markets behave and the major financial crises I have witnessed. Many of these macro crises were off the scale in so-called standard deviation moves and impacted many investors and hedge funds. Although the narrative is somewhat biased, I believe a historical perspective is important to understand where the market is now and how investment strategies might perform. The clear causal linkage between economic crises demonstrates that financial history is not a random walk or Markovian. History influences the present and the opportunities and perils are different with each bull and bear market.

Chapter 3 *Discretionary Adventures* concerns discretionary trading and, in particular, discretionary trading of corporates. For many years, I founded and managed a quantitative, event driven and arbitrage fund. The corporate focused fund traded across the capital structure, from equities to leveraged loans. In my opinion, the majority of discretionary trades are driven by a catalyst, which involves an event or a relative value opportunity or a combination of both. I cover strategies from merger arbitrage to curve and basis trades and give examples of actual trades that I carried out. The chapter is based on a talk I gave some years back at Oxford University.

Chapter 4 *Systematic Profits* outlines the operation of systematic hedge funds and, in particular, CTAs. Systematic hedge funds are based on scientific data analysis and computer algorithms to exploit inefficiencies and anomalies in markets. For a while, I represented Man AHL, one of the World's most successful fully systematic CTAs at the Oxford-Man Institute, Oxford University and was head of their flagship multi-strategy AHL Dimension fund. It is based around a public talk I prepared entitled

Managing a Systematic Hedge Fund: A Bold Application of Statistics. The title pretty much says it all.

Chapter 5 *The Factor Game* focuses on the rise of factor investing in long/short equity funds. Although you might want to ignore it, linear factor investing has become a mainstream systematic approach for equities. After the decline of the EMH, much of the academic finance community, at least the part not doing stochastic calculus, has been focused on "discovering" the numerous factors that influence equity markets. I discuss the origins and the applications of the most significant factors, including value, size, momentum and quality.

Chapter 6 *AI Again* has origins in a few talks on AI approaches I gave in recent years. These included a Ravenpack conference (there is a good Youtube video on this) for the Technical Analyst, Marcus Evans and others. AI trading is full of hype and expectation following the successes of AI in other domains such as Alphabet's AlphaGo and IBM Watson winning *Jeopardy*! I illustrate the key issues in applying AI to financial market prediction by considering neural net and simpler kNN methods.

Chapter 7 *ESG Investing* provides a brief introduction to modern environmental, social and governance (ESG) investment techniques. In the past couple of years, following Greta Thunberg and the Extinction Rebellion, ESG investing has become very fashionable. All the major investment houses on the long-only side now have serious offerings and gradually the influence of ESG is reaching the hedge fund world. However, the application of ESG techniques and, in particular, the ratings methodologies used are highly subjective, and careful consideration is required before applying them to any investment process.

Chapter 8 *Towards Quantamental* outlines the "new" world of alternative data and its application to the future of so-called quantamental investing. Alternative data sets from social media to private jet information have started to transform the world of quantitative trading. Alternative data can provide improvements to our current knowledge of the world and more accurate nowcasting techniques, but is it better suited to systematic or discretionary trading? The issues of integrating alternative data into the investment process is based on a 2018 conference panel I moderated: *Leveraging Data Sets to Generate New Sources of Alpha* with representatives of Goldman Sachs, JP Morgan and State Street.

Dr Richard D Bateson
Esher, Surrey
September 2021

About the Author

Richard D Bateson is the founder and CEO of Bateson Asset Management, an investment management and advisory company, based in London, specialising in quantitative strategies.

Richard has almost three decades of trading and investing experience across all major asset classes using a diverse range of discretionary and quantitative strategies at major fund managers, hedge funds and banks. Richard worked at $120bn Man Group plc, one of the World's largest hedge funds, and was the head of Dimension, AHL's $5bn multi-strategy systematic fund, including the award-winning Evolution fund. He was also the senior quantitative research strategist for all discretionary macro, fixed income and emerging market funds at GLG Partners. Richard was the founder of MGIM, a quantitative corporate event-driven and relative value hedge fund manager and managing director at Royal Bank of Canada.

He is a Visiting Fellow at the Cavendish Laboratory, Cambridge University, and has worked at several leading European research institutes including CERN, the European Synchrotron (ESRF), the London Centre for Nanotechnology (LCN) and the Institut Laue Langevin (ILL). He holds a first-class degree and a doctorate in physics from Cambridge University. He was a research committee member of the Oxford-Man Institute of Quantitative Finance at Oxford University. Richard is the author of *Financial Derivative Investments* (Imperial College Press, 2011), an introduction to structured products and derivatives.

Richard is an industry expert in financial AI and alternative data in financial markets, and he hosts panels and is an invited speaker at major conferences in London and Europe on such matters. Dr Bateson has been engaged as an expert witness on major legal cases in the US and UK involving AI/systematic trading, hedge funds and financial markets.

Contents

Guide to Acronyms

ABS	Asset backed security
ANN	Artificial neural network
API	Application programming interface
ATM	At-the-money
AUM	Assets under management
BtM	Book to market value
CAI	Goldman Sachs current activity indicator
CAPM	Capital asset pricing model
CAPTCHA	Completely automated public Turing test to tell computers and humans apart
CDO	Collateralised debt obligation
CDS	Credit default swap
CDX IG	Credit default swap index investment grade
CDX HY	Credit default swap index high yield
CFD	Contract for difference
CFNAI	Chicago Fed national activity indicator
CLO	Collateralised loan obligation
CoVaR	Covariance from VaR
CS01	Present value of 1 basis point credit spread
CTA	Commodity trading advisor
DJ	Dow Jones
DV01	Delta value of 1 basis point
EBITDA	Earnings before income, taxes, depreciation and amortization
EM	Emerging market
ERM	European exchange rate mechanism

ES	E-mini S&P 500 futures contract
ESG	Environmental social governance
ETF	Exchange traded fund
EURIBOR	Euro Interbank Offered Rate
FANGS	Facebook, Amazon, Netflix and Google
FRA	Forward rate agreement
FRN	Floating rate note
FTD	First-to-default
FTSE	Financial Times all shares index 100
FTW	Factors to watch
FUM	Funds under management
FX	Foreign exchange
GDP	Gross domestic product
GDPR	General Data Protection Regulation
HJM	Heath, Jarrow and Morton model
HNW	High net worth
HML	High book-to-market ratio minus low
HY	High yield
IG	Investment grade
IRD	Interest rate differential
IRR	Internal rate of return
ISDA	International Swaps and Derivatives Association
ITM	In-the-money
JGB	Japanese government bond
KNN	k-nearest neighbours
L/S	Long short
LBO	Leveraged buyout
LCDS	Loan credit default swap
LCDX	Loan credit default swap index
LEP	Large electron positron collider
LIBOR	London interbank offered rate
LMM	LIBOR market model
LSE	London School of Economics
ML	Machine learning
MNIST	Modified National Institute of Standards and Technology
MSE	Mean square error
NC	Non-call period
NDA	Non-disclosure agreement
NFL	No free lunch theorem

NINJA	No income, no job, no asset loan
NLP	Natural language processing
NQ	E-mini Nasdaq futures contract
OTC	Over-the-counter
OTM	Out-of-the money
P&L	Profit and loss
PB	Prime broker
PCA	Principal components analysis
PDE	Partial differential equation
PIGS	Portugal, Ireland, Greece and Spain
PIK	Payment in kind
PV	Present value
PV01	Present value of 1 basis point
QMJ	Quality minus junk
RNN	Recurrent neural network
RP	Risk parity
S&P	Standard and Poor's
SFDR	Sustainable Finance Disclosure Regulation
SMB	Small market capitalization minus big
SPC	Special purpose company
SPV	Special purpose vehicle
SVM	Support vector machine
TLA	Term loan A
TLB	Term loan B
TLC	Term loan C
TRS	Total return swap
VaR	Value at risk
VIX	CBOE volatility index
VRP	Volatility risk premium
VWAP	Volume weighted average price
XOVER	iTraxx crossover index
YTM	Yield to maturity

Glossary of Notations

The most commonly used notations in alphabetical order with non-Latin symbols at the end. Some have several uses but are distinguishable from their context.

A, a Firm value. Mean reversion parameter. General parameters.

B Debt value. Bond price. Duration.

C, c Fixed coupon. Copula function.

D, d Discount factor. Dividend. Parameter in BS equation. Day count. ML distance measure.

E Expectation.

F, f Futures price. Forward interest rate. Floating rate. A function. Response function. Equity factor.

g Growth rate.

h Accrual factor. Coupon period. Interest period. ML prediction function.

K, k Strike price of an option. Index.

L Survival probability. LIBOR.

M Month.

$M( )$ Multivariate cumulative normal distribution.

$N( )$ Cumulative normal distribution. Notional.

P Price of an option, bond, equity.

Pr Probability.

Q Cumulative default probability. Order size.

q Dividend yield of an equity. CDS premium.

R Interest Rate. Redemption amount. Recovery rate.

r	Risk free interest rate. Spot rate. Asset returns.
S	Underlying asset price. Usually an equity price. Swap rate.
s	Credit spread. Asset swap spread.
t	Time in the future. Current time $t = 0$.
T	Time to maturity (in years).
U	Unemployment.
V	Value or price of a swap. Option value. Option payoffs. Volume.
X, x	Currency. Funding spread. Timeseries.
Y, y	Yield of a bond. Return of an equity. Timeseries.
Z, z	Z-score. Normally distributed random variable. Zero rate.
Λ	Diagonalised matrix in PCA.
Σ	Covariance matrix.
α	Alpha of portfolio. Coefficients.
β	Beta of portfolio. Coefficients.
χ	Probability indicator function (equals 0 or 1).
$\phi(\ )$	Normally distributed. A Gaussian distribution.
$\varphi(\ )$	Gaussian probability density.
κ	Normalisation coefficient.
λ	Hazard rate or Poisson coefficient. EMWA parameter.
μ	Drift of underlying asset. Vector of returns.
ν	Volatility of bond or discount bond.
π	Inflation.
θ	Interest rate curve. ML model parameters.
ρ	Correlation coefficient.
σ	Volatility of underlying asset. Value-at-risk.
τ	Default time.
ω	Weights.

Chapter 1

Efficient Markets

1.1 Introduction

The abstract world of *efficient markets* was where my rollercoaster financial career started, almost three decades ago. The *efficient market hypothesis* (EMH) and its offspring, the Black–Scholes (BS) equation, generated the theoretical rocket fuel for the fast-growing derivatives markets. This introductory chapter explores my front row experience of this remarkable revolution, where increasingly exotic derivatives were invented using human ingenuity, mathematical assumptions and evolving technology. With the pace of innovation, financial products became progressively more absurd and incomprehensible. Warren Buffett's warning "beware of geeks bearing formulas", proved prescient of the global 2008 financial crisis. However, the cracks in the tenets of EMH and the financial firmament had been already observed. Numerous market "anomalies" that violated EMH were being discovered and could be mined to derive investment alpha. The rest of this book describes the exploitation of these anomalies and the rise of quantitative hedge funds.

1.2 Brownian Motion

It is amusing that the financial theories which dominated financial markets in the 20th century originated from the study of plants and pesky mosquitoes. In the 19th century the British became mildly obsessed with botany. Many exotic plant specimens were shipped from all corners of the British Empire. One of the leading botanists who came back laden with samples from New Holland (now Australia) was Robert Brown, who was a friend of Charles Darwin. In 1827, he surprisingly observed the chaotic movement of pollen grains using a microscope. The endless, random movement, now called Brownian motion, appeared inexplicably devoid of any external stimulus such as light or temperature.

However, the observations lay ignored and without explanation for decades. As is often the case in science, there was simultaneous renewed interest by several parties. In 1905, Karl Pearson wrote a letter to *Nature* about mosquito infestations and proposed a simple model. That at each time interval, a mosquito would move a defined distance at a random angle. He called this a "random walk" and apparently this was the first use of the term. Lord Rayleigh neatly provided a calculation for the probability distribution of the number of mosquitoes after a certain number of steps. It seems that he had tackled a similar problem with sound waves in media in the 1880s.

Simultaneously in 1905, Einstein published his famous paper on Brownian motion, deriving a diffusion equation and using it to estimate the size of atoms. It was a great year for Einstein since he also published his seminal works on special relativity and the photo-electric effect but the most cited of these papers was the one on Brownian motion. Although Einstein dismissed Brownian motion as trivial compared with his other exploits, the concept of Brownian fluctuations has subsequently proved important to a huge range of applications from thermodynamics and cellular biology to traffic flow and finance.

However, the great Einstein was arguably beaten in his mathematical formulation of Brownian motion by the remarkable 1900 doctoral thesis of Louis Bachelier. Einstein was seemingly unaware of Bachelier's work. Bachelier was a mathematics student at the Sorbonne in Paris. Whilst studying the movements of bond prices on the Paris Bourse, he was inspired by the physics analogy and later revealing remarked that he "copied it from the physics of a gas in equilibrium". He proposed that prices followed a random walk and were impacted by the unpredictable flow of news and information. This important analysis was to form the core tenet of the efficient market hypothesis (EMH) many decades later.

1.3 The Efficient Markets Hypothesis

The pursuit of the efficient market hypothesis is largely credited to the academics at Chicago University. It grew in popularity in the 1960s and principal proponents included Paul Samuelson and Eugene Fama. The key "weak form" of the EMH was that all news is rapidly incorporated into prices and thus prices are entirely a random walk. A true random walk is Markovian and price changes at time t are completely uncorrelated to price changes at any later time $t + 1$.

Modern portfolio theory is based around asset returns following normal distributions scaled by a volatility factor (Appx. A.1). To avoid negative prices, the standard assumption, in most financial derivative applications, is that the relative returns follow standard normal distributions. This means that underlying price returns follow a lognormal distribution (Appx. A.2). It is widely assumed that the use of normal distributions is a fundamental aspect of the EMH but in fact Bachelier questioned this assumption in 1914, as did Fama in his 1965 thesis and together with chaos theory genius Benoit Mandlebrott. Real markets display much fatter tails than normal distributions but the convenience of mathematical manipulation of normal distributions has resulted in their pervasive influence in financial theory and practical applications from derivatives pricing to risk management.

1.4 The Black–Scholes Equation

The mathematical machinery of diffusion equations was required to describe random walks in a manner suitable for derivatives pricing. The field of stochastic calculus was quickly adopted by the EMH movement including techniques such as Ito's lemma (Apps. A.3–A.4). The famous Black–Scholes (BS) pricing equations for call and put options were first published in the landmark paper by Fischer Black and Myron Scholes in 1973 and Robert Merton in the same year (Appx. A.5). Scholes and Merton were subsequently awarded the Nobel Prize in 1997. The success of these equations has led to them being the industry standard pricing model for European options on a wide variety of underlying assets ranging from equities and equity indices to currencies and commodities.

In the Black–Scholes methodology the underlying asset diffuses randomly through time with a constant growth rate and a volatility. For a so-called European equity call option if the equity finishes above the option strike price at the option maturity, then the option contract pays to the holder the difference between the final equity price and the strike price. If the equity finishes below the strike price, then the option contract expires worthless and pays zero to the holder. Black–Scholes, by using a diffusion equation, averages over all the paths of potential option pay-offs and present values back to the initial investment date. The average or expected value provides the initial price of the option or the premium. This approach is equivalent to modelling the terminal probability distribution of the equity and multiplying by the option payoff at maturity. Although in hindsight, this seemed like a straightforward calculation, back in the 1970s, it was a revolutionary insight to apply mathematics from the physical sciences to finance.

The Black–Scholes analysis is dependent on several major assumptions that are considered to apply in efficient, deeply liquid markets. These assumptions include: (i) the stock price follows geometric Brownian motion with a constant volatility, (ii) the volatility is constant and not dependent on time and price level of the underlying and (iii) trading and hedging is continuous, not discrete and costless. Although these assumptions are only a theoretical ideal, a more detailed analysis on the effect of bid/offer spread, discrete hedging and other "real world imperfections" shows that the Black–Scholes analysis is remarkably robust. Most effects can be accommodated by slightly modifying the volatility used in the calculation.

The key argument in deriving the Black–Scholes equations is the concept of risk neutrality in options pricing. The argument is that if we can instantaneously hedge an option with an amount of equity over a small time period, we can always make a portfolio of options plus a certain number of equities, independent of the movement of the equity (Fig. 1.1). The portfolio of option plus equity is thus hedged against random price movements and becomes "instantaneously riskless" over the period. Obviously, for a hedged portfolio in an efficient market the investor in the portfolio cannot earn more than the risk-free interest rate. Thus, all option contracts can in fact be valued using the risk-free rate instead of the observed market drift of the underlying stock. This strange effect is

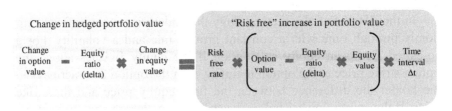

Figure 1.1:   The risk neutral argument.

known as *risk neutral valuation*. It simplifies derivative analysis and means that any solutions or prices we derive are valid in the real world provided our assumptions hold.

A little mentioned but major premise for options pricing theory is the *ergodic hypothesis* borrowed from physics and in particular, statistical mechanics for equilibrium systems (Appx. A.6). This mathematical sleight of hand allows us to integrate over the probabilities of all possible simultaneous price paths for an underlying asset to form an expected value. The discounted expected value is the price of an option in the BS formalism. This mathematical approach results in several notable financial paradoxes such as the St. Petersburg paradox (Appx. A.7). However, in reality there are no infinite, almost equivalent parallel universes but only one world path that prices actually follow. The number of possible paths and the probabilities assigned to them, particularly when markets are not in an "equilibrium" state, is in all likelihood much different from the ergodic ideal. It is surprising that the options pricing and dynamic hedging methodology is so robust under such conditions.

Although the BS equation was published in 1970s, it took a while for the knowledge to diffuse Brownian fashion across the globe and permeate all the investment banks. Whilst at university in the late 1980s I had a summer job with a great little software company in Leicester Square. The first index options only started trading in the US in 1983 and in London, knowledge of options mathematics and derivatives technology was scant. Effectively, nobody knew anything on the subject. Deltas and gammas etc. were really all Greek for everyone concerned. I was employed to go to the London School of Economics (LSE) library, photocopy the few published papers that existed and have a stab at designing a risk system for a leading US investment bank. Surprisingly we beat all the competition including the "Big 8" accounting and consulting firms. Attempts were made to bribe me to abandon my education but perhaps unwisely, I opted for an impoverished life in physics.

1.5 Interest Rate Exotics

Several years later I was lured from my cozy physics lab at the European Synchrotron (ESRF) to become an overly paid financial quant. To my surprise the derivatives field had moved on exponentially since my previous foray into finance. The exotic options business had been created. It was a green field site and was sucking up scientists, at a rate of knots.

An arms race of derivatives innovation was rapidly being established amongst the leading investment banks.

The first market to conquer was the interest rate derivatives market. The structured note market was booming. Instead of buying boring bonds, institutional investors could buy souped-up structured notes with all manner of embedded options to enhance yield. The great thing that investment bankers had discovered was that virtually no investors understood what a forward rate was or how to calculate one (Appx. A.8). This led to all sorts of shenanigans and investors buying unsuitable products with more risk than they could possibly imagine. Orange County in California blew up in 1994 as its treasurer binged on structured notes and suddenly lost \$1.6bn. It was the first really big casualty from the new derivatives era.

The technology required for interest rate derivatives was significantly more complex than just applying basic Black–Scholes. In Black–Scholes there is one forward rate but for structured notes, the whole interest rate term structure had to be modelled. No extensive literature existed for interest rate derivatives. There were a few early adaptations of Black's model but they lead to unsatisfactory mathematical arbitrages along the rates curve as the model evolved through time. Arbitrage free models such as the Vasicek, Ho–Lee and the Hull–White models with the latter incorporating mean reversion (Fig. 1.2) were developed. These were one factor models simulating movement of the short maturity rate or the spot rate (Appx. A.9). Later multi-factor models such as 2-factor Hull–White, Heath Jarrow Morton (HJM) and LIBOR (London Interbank Offered Rate) market models were introduced that allowed more complex movements of the interest rate curve to price more sophisticated derivatives.

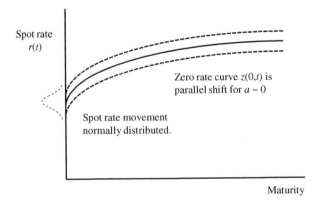

Figure 1.2:   The interest curve movement in the no-arbitrage Hull–White model.

Table 1.1:　Termsheet for a range chooser note.

USD RANGE CHOOSER NOTE	
ISSUER	: AA rated Issuer
CURRENCY	: USD
MATURITY	: 3 year
ISSUE PRICE	: 100%
COUPON	: 1 month USD LIBOR + 0.70% if 1 month USD LIBOR sets within RANGE otherwise no Coupon is payable.
RANGE	: Investor sets monthly 2 business days prior to each 1 month period an interest rate range of 1%. If 1 month USD LIBOR sets within RANGE, otherwise no interest rate payment will be made.
PAYMENT DATES	: Monthly Act/360
REDEMPTION	: The Notes are redeemed on the Maturity Date at 100%.

Since literature was scarce and fast developing, the quants at banks had to innovate to stay up to date and implement different technologies. It was an exciting time as banks innovated against each other to provide the latest products to their clients. The closed form solutions for pricing products could be pretty horrendous but there was much intellectual satisfaction in solving them. Products like the *range chooser note*, where the investor could pick a range for the next coupon period, and if the interest rate remained in the range, then they would receive an enhanced coupon, would prove particularly mind bending (Table 1.1) (Appx. A.10). American style options with early exercise on certain dates (often called Bermudans) were popular but these proved intractable for closed forms. To be more flexible and allow faster implementation, numerical finite difference approaches and Monte Carlo simulations were developed.

1.6 The Derivatives Ideology

Starting in the early 1990s, I was somewhat astonished at the over-confidence that my colleagues showed in the models. This confidence in the derivatives modelling framework ran through virtually every investment bank from the junior quants, risk management and to the senior management. The derivatives business was new and largely incomprehensible. Worryingly, the level of derivatives understanding was essentially inversely proportional to seniority of staff.

Initially, I was shocked that traders would quote prices to many significant figures. They would argue and fight over the last digit. In the physics world I came from every measurement or value came with a cautionary error bar. No such critical analysis was performed in derivatives trading. The business was led by an abstract mathematical framework, underpinned by stochastic calculus. Sorry to say, but as more mathematicians became involved, the more entrenched the methodology became. As it too often happens in theoretical physics, many quants started to believe the models reflected reality. The ideology prevailed over empirical measurement and common sense.

However, there was a good greedy rationale to favour the ideology — profits and bonuses. Assumptions were made that exotic trades could be hedged without costs until maturity. Profits were present valued and nicely paid out in traders, marketers and managers bonuses. The magic of present valuing never ceases to amaze, especially when your bonus relies on it. It was only after several headline blow-ups, that many years later, institutions started to seriously take reserves against potential future hedging issues in longer dated transactions.

The fact is financial markets are complex systems driven by news flow and the whims of multiple traders with different convictions and investment horizons. The option pricing models are a simplistic representation of market reality. Usually, the principal unknown in these models is the implied volatility of the underlying asset. Badly estimating the implied volatility used in pricing and hedging is problematic, though it is arguably a smaller problem than the mis-specification of the model. In practice, there exists a large set of unknown models of different complexity that could be used to model reality, but essentially, we end up using the simplest first order one. This has many advantages in terms of tractability, comprehensibility and standardisation but we must be aware that model risk is high. The error bars should be big but according to the Gospel of Derivatives, they don't exist.

1.7 Credit Derivatives

As people became more confident in modelling the interest rate term structure, a new market for credit derivatives began to develop. The essential business of banks is lending and this necessarily incurs borrowers' credit risk. By creating a credit derivatives market, credit risk could be transferred and hedged between different institutions. Credit derivatives and the associated credit insurance markets were the next natural step in derivatives technology.

By 1995 there were only a handful of players and the first active traders were cheery asset swappers who enjoyed a few beers every lunchtime. Credit derivatives grew from the older asset swap market, where fixed rate bonds were sold as a package with an interest rate swap. This process turned a fixed rate coupon into a floating rate coupon plus a fixed spread. The spread, despite including a measure of liquidity risk, was viewed as a measure of the market credit price. Although the theoretical spread derived from rating agency default risk was often markedly different, the asset swap spread was quickly taken as an approximation for the premium paid in a *credit default swap* (CDS). This allowed a visible liquid market pricing to be developed and CDS to be created for hedging assets and for speculation.

There however remained a couple of significant issues. The first was developing a standardised CDS contract and process between market participants. Providing a workable over-the-counter (OTC) contract was harder than it first seemed. Contracts initially differed between counterparties and basis risks appeared between contracts. On a company default or *credit event*, there was much debate over the actual credit event definitions, particularly the triggering of the restructuring clause. There was also the deliverability problem. On a credit event, physical delivery of the underlying asset was required in exchange for par. Sometimes, as with Indonesia in the *Asian crisis* (1997), a lack of bonds would cause a squeeze and the defaulted asset could rise above par in value. A cash payment mechanism was quickly developed based on an official bond valuation process to remedy the situation. After a year or so all the major banks agreed together with the International Swaps and Derivatives Association (ISDA) on a mutually acceptable framework that has not been tinkered with much since.

The second major issue for developing the CDS market was a pricing model. As the CDS spread moved significantly away from the initial traded value, what was the value of the swap? With an interest rate swap this modelling framework was well established but there was no consistent methodology for CDS in the early days. Arguments and haggling occurred between traders during CDS unwinds, particularly for a name like Thailand whose credit spread had ballooned out. What discount factors should be applied? Initial attempts to use a stochastic Black–Scholes type model were quickly abandoned. The model which everyone finally settled on was a hazard rate model where the hazard rate represented the probability of an immediate credit event over a given time period. This model was simple, clear and had the nice property that for flat rates and credit curves, the CDS premium was equal to the hazard rate multiplied by the expected loss on a credit event.

1.8 The Normal Copula

Developing vanilla CDS was however just the first stage on the road to an exotic credit derivatives market. The hazard rate model was extended to incorporate a range of products including basket notes and spread options. A popular product was the first-to-default basket in which investors were paid an enhanced spread to assume the first credit loss on a basket of around 5–10 names. Unfortunately, from a modelling perspective this required the introduction of correlation between credit events of different entities. Quants realised that actually the hazard rate model derived from a so-called Poisson probability distribution was not very good at incorporating correlations. Instead, the multi-variate normal distribution came to the rescue. By mangling the hazard rate model together with the normal distribution for time to default an acceptable basket correlation model was possible.

This technique became known as the *normal copula* approach (Appx. B.11). It allowed all manner of fantastic yield enhancing credit products to be developed for investors. However, the optimistic modelling framework was moving further and further away from the EMH of the original Black's model. CDS were much more illiquid than equities and rates. Could option structures be dynamically hedged and what were the costs? How would you hedge close to a default? Risk neutrality arguments, in practice, went right out the window. The dangers of modeling credit correlation were put on the back burner since the first synthetic *collateralised debt obligations* (CDOs) were appearing. Large portfolios of corporate CDS were sliced or "tranched" into different levels of risk for investors.

1.9 Equity Correlation

By 1999 the *dot-com* bubble was in full expansion. I had a brief interlude from the world of credit derivatives and became the global head of structuring for a European investment bank. There the primary focus was on equity derivatives and especially those of a super exotic variety. By this time, derivatives trading had been transformed from one where you would have to amateurly self-educate yourself in the library, to one where the leading business schools were training quant foot-soldiers en masse in stochastic calculus and financial engineering. I had recourse to large numbers of very smart Polytechniciens already trained in the dark arts of Ito's lemma and C++ programming. An arms race was developing between the leading pioneering French banks who all had the utmost confidence in the EMH and dynamic hedging.

Consequently, the Black–Scholes equation and stochastic modelling pushed the envelope as far as it would go. The new exotics included long dated maturities, trading volatility skew of highly out-of-the-money (OTM) options and nefariously difficult correlations. The vol "smile" was a large effect, time varying (Fig. 1.3) and not readily modelled.

The *reverse convertible* notes were arguably the most popular structure since they provided a high income through the investor effectively selling an embedded put on an underlying reference share. In the vanilla version if the share falls below its initial value at maturity, the investor is redeemed not at par but either in cash or physically in shares. Sounds like an asinine product? Maybe, but reverse converts were a hugely successful product for institutions and retail hungry for yield in a moderately bullish market. The non-vanilla versions developed rapidly including barriers, averaging and baskets of underlyings. For example, the knock-in reverse

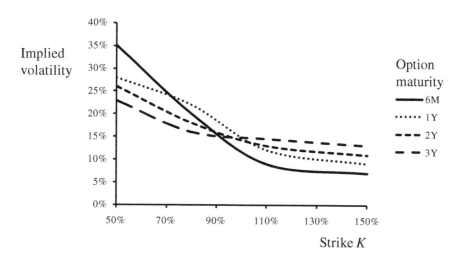

Figure 1.3:   Typical DJ Eurostoxx 50 equity index volatility smiles.

Table 1.2:   Termsheet for a knock-in reverse convertible.

13.0% EUR KNOCK-IN REVERSE CONVERTIBLE NOTES ON DEUTSCHE TELEKOM	
ISSUER	:	A rated Issuer
CURRENCY	:	EUR
MATURITY	:	1 year
ISSUE PRICE	:	100%
UNDERLYING	:	Deutsche Telekom
ANNUAL COUPON	:	13.0%
DENOMINATION	:	$100\% \times DTEL_{initial}$, the opening price of the Underlying on the Issue Date.
KNOCK IN LEVEL	:	$80\% \times DTEL_{initial}$
REDEMPTION	:	Each Note will be redeemed at maturity as follows depending on $DTEL_{final}$, the closing price of the Underlying 3 business days before the Maturity Date and $DTEL_{min}$ the lowest daily closing price of the Underlying observed between the Issue Date and 3 business days before the Maturity Date. If $DTEL_{final} > 100\% \times DTEL_{initial}$ redeemed at 100% whatever the level of $DTEL_{min}$. If $DTEL_{final} < 100\% \times DTEL_{initial}$ redeemed with 1 share if $DTEL_{min}$ is lower or equal to the Knock-in Level, or 100% if $DTEL_{min}$ is higher than the Knock-in Level.

convert where the put option knocked-in if the underlying fell beneath a deeply OTM strike (say, 80%) during the life of the note (Table 1.2) (Appx. A.11). This required dynamically hedging the barrier option through the life of the trade.

Fortunately, most reverse converts were short dated but longer dated 5–10-year exotic products rapidly became more widespread. Société Générale (SocGen), the leader in the field, developed "worst-of" products where performance was based on the worst performing equity in a basket. Everybody else swiftly copied to keep up. As you can imagine, depending on the correlation assumed, the worst-of call option or forward could be incredibly cheap since there is probably at least one duff equity in a basket (Fig. 1.4). The concept allowed many interesting products that were optically appealing to investors but totally opaque in terms of pricing (Appx. A.12). Margins were high which was what investment banks loved.

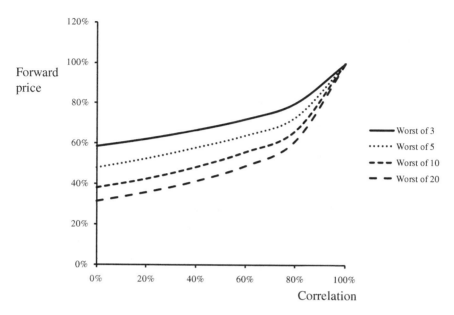

Figure 1.4:   Example worst-of forward versus basket correlation and size.

An extreme example, but a highly popular product, was the capital protected 10-year maturity "Pulsar" note initially developed by SocGen (Table 1.3). In my mind, it epitomises the ludicrous level of complexity and hyper confidence in the derivatives technology. The Pulsar references an underlying basket of 10 or so diversified stocks. The investor would be paid 300% in year 10 (equal to an effective yield of 11.6%) except if any of the stocks during years 6 to 10 fell below 60% of their initial values. If any stock fell this low, then the investor would be paid at maturity 200% plus the performance of the worst performing stock at maturity. The simple description sounds kind of comprehensible but actually structuring and trading the product is mind boggling. It includes (i) a zero-coupon bond redeeming 100% at maturity, (ii) a worst-of, knock-out digital option paying 200% with a barrier at 40% of the initial stock price of each stock and (iii) a worst-of, knock-in forward on the worst-of with a knock-in at 40% and forward strike at the initial stock price (Appx. A.13). The product necessitates dynamically hedging over 10 years options involving deeply OTM continuous barriers and managing volatility and correlation risk between multiple underlyings. Amazing faith is required in the derivatives methodology and infrastructure since well before the maturity date the original group of traders and structurers who conceived the horrific

Table 1.3:   Termsheet for a Pulsar capital protected basket note.

EUR "PULSAR" PROTECTED NOTES ON A BASKET OF EUROPEAN BLUE CHIP STOCKS	
ISSUER	: A rated Issuer
CURRENCY	: EUR
MATURITY	: 10 year
ISSUE PRICE	: 100%
UNDERLYING BASKET	: An equally weighted basket composed of

BASF   Nokia
BMW   Elsevier NV
Akzo Nobel   Novartis
Dresdner Bank   Telefonica
LVMH   Total Fina

COUPON	: Zero coupon

KNOCK-IN EVENT : Between Year 6 and Year 10, if the lowest daily closing price of any of the 10 underlying stocks ($STOCK_{min}$) is lower than or equal to 60% of their initial values ($STOCK_{min} \le 60\% \times STOCK_{initial}$) then a Knock-in Event will occur.

REDEMPTION : Each Note will be redeemed at maturity as follows:
If the Knock-in Event has not occurred a Redemption Amount equal to 300% (annualised yield 11.6% equivalent).
If the Knock-in Event has occurred a Redemption Amount equal to 200% plus the return of the worst performing stock at maturity.

$$200\% + Min\left[\frac{S_1(T)-S_1(0)}{S_1(0)},...,\frac{S_i(T)-S_i(0)}{S_i(0)},...,\frac{S_{10}(T)-S_{10}(0)}{S_{10}(0)}\right],$$

where
$S_i(T)$ is the closing price of the ith share ($i = 1,...,10$) 5 business days before the Maturity Date.
$S_i(0)$ opening price of the ith share on the Issue Date.

product will certainly not be around. Fortunately, however, these products included a massive theoretical profit of 8–10%, which was of course present valued upfront and nicely contributed to the bonus pool.

Innovation continued and in 2000 my equities team started developing certificates based on dynamic trading strategies and options on funds. In developing the novel strategy certificates, we noticed surprising departures from the traditional EMH that formed the core tenet of our highly profitable derivatives business. Chief among them was the "momentum" effect or the observation that buying the recent winners and selling the losers proved a highly profitable investment method. Termed the "premier anomaly" by Eugene Fama, one of the principle academic proponents of the EMH, it was published by Mark Cahart in 1997. However, its original academic publication, which was seemingly swept under the carpet by EMH theorists, extended far back to an original 1967 paper *Relative Strength as a Criterion for Investment Selection* by a Robert Levy. Hunting around we discovered several other statistically significant anomalies that could be exploited. The experience, for an EMH indoctrinated derivative specialist at least, was an eye opener.

1.10 Structured Credit Trading

By the time I returned to credit trading, the growing synthetic CDO market had evolved into a massive ratings arbitrage. Large portfolios of 50–200 underlying credits were assembled and tranched into levels of risk from AAA to unrated high yielding equity tranches. Investors would buy the tranches at yield levels slightly above that of other rated *asset backed securities* (ABS) such as *collateralised loan obligations* (CLOs). A typical capital structure of a synthetic CDO and the attribution of credit losses is shown in Fig. 1.5. The arbitrage lay in the fact that the effective spread

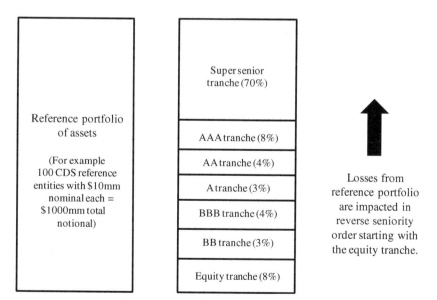

Figure 1.5:   Capital structure of a typical synthetic CDO.

paid to the investment bank from the hedges significantly exceeded the spread paid to all the tranche investors. Structured credit trading as it became known was massively profitable and became more so with new innovations.

The first innovation was creating super-AAA or "AAAA" rated tranches which paid far less spread (say 5–10 bp) relative to 30–50 bp for normal AAA. This required carving the usual top of the CDO capital structure into a large super-AAA tranche and a wafer-thin AAA tranche (Table 1.4). Being paid hundreds of thousands to rate each trade, the ratings agencies arguably facilitated this maneuver by the investment banks. Various counterparties like AIG and the monoline insurers (AMBAC, MBIA ...) loved these tranches, since according to their erroneous

Table 1.4: Termsheet for an investment grade synthetic CDO.

INVESTMENT GRADE CORPORATE SYNTHETIC CDO					
NOTIONAL	:	USD 1000mm			
MATURITY	:	5 year			
PORTFOLIO	:	Static Portfolio Number of Obligors: 100 Exposure per Obligor: $10mm Moody's Diversity Score: 60 Weighted Average Rating: A3 Type of Obligations: Bonds or Loans Seniority of Obligations: Senior and Unsecured			
TRANSACTION STRUCTURE	:	Tranche	Amount	%	Rating	Spread

Tranche	Amount	%	Rating	Spread
A	916mm	91.6	NR	10 bp
B	30	3.0	Aaa	60
C	23	2.3	Aa3	110
D	12	1.4	Baa2	320
E	22	2.2	NR	1600

CREDIT EVENTS	:	Bankruptcy, Failure to Pay, Restructuring
ISSUED NOTES	:	Floating Rate Notes for B, C, D, E Tranches issued from a SPV Issuer based in Cayman Islands with AAA ABS underlying collateral with AA rated swap counterparty.

rating-based and actuarial style models they were essentially risk-free and money for old rope. The "successful" salesman at one counterparty shipped in billions of dollars of our notional risk whilst building his villa in St. Barths and ski lodge in Whistler. In fact, they so underestimated the risk that there was enough profit for us to hedge by first insuring the tranches with a monoline and then double "wrapping" the tranche with a second reputable retail bank. If both the portfolio and insurer defaulted one after another, the solid retail bank would cover us for the credit loss. A massive mispricing of risk was occurring which would later prove problematic in the great *credit crisis* of 2008.

As CDS became more liquid, the next credit derivatives innovation was applying delta hedging tech based on the normal copula approach to the hundreds of names in a CDO. Somehow, we obtained risk approval for our CDO delta hedging model before virtually anybody else in the market. Even the great Goldman and Morgan didn't have the delta hedging model and the single tranche technology. We knew a window of just 6–12 months existed before it became market standard and old hat. By risk managing and dynamically delta hedging the individual names in CDOs using vanilla CDS at a trading book level, individual tranches of CDOs could be synthetically created for individual investors on demand. There was no requirement to place the senior and equity tranches, which was a tedious and uncertain key to previous synthetic CDO deals and reduced profitability on trades. We had several orders for mezzanine tranches from clients and could provide enhanced spreads for ratings compared with existing deals (20–30% or higher). Certain credits could even be omitted from each tranche if investors wished. Spreads had widened and it was possible on the first $1000m portfolio to achieve at a very conservative correlation level an amazing 2% margin (around $20m) for just $80m of notes placed with investors. Sensibly due to the uncertainties that remained in re-hedging the deal a large reserve was taken for future hedging risks. Within a year the technique was widespread amongst several investment banks and the arbitrage gradually closed. To maintain margins in the arms race, a new structured credit product had to be developed.

For a while we were arguably the biggest buyer of asset backed securities and primarily CLOs in London. We focused on the senior tranches but bought in volume. The other investment banks such as the now defunct Bear Stearns loved us for buying all their product. The rationale for us for buying portfolios of ABS was simple. We could efficiently term

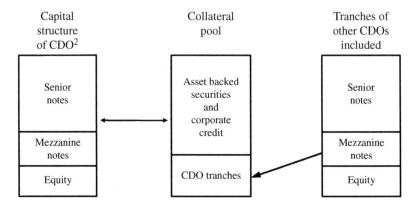

Figure 1.6:   Typical "CDO-Squared" or CDO^2.

finance the cash bonds at LIBOR minus a spread by employing the banks' credit rating, re-tranche and sell-off all the credit risk to 3rd parties via synthetic CDOs. These new CDOs were thus essentially CDOs based on diversified, already tranched and rated CLOs. This was profitable for a while, but ABS spreads were tightening as others started to pursue the same strategy. Luckily, a new innovation was right before our eyes. If we stuck the delta hedged synthetic mezzanine CDO tranches that we created ourselves directly into the ABS portfolios, then the profitability of the trades could be increased. This unwieldy structure was a synthetic CDO within a synthetic CDO and became infamously known as the CDO^2 or "CDO-squared" (Fig. 1.6).

1.11 Towards Real Markets

At this point I was a managing director of structured credit trading at a leading North American bank. The business was incredibly profitable but derivatives and their ever-increasing complexity was in my mind close to reaching a conclusion. The trajectory of derivatives innovation was nearing its apex. The coverage of major asset classes including equities, interest rates and credit was close to complete. What asset class or innovation was left? In too many cases, the spiralling incomprehensibility of products seemed to be a method for investment banks to confuse investors and empty their pockets. Also, I felt increasingly uncomfortable with the model of ratings arbitrage where the investment banks had seriously outwitted the semi-compliant rating agencies.

Importantly, the banks themselves were running ever increasing risks as new innovations in derivatives technologies departed more and more from the simple assumptions of the Black–Scholes model. Trading skew, correlation and long maturities in increasingly illiquid markets seemed a massive departure from the EMH, the original theoretical bedrock of the derivatives industry. It seemed that the push for profits and innovation coincided with a mass delusion in quant finance and its acceptance from risk managers in banks.

The fact is that real markets did not visibly behave like stated in the EMH. I had witnessed too many market bubbles, crises and corporate mishaps to believe that markets were entirely random and that we could naively apply the normal distribution and expected value approaches to every problem encountered. Market opportunities, in-efficiencies and anomalies abounded across equity and bond markets. The plain vanilla derivatives, such as CDS, could be visibly used to exploit these opportunities and, realise alpha. I decided to move from the theoretical planet of efficient markets and enter the messy, real market world of hedge funds.

Chapter 2

Real Markets

2.1 The Federal Cavalry

The story of real markets over the last few decades is one of state intervention. Although one might like to believe in the animal spirits of numerous buyers and sellers creating an efficient market, as outlined in the EMH, the financial reality has proven somewhat different. The real market is a complex system that provides an emergent series of booms and busts, all causally linked and loosely connected to the broader economy. In all likelihood, the idealist Western capitalist system is akin to a mere fairy tale. The global markets would have spiralled totally out of control on numerous occasions if left to their own devices. The balancing act to keep the show on the road and stop the wheels periodically falling completely off has been led by the G7 governments and their stalwart, underappreciated financial institutions — the central banks.

The deadly coronavirus (COVID-19) pandemic is a severe health crisis that will be hopefully resolved in the near future with the help of vaccines and sensible public health policy. Importantly, once again the US Federal Reserve Bank (the Fed) cavalry has ridden to the rescue and "saved" the financial markets from a doomsday scenario. However, the influence of the Fed in capital markets and the subsequent hangover will possibly take several decades to unwind and we must live with the unexpected consequences.

The side-effects of the unprecedented levels of central bank intervention are multi-faceted and sometimes undesirable. They include inefficient markets, bad allocation of capital, perpetuation of crazy bubbles and *enrichissement* of the "in-crowd". For most of my financial career there has been a long and increasingly tortuous path of Fed interference and adventurism in capital markets which inexplicably rises exponentially in scale with each crisis. Unfortunately, the sustainability of these continually increasing central bank interventions underpins the survival of global markets and economies.

To have an idea of this encroachment and impact on the romanticised free markets, we need to rewind slightly and play my often myopic and highly biased version of market history.

2.2 Once "Greed was Good"

Back in the early 1980s, the world was in convalescence from a large bout of inflation from the 1970s oil crises and US interest rates were above an eye-watering 10%. I don't really remember the oil shocks since I was too young, but I recall the 1970s summers being hot and seemingly extending forever (probably a childhood illusion). Adults spoke ominously of industrial strikes and trash in the streets on the TV.

In the 1980s, pop music arguably improved, interest rates fell and stock markets soared in a chaotic free-wheeling market. The high yield bond market was invented by Michael Milken (who later went to jail for pushing the envelope a bit too far). Gordon Gekko appeared in pinstripes with a brick sized mobile phone in the movie *Wall Street* and cited "greed is good".

In the UK, Margaret Thatcher was either loved or hated for her social and economic policies but was a fervent supporter of free markets. Perhaps her ideology was too extreme if you were a coal miner or union member but an economic boom ensued. The property market went crazy, entrepreneurship became trendy, more restaurants opened up and flashy money appeared. I even remember seeing an entire transporter full of Ferrari Testarossas driving past my school. Bizarrely, comedian Harry Enfield improbably reached number 4 in the singles chart with the song "*Loadsamoney*".

Thatcher's privatisation program, although you might dislike cramped franchise run commuter trains and buying electricity off the EDF (an inspiring attempt to hide "*Electricite de France*" from the Brits), was overall a short-term success. In contrast many European countries still have not bitten the bullet and have highly unionised, state-run inefficient, bureaucracies constantly demanding tax-payer funded bail-outs (I am thinking France and Italy which mainly defy all the laws of economics).

2.3 The Great Japan Crash

However, perhaps the most beneficial long-term policy of the Thatcher years was enticing foreign inward investment, particularly the Japanese. It was a bold attempt to make the native British industry "pull their socks up". As a teenager one of my friends had a crappy yellow Japanese Datsun car that smoked a lot, with bits that fell off, and it did not impress the girls. Everything rubbish was an import from Japan.

Overnight this somehow changed. Everyone was discussing VHS and Betamax, buying the latest Sony Walkman and the latest high-tech Japanese gizmos. A few people moaned that all the indigenous British TV manufacturers were being driven out of business as the Japanese had somehow mastered the knack of building great products, with high quality and surprising efficiency which actually made money so nobody cared. They even had fairly enlightened personnel policies (if you could put up with the daily corporate exercise routine). Japan was booming.

The raging Nikkei rose from around 7000 in 1985 to over 36,000 in 1991. The Tokyo property market was so overvalued that the land on which the Emperor's Palace was built on became supposedly worth more than all the real-estate in California. The Japanese loved playing golf and they bought every golf course they could lay their hands on.

Actually, everyone was terrified they would buy everything in sight. I was in Japan doing a big physics experiment on a particle accelerator and bought a book "*Japan, The Coming Economic Crash*" or some such which seemed pretty far-fetched at the time.

I remember a Sean Connery film in 1993 — *Rising Sun*, about an evil, dastardly Japanese conglomerate operating in California, murdering hookers and thinking they were above the Los Angeles Police Department (LAPD). However, by the time the movie came out the asset bubble had burst as the Bank of Japan (BoJ) raised interest rates from 2.5% to 4.25% in 1989 and to 6.0% in 1990. Crude government intervention crushed the bubble. The 1990 Gulf War I, despite the Standard and Poor's 500 (S&P 500) temporarily stumbling to a 20% decline, paled in comparison with what was going on in Japan.

The Nikkei crashed and the "lost decade" started in Japan (Fig. 2.1). In fact, a lost decade is an understatement since the bear market never

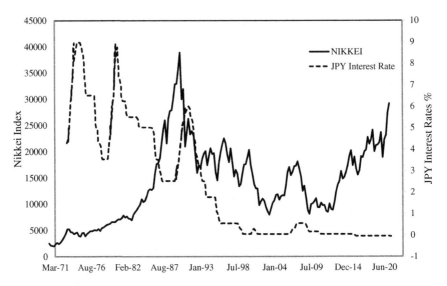

Figure 2.1:   The Japanese boom and bust.

really stopped. The Nikkei has never fully recovered despite three decades and massive economic stimulus in the form of *quantitative easing* (QE) of all forms. The scale and length of the declines are like nothing we have seen in the West. I think the market bottom was below 8000 in 2008 and still not back to 1989 levels over 30 years after the initial crash.

To prop up the market and economy during this time, the BoJ has become the master of QE — buying bonds, equities and just about anything else but to no avail. Ironically my first job in finance was for a behemoth Japanese bank. I had first-hand exposure to what a portfolio of bad loans was and how they could be optimistically marked and juiced up to make them look better for regulators and accountants. My boss, when he was not snoozing at his desk, was arguably the smartest in the bank and the best at putting lipstick on a pig.

2.4 Black Monday

A major equity market event in the 1980s was the 1987 stock market crash or "Black Monday". The Dow Jones fell an impressive 22% in several hours and was a dramatic event in the recent history of crashes. Nobody has ever given me a convincing explanation for the origin of the crash, but it may have been exacerbated by computerised portfolio insurance hedges, that reduce risk by selling in a falling market, which became popular at that time. Arguably, this event was a largely ignored red flag for the impact of automated trading on market stability. However, we can really label 1987 as a correction since the recent rise in the market in the previous 12 months was a massive 45%. Interestingly, for all those investors that assume these days that Treasuries are an inversely correlated hedge, in 1987 they too fell with equities.

Importantly, for our story the Fed market reaction to stabilise markets was limited in scope but highly efficient. Recently appointed Fed Chairman Alan Greenspan made a succinct statement that the Fed "affirmed its readiness to serve as a source of liquidity", rates were cut by 0.5% and the Fed made some limited purchases on the open market. Global markets were calmed relatively easily. The Fed had demonstrated its ability to support markets and they recovered over the next couple of years.

2.5 George's Black Wednesday

In the 1990s there followed a series of secondary crises which had limited global impact. In 1992 the UK was snookered into the politically motivated *European exchange rate mechanism* (ERM) that unwisely obliged Sterling to float in a narrow band. Speculators like George Soros made billions and became infamous household celebrities by breaking the currency band on "Black Wednesday".

In a futile attempt to defend the band, UK rates were raised to a massive 15% which unsurprisingly caused a major housing crash. The words "negative equity" entered the English dictionary and people left, right and centre were posting the keys through the letterbox and legging it. In the end, thanks to Gordon Brown sensibly ignoring Tony Blair, the UK never did join the Euro.

2.6 Tequila and Tigers

A series of well contained emerging market crises followed. In the 1994–1995 Mexican Peso crisis or "Tequila crisis", Mexico was effectively bailed out by the Fed. Our exuberant investors that had bought 2–3x leveraged emerging market bonds took a bath as liquidation triggers were hit but life continued as normal.

In the 1997 *Asian crisis*, the (too) fast growing "tiger" countries of Thailand, Indonesia etc. hit a pothole in the road. The crisis was mainly caused by sovereigns issuing Eurodollar debt in USD and their local currency plunging when people spotted that all the borrowed money had been spent on empty office blocks and unfinished infrastructure.

This was my first experience of using credit default swaps (CDS) to short sovereigns and it led to big arguments about what constituted a credit event, especially when Indonesian companies just refused to pay their debts, kept on operating as normal and ignored all the western lawyers. One large Indonesian taxi company just defaulted, kept driving and never looked back.

2.7 The Russian GKO Bust

In the 1998 Russian crisis, Russia unexpectedly defaulted on its local currency debt, which although very traumatic for the Russian people was extremely annoying for all those investment banks that had been putting theirs and their clients' money into Russian GKO bonds. These bonds were seen as magic "free" money guaranteed by the Russian state that paid 30–50% per annum when hedged into USD (Fig. 2.2).

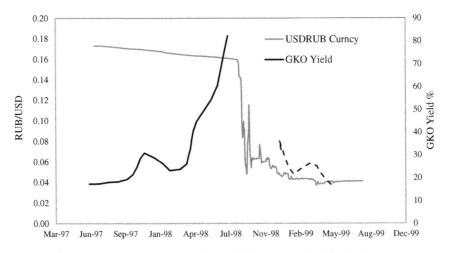

Figure 2.2:   Russian GKO yields and RUB Russian Rouble devaluation.

My friends at one major Swiss bank actually had "cleverly" invested most of their bonus pool into those GKOs which made us all laugh at the time. For Russia it marked a post-soviet low as a drunken Yeltsin presided over a plummeting, gangster economy, where even the $5bn of IMF/World Bank funds were apparently stolen on arrival. Surprisingly, after a massive Rouble devaluation, they started trading GKOs again several months later whilst achieving lower yields than before.

2.8 Too Big to Fail

Now, between 1997 and 1998, the Fed was not super concerned about the Russia crisis itself but by a spin-off crisis involving a high-profile hedge fund called Long Term Capital Management (LTCM). LTCM employed high leverage arbitrage strategies, mainly in fixed income instruments like bonds and associated derivatives. They were viewed as a market leader, employing the most sophisticated technologies.

There were even two future Nobel prize winners, Myron Scholes (co-author of the famous Black–Scholes model) and Robert Merton as founders. All my friends at the investment banks who helped them put on complicated "arb" trades raved about them as pure geniuses. What could possibly go wrong? Well, they blew up totally and their trades were so intertwined with all the other major names on the Street that the Fed viewed them as a major systemic risk to the financial system.

A major rescue was secretly initiated involving a slew of banks (which also curiously had many of the same trading positions on). Russia etc. was a side show. LTCM was closer to home, was about 25× leveraged in 1998 had $4.7bn of equity and had borrowed $124.5bn for total assets of around $129bn. $4.7bn sounded amazingly big at the time but later in our story, the numbers will become unfeasibly larger.

When all the positions were finally liquidated the loss was almost 100% of the original investors' equity but no US tax-payers money was injected (Fig. 2.3). However, the implications of the event would set the stage for future government interventions. LTCM was viewed as "too big to fail" and the Fed was prepared to use its power (even persuasive and arm twisting) to protect the markets and other investors from reckless 3rd parties (including the investment banks that helped them out).

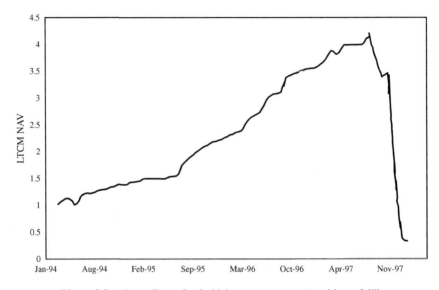

Figure 2.3:   Long Term Capital Management was "too big to fail".

2.9 The .Con Bubble

The .com (or .con) bubble was a marvel of human gullibility and a spectacle to behold. The arrival of the internet and start-up mania arrived suddenly. Small companies with rubbish websites that took minutes to load were set to take over the world overnight and destroy dinosaur bricks and mortar retailers. It was a compelling story and somehow nearly everyone (Warren Buffet excepted) believed it.

I ran an equity derivatives team at the time and all work on the trading floor stopped for several months whilst everybody speculated on the latest .com offerings with their own money. Nobody was interested in serving clients, much to the frustration of the senior management who sent round memo after memo telling staff not to use the banks' trading systems to trade equities for themselves.

All the guys working for me, however junior, were using all their spare cash looking for instant massive gains. The guy next to me had a huge position in Pets.com (soon to be worthless). Even I bought 5k of some stupid bookstore called Amazon (what would that be worth now?). Some colleagues had quickly made several hundred thousands of paper profits. I cashed in and went on holiday to New Zealand. When I came back the trading floor all had long faces and were a bit more subdued since the market had crashed (Fig. 2.4).

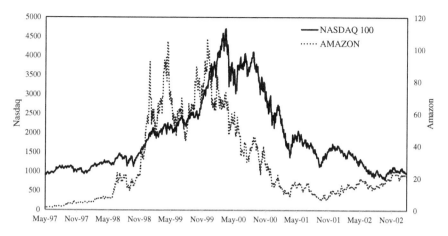

Figure 2.4: Nasdaq 100 and the great survivor Amazon.

Despite hopes for a rally, the crash continued for some time and many .coms were annihilated. Everyone was more philosophical and realised that the companies they had bought were mostly rubbish with rubbish business plans. In my mind this was a perfect semi-irrational bubble and the subsequent well-deserved crash worthy of capitalism at its best. The bubble created lots of ideas and in the process eliminated those business models not worthy of future investment. Now, great names such as Amazon, eBay, Expedia etc. survived the crisis and created the internet revolution that we now enjoy. Importantly there was little government intervention. Interest rates were cut but nobody was rescued with tax-payer money.

When equities hit bottom at the end of 2002 after the .com crash, there followed a bull market until 2007. Rates had fallen from around 6.5% at the end of 2000 to 1% by 2003. Everybody now knew that the Fed had their backs and the Fed chairman "Greenspan put" became widely discussed amongst traders, who laughed about it outside the City watering holes. If the Fed had your back, how could you possibly lose, right? The S&P 500 index accelerated back to the .com highs by the autumn of 2007.

2.10 The Lehman Moment

By this time, rates were pushed by the Fed back to over 5% to slow things down a bit. Financial innovation and easy access to leverage and credit had led to a significant bubble forming over several years in many asset classes. Early in the decade I had been structuring and trading a new-fangled financial instrument called collateralised debt obligations or CDOs, where portfolios of bonds would be sliced into different tranches of risk for investors. Portfolios would have to contain diversified assets to reduce the risk but by 2007, the only collateral available for these trades with enough spread were so-called subprime mortgages.

A visit by Barclays super-keen, head derivatives salesman telling me to sponsor a CDO and that 100% US subprime would supply the "juice" made alarm bells ring. These were based on essentially highly risky mortgages and often NINJA loans (No Income, No Job, No Assets and cynically No Money back). The ratings agencies were cunningly "persuaded" by several eager investment banks to unwisely allow US subprime mortgage only CDOs.

The dubious rating agency theory was that "property prices never fall across the US at the same time" and correlation risk was low. However, this unfortunate assumption was to ignite the global *credit crisis*. By the end of 2009, with the BBC's Robert Peston gleefully moaning on TV every night about the forthcoming apocalypse, even my cleaning lady knew that maligned CDOs were deadly toxic waste and contributed to global warming, ozone hole depletion and every other known affliction.

During the credit crisis, major financial institutions astonishingly failed like dominos as their internal leverage unravelled at breakneck speed. Massive declines in financial equity prices were occurring (Fig. 2.5). The Fed intervened early to help find a solution for Bear Stearns (an early casualty) but blinked when confronted by the highly leveraged Lehman Brothers. Based on past LTCM form, the market expected a bailout.

I rang Lehman the day they closed hoping to speed them up to wire the money they owed me from a swap unwind. Only one week before, their credit people were checking if our hedge fund was credit-worthy and assuring us they were safe as houses. Someone picked up and screamed down the phone "It's all over. Everyone is gone. It's finished … aaagh" then stone silence.

On TV there was immediate chaos of watching people run out of their building holding cardboard boxes and carrying stripped office fixtures but then absolute calm reigned. Everyone was left wondering what all the fuss had been about but a couple of days later all hell broke loose and the rollercoaster took another leg down.

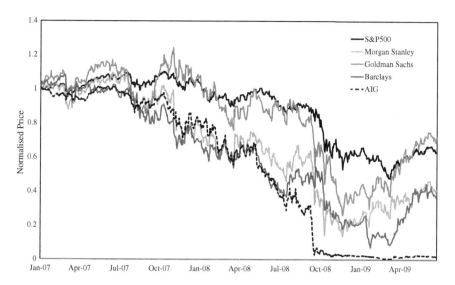

Figure 2.5:   Financial chaos: Share prices of major brokers and financials.

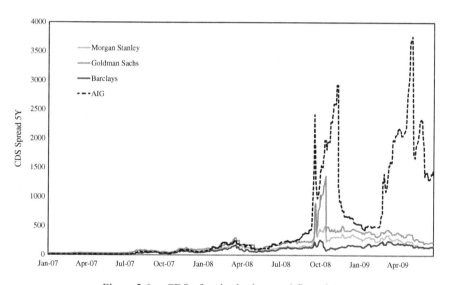

Figure 2.6:   CDS of major brokers and financials.

The Fed, making things up as it went along, was forced into saving a string of companies and the whole financial system on an unprecedented scale. Credit default swap (CDS) spreads exploded as everybody tried to guess which bank or insurer would be the next victim (Fig. 2.6).

Many mighty financial institutions succumbed to the pandemonium in equity and credit markets and were rescued. All my fund's money was stashed in a couple of Wall Street investment banks that would go bust by Monday if they were not saved by the Fed during the weekend.

Even the great AAA rated AIG insurance company, with whom I had often traded super-AAA CDO tranches, blew-up as they were forced by accountants to inconveniently mark-to-market their CDO trading book just as the buyers (and the market) suddenly disappeared and ran for the hills.

The Anglo-Saxon institutions "took the losses on the chin" and painfully realised all their mark-to-market losses. However, in mainland Europe the immediate, inextricable problems were papered over by bureaucrats in quasi-Japanese style as all those worthless loans were moved to the banking book, marked at par (100%) and hidden from shareholders to fester and nastily mature for the next decade.

The scale of the central bank intervention was unprecedented in modern times as global attempts were made to prevent a chain reaction of banking failures and avoid spill-over to the wider economy. The Fed slashed interest rates to their lowest ever levels (0.0–0.25%) and injected over \$2tr in financial stimulus by mainly buying bonds off the various financial institutions and providing them unlimited liquidity to stave off disaster.

The BoJ went further, loading up on most of the Japanese stock market and then deciding that was not enough, greedily entered the US market by becoming the biggest buyer of US ETFs. The Swiss SNB (which often suffers from the delusion it's a hedge fund) even decided that it was fair play to buy tech stocks like Apple on the dips. Luckily it seemed to work and markets stabilised and recovered.

Quantitative easing (QE) entered the public lexicon and became the new paradigm which left the majority of economists scratching their heads and wondering how it was possible that a country could issue bonds with one entity like the Treasury and purchase them with another like the Bank of England? Surely this was unfair, not playing by the rules and defeating the "laws of economics"?

Working at a leading Mayfair hedge fund, I spent ages arguing that as a physicist (who thinks most economic "laws" are plain daft), I could see no immediate contradiction. Those economically trained and their leading Harvard advisers insisted that under the circumstances, shorting Japanese Government Bonds (JGBs) was a good idea and that one day soon,

Treasuries would crash, obviously since the Fed would have to sell all the bonds they bought in haste.

Anyways, the JGB trade continued to be the "widow maker" and the Fed just bought more bonds as the old ones matured. The economists reluctantly came up with a new name for it called *modern monetary theory* (MMT) and consigned the old economics textbooks to the dustbin. The rule of thumb now seems to be that if every other G20 country is economically screwed, MMT works a treat but don't try it home alone and don't tell the newspapers how the magic really works.

The extensive use of QE led from 2010 to a self-sustaining bubble for almost 10 years (Fig. 2.7). Low interest rates became rocket-fuel for the markets and the trader's motto became "don't fight the Fed". Bad economic data was overlooked and the best investment strategy became 100% long equities (or even more since you could borrow at super low rates). A riskier but apparently market guru winning strategy was "buy the dips" since everybody knew that the Fed would step in and support the market if things went too awry.

In 2010 the curious *flash crash* occurred, as for a brief 36 minutes the major US indices crashed by almost 10% and then rebounded. It was apparently caused by a breakdown of liquidity and a sudden disruption of the microstructure of the market. All the automated market makers and their algorithms backed away in a gigantic feedback loop as the market quickly plunged, leaving no support to the market. Later, the catalyst for

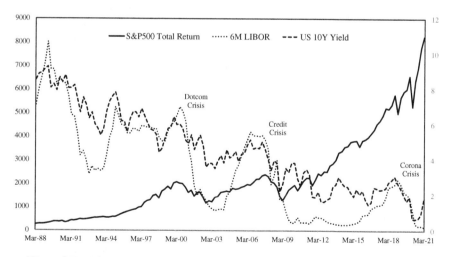

Figure 2.7:   The exponential rise of the S&P (total return) and the decline in rates.

the event was strangely pinned by US authorities on an amateur British trader working from his parent's home, who had perfected the art of "spoofing" — placing orders to spook the market and cancelling them before they are filled. The fact was that for many institutional high-speed algorithmic traders, spoofing was the norm and actually a major trading strategy was somehow overlooked by regulators.

Curiously, throughout the entire decade, inflation never reared its ugly head to spoil the low interest rate party. This too confounded every economic pundit. Politically motivated austerity (which now seems ridiculous in the new coronavirus era) was flavour of the decade and led to subdued consumer demand. Instead, civil servants had their salaries frozen, sick people had their benefits taken away and joe consumer was skint and had no money to spend.

The yacht elite had more money than they knew what to do with and money flowed in bubble quantities into all questionable "investable" asset types from risky covenant-lite leveraged loans to impressionist paintings and rusty vintage Jaguars. The inflation supply side was also impacted as the relentless improvement of technology increased productivity and the biggest deflator of all — China succeeded in its quest to be the #1 producer for the planet.

2.11 Taper Tantrums

The post credit crisis bubble eventually started to lose steam as even unlimited QE eventually loses its lustre and becomes boring. Investors began to worry what would happen when the QE punch-bowl was finally taken away? The market was already a complete QE junkie and in 2013, the first "taper tantrum" in the markets occurred, leading to a brief sell-off. By this stage the Fed had acquired over $4tr of financial assets. The central banks now effectively controlled the market and needed to supply the QE "drugs" to keep the show on the road.

There was an interesting Eurozone debt crisis side-show taking place during this period at the general pace of a typical bureaucratic EU escargot. In a nutshell Greece had economically exaggerated (aided by the notorious vampire squid bank) to facilitate joining the Euro, the Germans reluctantly dragged their feet on bailing them out and a few investors who had leveraged up on PIGS (Portugal, Italy, Greece, Spain) bonds for the great Eurozone convergence trade were slaughtered. Otherwise, the bulls were 100% in control and the market drove even higher.

The Fed backed away from confrontation with the markets and kept rates low and was only brave enough to attempt to normalise rates to 1.5% by the end of 2017. In early 2018 a short-lived VIX volatility index crash (involving a painful spike in implied volatility) attested again to the market's nerves of the QE bubble being punctured.

Twitter crazy POTUS, Donald Trump, griping about the irritating interest rate rises, promised US corporate tax cuts which kept the market alive for a final gasp. The promised reduction in red tape and the thought of those big tech companies repatriating their hoards of money from "dodgy" tax havens boosted the market again. Share buybacks in the low interest rate environment also nicely bolstered the market as altruistic US CEOs were rewarded by higher share prices.

By mid-2019 the Fed became more cautious as Trump's trade war with China finally crystallised and market volatility increased. Rates maxed out at a totally unimpressive 2.25% before being cut in panic. Any attempt at the Fed attaining a normalisation of interest rates and loose monetary policy was abandoned. The inability to normalise rates and the failure of many global economies to eliminate QE life support in the decade following the credit crisis left them ill adapted to cope with the next economic problem.

2.12 The Corona Crisis

We all know what happened next. At the time of writing, the coronavirus pandemic is a continuing disaster that was visible coming down the tracks from January 2020 as we witnessed Chinese citizens being mercilessly boarded up in their apartments on the evening news. But in the West, the politicians suffered a collective failure of imagination of what would be the effect in our more open economies. Evasive action like limiting flights from China, quarantine and stockpiling PPE Personal protective equipment was not taken. Somehow humans (at least the ones we put in charge) think linearly, unlike viruses that behave exponentially.

To avoid slipping into the abyss the economic support package is enormous and includes corporate loans, furloughing benefits, QE (again) and unashamed printing of money. The fiscal stimulus in the US encompassed purchases of corporate bonds and high yield (via ETFs) and the injected liquidity is reportedly over an eye-watering $6tr. After Trump, President Biden was soon busy adding another $2tr (Fig. 2.8). According to excited, nerdy economic historians, we now proudly have the lowest

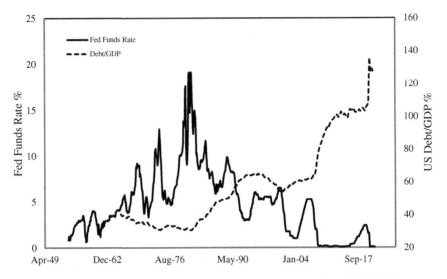

Figure 2.8: Endless US fiscal stimulus with near zero rates and high debt.

interest rates since Stonehenge was constructed and have experienced the worst recession in 300 years.

That sounds really, really bad right? But don't worry since the concerted G20 central bank intervention succeeded in stymieing the death spiral of the equity and debt markets. In fact, they quickly rebounded to new highs despite horrendous corporate fundamentals. Remember the infantile Gordon growth model from primary school (Appx. B.1)? Every equity with a finite dividend should have an infinite value in a zero-interest rate world as discounting disappears. More than ever the bullish markets are in the hands of the Fed and policy makers. Liquidity abounds and apparently around one-third of US pandemic cheques (at least those not invested in bitcoin) were recycled into the markets. Market inflows in 2021 have exceeded the sum of the several previous years.

2.13 "The Best of All Possible Worlds"

The coronavirus crisis and the numerous variants will soon hopefully come to an end. Amazon and Netflix will have taken over the World and we will have eaten too many Domino's take-aways, but the financial markets will be left in a massively dysfunctional funk. What's the problem, you might ask? They are at all-time highs, which is the Panglossian "best of all possible worlds". But beneath the surface lurks the murky intractable issue that markets are more highly controlled by the central banks than any other time in my career. The Empire with their stormtroopers and quasi-infinite financial firepower are now in total control.

Conventional wisdom (held by anybody now retaining any sanity after the recent events) is that an efficient market should be composed of independent clued-up investors (or "agents") with different views that allow a coherent price discovery mechanism including some element of fundamental value. Although this complex and unpredictable process might have periods of "irrational exuberance", occasional corrections and severe manic depressions, the collective action of multiple "free" agents is what comprises a free market and provides objective valuation. Now, bizarrely, central banks hold all the cards and control this market valuation, in almost a cartel-like fashion, whether they like it or not.

2.14 Will Chaos Theory Rule?

The influence of the Fed now dwarfs all the other investors and could paradoxically lead to highly unstable markets (remember chaos theory and that butterfly?). Any false move or bad policy decision could provoke catastrophe for other investors. The central banks do not readily desire this responsibility and wholesale "sovietisation" of the markets but they are caught between a rock and a hard place. How to reduce the level of intervention and return to "normal" free markets without crashing the entire financial system on a scale never before witnessed?

Optimistically, extricating themselves and reducing state influence in financial markets could take several decades of nimble footwork even if the Fed was resolute. However, as we have seen in this story, Fed interventions are haphazard, have amazingly never regressed in size and indeed expanded in a mind-boggling exponential trend. The once terrifying LTCM debacle was a measly $4.7bn and now we are at over $8tr and rising, real rates are negative and the money printing presses are still rolling.

Unless there is an unwelcome, unexpected reckoning, it appears to be a predictable one-way street of Fed interventions and ballooning state balance sheets with each subsequent crisis. Arguably they are now running out of tarmac for successful future interventions and bailouts.

In the meantime, as an investor, best stay on the sunny side of the Fed for your asset purchases and keep your eyes skinned for the "true" reflation trade. As the economy recovers in 2021, US labour markets look tight, commodities such as copper are rising and there are severe shortages of semi-conductors. Bond yields are rising but does this really mark a fundamental turning point in the ever-decreasing long term trend of interest rates? The most recent US CPI data are pointing to more inflation, but a sensible question is whether this is transitory or more permanent? The central banks claim the former and this could be true. As with Newton's Laws of Motion, a car accelerating requires a force and the foot on the pedal. The rapidly recovering US economy requires "gas" to reaccelerate to cruising speed. Once at cruising speed and supply chains are normalised, maybe we return to the former status quo — low consumer demand and deflationary China — and low inflation. This is arguably an optimistic scenario but there exists worrying stagflation alternatives. The central banks have printed enormous amounts of money during QE which could lead to a sustained bout of inflation. Also, already fragile global supply chains are vulnerable to further disruption by an unexpected macro shock. Many unpredictable but minor shocks would probably suffice from new virus variants and badly implemented Fed tapering to domestic Chinese property defaults and international conflict. The jury is still out on the coronavirus recovery, its final impact on the global economy and the Fed's next steps.

Chapter 3

Discretionary Adventures

3.1 Catalyst Trading

When the teenage-looking investment analyst comes round to your Mayfair office with his boxes to tick, you need to quickly decide what strategy ship you are on. Are you long/short equity, event driven, relative value or macro? Who knows exactly what these artificially invented definitions and abstract classifications are? The overlap between them is large. What is flavour of the month amongst faddish investors? Cap structure arb, relative value or even a smattering of macro might please them this quarter.

All you want to do is get back to trading and make money. Who cares about the precise definition. Any well studied "punt" or opportunity is acceptable in your book provided the odds and risk are in your favour. The role of a discretionary hedge fund manager is to identify and manage a portfolio of these bets, eke out profits and not be too mentally scarred by the (un)expected market turmoil.

The boundaries between the "formal" strategies are blurred. Most hedge fund managers do not want to limit their opportunity set if possible. Market opportunities evolve with time and any "free lunch" that presents itself is worth eating. The feature that all good trades possess is a rationale and a catalyst that triggers an event.

The rational for the event could be fundamentally driven or simply a relative value mispricing (Fig. 3.1). Fundamental trades could include company restructurings, profit announcements, rights issues and merger

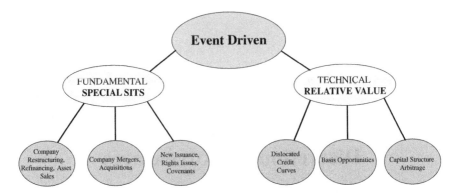

Figure 3.1:   Event driven trades span from fundamental to technical.

and acquisitions activity (M&A). Formally, only M&A are "special sits" but that lacks imagination since in reality, the list of corporate "situations" that can be exploited, as I shall describe later, is extensive. Relative value trades instead involve technical mis-pricings or arbitrages. These could include closely correlated equities or pairs moving out of whack, dislocated credit curves or basis opportunities. Relative value trades require a reversion event to make a profit and require a catalyst to close the arbitrage. Thus, some anticipated volatility in the trade is required, unless of course they are intrinsically "positive" carry since everybody loves positive carry.

A near-term catalyst to precipitate the desired change of asset prices is favoured. Capital is scarce and must be deployed efficiently in the trades that will evolve quickly. Nobody has patience for "dead" trades that take months to reach a conclusion. Most trades employ leverage to magnify small potential profits while long-term financing costs are important and must be optimised.

As you might guess, the financial instruments that allow one to exploit the opportunity are numerous. In corporate land we have cash equities, bonds, and loans plus all the nefarious derivatives associated with them. For our macro views on indices, rates, fx and commodities, we can use futures, government bonds, fx and various over-the-counter (OTC) swaps, caps and floors. The list of instruments employed is considerable and is limited by experience, liquidity considerations, financing costs, investment mandate and occasionally by what your boss (if you have one) allows you to trade.

3.2 Classifying Event Driven Trades

According to highly reliable hedge fund databases, only around 7% of hedge funds are apparently "event" driven. However, now you know better than to trust this meaningless statistic. As the CEO of one of the World's biggest macro hedge fund managers told me (before totally panning systematic trading), "people mistakenly think we are investors but in fact we are traders". In my experience this is entirely true. Discretionary hedge fund managers are continually scanning the markets to put on trades that will be driven by a causal series of events. These can be an anticipated chain of macro or corporate events. For a recent example in 2020, the airline industry is in dire straits, so aircraft orders will be down. Rolls-Royce makes aircraft engines, will burn loads of cash, and will need to do a rights issue, so let's short Rolls-Royce versus another stronger name in the engineering sector. The logic for the chain of events is often highly subjective, but managers must make reasonable assumptions based on the available and often sketchy information to quantify the opportunity. The events can also be macro-orientated. For example, expected big falls in US GDP will provoke (another) Fed rescue package, more QE and Treasury buybacks and long-term yields will tighten further. Without events or catalysts, discretionary fund managers have no sand pit to play in.

Corporate event driven trades have a huge diversity, particularly in the high yield space where importantly they span the entire capital structure of companies. Some like mergers, rights issues, initial public offerings (IPOs) and spinouts are better suited to long/short equity strategies. Others like restructuring, asset sales and covenant waivers are more debt related strategies. Many such as new issues, refinancing and leveraged buyouts influence both equity and debt and arguably lie in the domain of *capital structure arbitrage* (Fig. 3.2).

Some companies are subject in their history and life cycle to numerous events. They can be enjoying using excess cashflow to deleverage, then for share buybacks, be suddenly acquired and leveraged in a *leveraged buy out* (LBO), later revalued to pay a special dividend and then IPOed to be taken public again. As a trader you need to follow these evolving stories with an eye on the historic path of the company. Being an amateur historian is an important part of the job description for a discretionary trader.

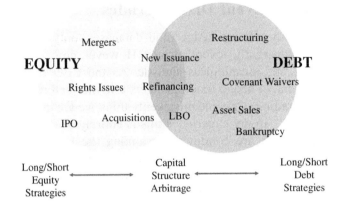

Figure 3.2:   Special situations span the capital structure.

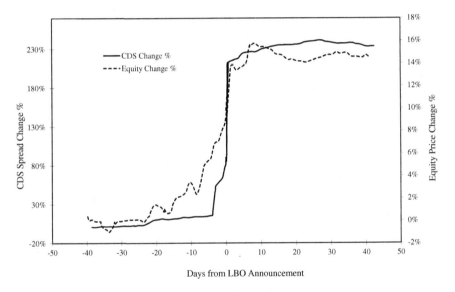

Figure 3.3:   Typical equity and CDS moves on an LBO announcement.

The impact of various corporate events can have markedly different impact on the asset pricing across the capital structure (Appx. B.2). M&A events can be positive for share prices and either positive or negative for debt holders, depending on the final post deal leverage. LBO events result in large equity and credit moves as purchased companies are massively releveraged. Figure 3.3 shows the associated widening of credit default swap (CDS) and equity rise averaged across a large sample of LBOs. Spin-offs usually benefit equity holders, and the proceeds could result in a special dividend or debt reduction. Company rights issues where new shares are issued are commonly negative for equity holders but positive for debt holders. Share buybacks use cashflow for repurchasing equities and are most likely to keep equity prices buoyant but at the expense of paying down company debt. A multitude of possible corporate events can be exploited for different trading opportunities. Moreover, these opportunities have the advantage that they are company specific and idiosyncratic. If prepared in the right way these trades can allow overall market or systemic risk to be hedged out and the specific event to be isolated.

3.3 Corporate Capital Structure

The firm value or enterprise value of a company is given as the sum of the debt and equity value of a company. Approximately this should equal the assets of the company, but this may include intangible assets and other factors such as goodwill. The company's capital structure is typically composed of several layers or tranches (Fig. 3.4). Equity is at the bottom, followed by tiers of debt increasing in seniority from subordinated debt, senior unsecured debt to secured debt. Most bonds fall into the category of senior unsecured debt and bank loans are the upper most secured debt.

High quality companies may have very little or no debt and most of their capital structure is dominated by equity. However, more credit risky

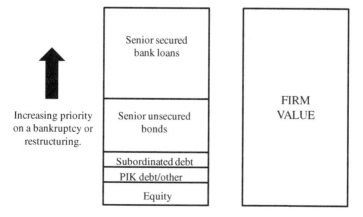

Figure 3.4:   Typical corporate capital structure.

high yield companies could have small equity cushions of around 10–20% of the capital structure.

For some highly leveraged companies, the effective equity is illusory. This is particularly true for some leveraged buyout companies that have been releveraged multiple times. In the same way that after you have bought a house you might have it revalued upwards to increase the equity to allow a remortgage and additional borrowing, private equity companies often do the same thing. A few cosmetic changes, EBITA home improvements, intangible revaluations and hey presto, another releveraging is possible. In Fig. 3.5 the French shoe retailer (a) only has a true equity tranche of 1.4% whereas my old cable company Virgin Media (c) has an effective equity of 28%. Moreover, the bonds and equities of Virgin Media are publicly traded, providing increased transparency of the company's performance. Unsurprisingly, the LBOed French shoe retailer soon ran into problems and endured three restructurings from 2014 to 2020, wiping out nearly €3.3bn of debt.

Table 3.1 shows a typical analysis of a company's capital structure. Here we consider a much-traded favourite, Virgin Media or previously NTL. As a company it had a rough start with a bankruptcy after digging

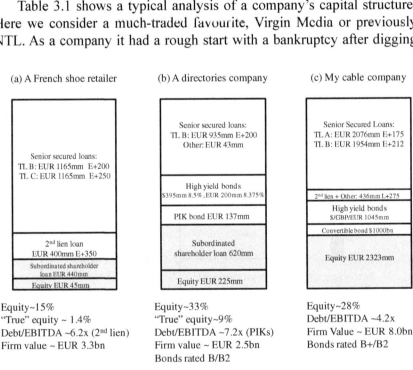

(a) A French shoe retailer   (b) A directories company   (c) My cable company

Equity~15%
"True" equity ~ 1.4%
Debt/EBITDA ~6.2x (2ⁿᵈ lien)
Firm value ~ EUR 3.3bn

Equity~33%
"True" equity~9%
Debt/EBITDA ~7.2x (PIKs)
Firm value ~ EUR 2.5bn
Bonds rated B/B2

Equity~28%
Debt/EBITDA ~4.2x
Firm Value ~ EUR 8.0bn
Bonds rated B+/B2

Figure 3.5:   Example capital structures for different companies.

Table 3.1: Virgin Media capital structure and leverage (*ca.* 2007).

	Notional	Used (£)	Spread	Maturity	Leverage
Virgin Media/NTL — UK Cable Company					
Capital Structure					
Bank Debt					
Revolver	100	0	175	Mar 11	
A	3,525	2,076	175	Mar 11	
B		1,981	212.5	Sep 12	
C-2nd Lien	300	300	275	Mar 13	
Senior facility		**4,357**			3.34
Other/capital leases		179			
		4,536			3.48
Senior Bond					
Senior notes 2014	€225	178	8.75%	Apr 14	
Senior notes 2014	$425	239	8.75%	Apr 14	
Senior notes 2014	£375	375	9.75%	Apr 14	
Senior notes 2016	$550	309	9.13%	Aug 16	
		1,101			
USD Convertible		562	6.50%	Nov 16	
TOTAL DEBT		**6,199**			4.76
Cash		−521			
NET DEBT		**5,678**			**4.36**
Equity	**1,456**				
	20%				
EV	**7,134**				**5.48**

lots of unprofitable holes in the road before reemerging as a new NTL, which then Mr Richard Branson cleverly merged with his Virgin Mobile to become the UK's most successful cable company. Through each level of debt from bank debt to bonds, convertible bonds and equity, the leverage as a multiple of EBITDA (earnings before interest, taxes, depreciation, and amortization) is calculated. This provides a view on the level of protection accorded to each tranche. The bank debt includes a revolver, a term loan A, a large B tranche and a more subordinated C second lien (2nd Lien). The loan tranches pay a floating rate and a spread (in bp). Below the loans sit a series of pari-passu senior unsecured fixed rate bonds plus a convertible bond. The total debt is 4.76× EBITDA but there is cash on the balance sheet which reduced the effective debt to 4.36×. At the time of the calculation, the equity provided a 20% cushion giving an overall enterprise value of 5.48× EBITDA.

The seniority of debt is important in a bankruptcy. On bankruptcy or default of an issuer, holders of obligations will be paid out in order of seniority. Debt holders will always rank above equity holders who take the first loss. After the equity has been eroded, losses in a bankruptcy are then applied from the equity upwards to the debt layers in the capital structure (Fig. 3.4). Senior debt holders rank higher and will take losses after the subordinated debt holders. Senior secured loans have ultimate security over the assets of the company.

That is the theory anyways. In practice rarely does a company go bust overnight with no warning. There are notable recent exceptions such as WorldCom, Enron, Parmalat and even the extenuating market circumstances of Lehman Brothers. Some of these sudden bankruptcies involved fraudulent accounting which was "discovered", sending companies instantly insolvent. The German fintech company Wirecard was the most recent example in 2020.

However, the usual state of affairs when a company starts to run into trouble is that various debt covenants are progressively triggered. Generally, debt covenants (such as maximum debt/EBITDA, interest coverage etc.) are written into debt terms to protect lenders. As covenants are neared or breached, negotiations start between the debt holders, the company and the other shareholders. The loan holders probably have the tightest covenants, and they will be in the driving seat to determine what actions should be taken. Sometimes a covenant waiver can be agreed by the company with the lenders or a reset whereby a fee is paid to lenders. A company restructuring could be proposed. It could be a "friendly" recapitalisation whereby new equity is injected into the company by a private equity sponsor. A less diplomatic "unfriendly" restructuring may consist of loan holders dictating terms, wiping out existing equity holders, changing terms on existing debt (lower coupon and longer maturity etc. to make it less onerous) and performing a debt for equity swap. In a debt for equity swap, the lenders take control of the company and become the new equity owners of the company. There are numerous options and hard bankruptcies with appointment of a receiver and asset sales to redeem loan holders is a last resort.

The detailed nature of the bankruptcy process is highly dependent on jurisdiction. In several jurisdictions a company can place itself into voluntary bankruptcy to attempt a proposed restructuring as with Chapter 11 in the US Bankruptcy Code. A judge is appointed with all parties involved, from debt holders to workers and suppliers having a say. This can result, in some countries, in a rather tortuous, lengthy process if you are a debt holder and just wish to get your money back, but instead the company is allowed to plod on as an irrelevant zombie company. This means that some jurisdictions like the UK and Germany are seen as more bankruptcy friendly for debt holders than say, France.

The value of a bond after a default is often called the recovery rate. The rating agencies have studiously complied recovery rate statistics for defaulted debt over many years. As expected, the average recovery rate is higher as the seniority of debt increases. Senior secured debt has a recovery rate of around 65–75% compared with 35–45% on senior unsecured debt. Averages can be misleading though and in recessionary periods, recovery rates can be lower. Recovery rates can depend strongly on the industrial sector and if a company has hard assets.

Whether by fluke, skill or uncanny credit analysis, I am fortunate enough to never have been long an asset on a default. For those colleagues who have experienced an unexpected default in size, it is often sufficient to induce mild PTSD and can swiftly curtail one's trading career. For one of my first introductory trades with my prime broker, I was "encouraged" to buy a new issue bond to ensure I received future favourable treatment. It was a horrid European bus company that I quickly and quietly sold on. The broker would periodically ring to enquire if I still had the bond, reassuring me it was a great purchase. One day it suddenly went bust at a low recovery rate. They stopped calling and the incident was swept under the carpet. However, my most annoying exposure to a default was while working at an investment bank, an overconfident credit trader, a few desks away, doubled up in size on WorldCom as it dropped from near par to the $80s in price. A few days later it spiralled down to the $20s, the position was cut and blew a massive hole in our P&L and bonus pool. From a historical recovery rate perspective, WorldCom was valued at 11% at the time of the credit event, then the bonds rose several months later towards 30% and in a final legal settlement, a judge awarded a payout of 43% to bond holders. The fact is that any amount of credit analysis can fail to spot complete credit turkeys, especially if a firm has quasi-negligent accountants. As an example, on another occasion I structured a bespoke CDO equity tranche for a sophisticated French insurer, who spent months choosing and agonising over a small portfolio of corporates and performing extensive relative and fundamental single name credit analysis.

Nevertheless, within 18 months the trade had turned sour as Enron, WorldCom and British Energy, in the portfolio, all suffered credit events with very low recoveries.

3.4 The Instruments of Torture

A company's capital structure is built up from equities, bonds and loans. As we ascend the capital structure the liquidity decreases from the liquid, electronic trading venues of equities to high yield (HY) bonds traded by phone and Bloomberg IB chat messaging, to loans which are almost traded "by appointment only". In most investment banks and brokers, the different layers of the capital structure are often traded by teams sitting at different locations on the trading floor. Fortunately, this segregation of views and information provides trading opportunities for hedge funds. Integrated desks, trading expertly all instruments of a particular name in a synchronized manner are rare. If you are reading this book, you are probably conversant with equities and perhaps corporate bonds, but it is worth recapping their important qualities for hedge fund trading. In particular, I will dwell on trading corporate loans as it is a relatively murky, opaque market for most outsiders.

3.4.1 *Equities*

Equities are the most widely traded and liquid corporate instruments and commonly employed by hedge funds in a long/short portfolio format to hedge out systemic market risk. Indeed, the equity investment philosophy of legendary hedge fund manager Julian Robertson was to "find the 200 [best companies in the World] and go long and invest in them and find the 200 worst companies in the world and go short". Although portfolio sizes and equity selection processes vary hugely, this sentiment forms the essence of long/short equity (L/S equity) hedge fund investing.

Equities form the base of the capital structure and are more volatile and riskier than company debt. From a theoretical perspective they are a call option on the firm value where the option strike value is the level of company debt (Appx. B.7). If the company value falls too low, the equity becomes worthless and the debt holders assume control of the company. If the company value rises, then the equity holders reap the increase in value.

The most common form of equities are ordinary shares that confer voting rights. These voting rights are often used by so-called activist hedge funds (e.g., TCI, Elliott etc.) to pressure company management into following their plans to "unlock" value and increase the share price. Other types of shares exist but are less frequently traded. These include preference shares which have priority of payment over ordinary shares and sometimes have different voting rights. A widely traded preference share is VW prefs which are sometimes traded as a reversion pair-trade versus the VW ords. Also, different ordinary share classes can exist with various voting rights and these can be used by some shareholders to retain overall control of the company. Viacom and even Google/Alphabet are examples. One should be aware of such structures when investing.

Shares can be simultaneously listed on different global exchanges. In principle, arbitrage trading should keep these different listings in line but some like the Carnival US and London line (CCL US and CCL LN) are traded by hedge funds due to the frequent size of mis-pricings, low trading cost and high mean reversion. American depositary receipts (ADRs) are also a large market where foreign companies can effectively list their foreign listed shares on US exchanges and can be used for arbitrage trades.

Most hedge funds invest in liquid equities that are listed on major exchanges and can these days be traded electronically across different global venues (NYSE, Nasdaq, Euronext etc.). There is price visibility and liquidity can be clearly monitored. If equities are unlisted their valuation is often established by auditors or worse, a dubious "last historic trade" pricing rather than a proper mark-to-market method. This can lead to great subjectivity and price manipulation. If a hedge fund has a dominant position in the equity there is always the possibility of mismarking positions to smooth out P&L. Regrettably, there is frequently a "ratchet" effect where price up moves are taken at convenient moments while down moves are ignored until better days arrive or, as numerous hedge fund scandals attest, never.

I have worked on funds that have invested in obscure, unlisted emerging market investments that include opaque Chinese gold mining companies which are hard to pinpoint on the map. These are virtually impossible to value, especially when nobody in the office can remember why the previous manager bought the equities. Often these unlisted equities seem great investments in bullish markets but in bearish markets, or when the underlying has corporate problems, exiting the investments in a timely manner is virtually impossible. If there is a mismatch between the liquidity of the fund and the equity holdings, this can prove a problem for investors and "gating" may result. Recently, in the UK, several long only retail funds (such as Neil Woodford in 2019) seeking small company alpha, have fallen foul of these liquidity problems when numerous investors have wished to redeem.

Finally, if like Mr Robertson, you want to adopt a short position you must first remember to borrow the equity and reluctantly pay the borrow interest. The lenders of the equities are large institutions like banks, insurers and traditional fund managers, who are naturally long the equities. They participate in securities lending to enhance portfolio returns by being paid the stock loan fees. Your broker generally provides a screen with all the borrow costs and sizes available. Most equities are classified as *general collateral* (GC) with standardised low rates. However, some highly shorted or smaller stocks become so-called "hard to borrow" or non-GC and either demand a much higher rate or become unavailable to borrow. For example, Lufthansa in 2021 was quoted at 15% per annum due to the high demand and Wirecard, plunging to bankruptcy in 2020, became unborrowable.

Many weighty financial tomes have been written on theoretical methods for equity valuation. Unfortunately, none are entirely satisfactory and true objective valuation remains elusive. Equities are the most speculative part of the capital structure, and their price is determined not on any fully rational basis but instead by Mr Market. Their valuation is subjective and purely a matter of supply and demand. However, if we want some theoretical benchmark then there exists a range of models. The most basic equity valuation model is the *Gordon growth model* developed in 1959. It essentially values an equity price today as the discounted future value of all the expected dividends of the company (Appx. B.1). Obviously, this is an oversimplification and runs into numerous problems with dividendless growth stocks and low interest rates. However, the fact is that it represents a fundamental starting point for absolute equity valuation. Many more modern equity valuation models used by investment managers are simply variations of Mr Gordon's methodology or based on component-based approaches using the balance sheet and various additional measures such as EBITDA, free cashflow etc.

3.4.2 *Corporate bonds*

Corporate bonds are usually senior unsecured debt which comprise the middle of the capital structure, sandwiched between the equity tranche and senior secured loans. They are generally less volatile than equity, pay a coupon and aim to redeem investors capital on a scheduled maturity date. Electronic platforms exist for certain liquid bond issues, but these are usually for small sizes and often destined for retail investors. For the best pricing and institutional sizes, the corporate bond markets still remain a predominantly OTC market controlled by a handful of major brokers and investment banks which provide liquidity. In the bazaar of high yield bonds, the occasional haggling with vendors is still commonplace.

As soon as anybody starts talking about bonds, you remark that they never talk about prices but instead yields. The next thing you remark is that the person confidently talking about yields does not probably really know what a bond yield is and, most likely cannot give you even a remotely imprecise definition of one. In fact, there are several different kinds of yield but the most widely used is the *yield to maturity* (YTM). This is the effective rate of return on your investment if you buy the bond and hold on to maturity. YTM is a mathematically derived value based on the current price of the bond and bond's structure, that in the simplest sense includes all the periodic future coupons and the principal to be redeemed at the maturity by the bond's issuer. The YTM is the internal discount rate applied to all the future bond payments to give today's price and it can only be found through an iterative process (Appx B.4).

If you survey the bond markets for a given currency you quickly see that the bonds of corporate issuers, for various maturities, demonstrate different yield curves. The major variations are primarily due to different market credit risk perceptions. Although liquidity effects are important, in a relatively efficient market, the yield of a bond is comprised of two major components — underlying interest rates and a premium for credit risk. The spread of the yield curve above the "risk-free" government curve is the credit curve. It is a measure of the credit risk or risk of default of an issuer of a debt obligation. Typically, the curve is concave, and investors will require a higher premium to hold a bond for longer (Fig. 3.6). However, this is not always the case since some speculative bonds, close to default, have a high probability of default in the near term. This leads to inverted term structures since if the company survives the near term, then maybe there will be future improvements in credit quality.

In practice, the convention for the "riskless" credit curve is taken as the market swap or LIBOR curve. The use of the swap curve and not the government bond or Treasury curve is a hangover from the origins of the asset swap market. The interbank swap curve is traditionally viewed as an

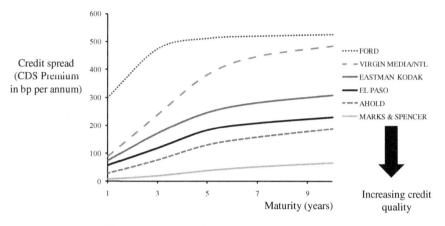

Figure 3.6:   Example of corporate credit curves.

AA rated bank curve and is obviously not entirely risk-free since we have seen in the *credit crisis* (2008) that the major banks themselves are not riskless and have spread curves with significant volatility. Perhaps by using risk management principles such as mark-to-market margining, the swap curve is a good enough proxy for a "risk-free" curve. The credit spread above LIBOR as we shall see for most debt issuers is approximately equal to the *credit default swap* (CDS) premium.

Thus, there are multiple confusing definitions for bond credit spreads, and we should be careful in what we are presented with. If for example a 5-year USD Xerox bond is said to yield US Treasuries + 180 bp (or "T + 180"), then the 180 bp is a measure of the credit risk above the USD Treasury curve. But the swap curve might lie 60 bp above the Treasury curve and thus the bond might be quoted as LIBOR + 120 bp (or "L + 120"). There are numerous other definitions of spread such as the asset swap spread, the I-spread and the Z-spread and that is just for bonds with well-defined maturities and no call features. The mathematics are subtly different. For example, the I-spread is the bond yield minus the underlying interpolated rate of the swap curve and the Z-spread is the amount of spread that must be added to the zero curve (not the swap curve) to correctly price the bond. Market participants are very careless about what spread they are quoting and salespeople often do not know the differences, simply spouting the number that their own trader has just told them. One must remember to be very careful when trading just off a spread rather than a price.

Depending on the credit quality of the issuer and their positions in the bonds in the corporate and capital structure, bonds are assigned a credit rating by the rating agencies. The triopoly of leading rating agencies are Standard & Poor's, Moody's and Fitch which use fairly similar rating scales. If we consider S&P/Moody's ratings, then AAA/Aaa is the highest rating and CCC /Caa2 are the lowest ratings. Anything below this and the company is unfortunately in various technical stages of default. The rating agency scale bifurcates the bond world into *investment grade* or IG (AAA/Aaa to BBB/Baa3) and *high yield* or HY (BB+/Ba1) and below. Although this bifurcation is entirely artificial it does lead to different market behaviour and norms. IG and HY are often traded by different traders in banks and brokers, investment guidelines often feature limits imposed on IG/HY and there are credit indices and ETFs that are exclusively one or the other. Sometimes this can lead to awkward investor reactions in stress situations. For example, once I launched a CDO with investment grade collateral, some of which was slightly downgraded. The Japanese investors that bought the mezzanine Baa3 tranche, due to their investment restrictions, were forced to immediately sell the notes at a loss, when the agency downgraded their tranche to Ba1. Eventually the notes would have redeemed at par.

Most bonds are fixed rate with a periodic coupon paid annually or semi-annually. A proportion however are floaters or *floating rate notes* (FRNs) that pay a variable coupon (usually based on LIBOR) plus a fixed spread (Appx. B.5). Importantly for trading, fixed rate bond prices are subject to variations of government interest rates and not just credit quality. Although bonds "pull to par" (100%) towards their maturity date, in the interim higher/lower interest rates produce lower/higher prices. The sensitivity of a fixed rate bond to rate moves is expressed as duration or DV01 (the delta price movement of the bond for a 1 bp parallel move in rates across the current interest rate curve). Thus, unless you specifically seek exposure to rates for carry and a macro view, fixed rate bond portfolios should be hedged by shorting treasuries of a similar duration or using fixed/floating interest rate swaps. Using swaps to hedge the interest rate risk in bond portfolios led to the creation of asset swaps.

The *asset swap* market was the precursor to the *credit derivative swap* (CDS) market. Asset swaps provided the benchmark credit pricing for the CDS market and when the CDS market was still a toddler, cash prices drove CDS prices. An asset swap allows an investor to swap a fixed rate bond into a floating rate instrument, removing the interest rate risk.

This creates a LIBOR plus spread instrument that, like a floating rate note, is pure credit risk. Typically, the underlying bond plus swap are sold together as an asset swap package (Appx. B.6). The creation of the asset swap market drove transparency in credit pricing as the spread of the asset swap above LIBOR was indicative of the credit risk premium. Asset swaps allowed investors to arbitrage different credit risks between different markets. For example, an illiquid bond of an issuer trading in Euro might be cheaper when swapped into USD than the regular USD denominated asset of the issuer. This created more efficiency for asset pricing and allowed spread to become the proxy for credit risk.

3.4.3 *Credit default swaps*

The *credit default swap* (CDS) market has exploded since its creation in the mid-1990s. According to a 2019 analysis by ISDA the gross outstanding notional in 2021 was $9.4tr and that almost 1300 unique credits had been traded with a significant core of around 500 names. HY names represented about 20% of IG contracts. The leading single names traded in that year ranged from ArcelorMittal and UniCredit to the sovereigns like Brazil and Turkey. Often the leading names traded in each year are a function of the popular credit concerns of the time. In 2019 Italian bank solvency and Brazil and Turkey political and economic issues were frequent headlines.

The basic methodology for CDS is standardised and well defined. In a plain vanilla CDS, one counterparty (the protection buyer) pays a spread or premium to the other counterparty (the protection seller) for credit protection on a particular credit (the reference entity). In the event of a credit default or *credit event* associated with the reference entity, the protection seller will pay 100% cash to the buyer who will then deliver a par nominal amount of the defaulted underlying asset to the seller. The premium payments will then cease, and the swap will terminate (Fig. 3.7). The CDS thus superficially appears as a form of insurance and indeed many specialised CDS are actually traded in the form of insurance contracts, particularly with insurance counterparties. In the settlement process, the buyer, assuming he originally purchased the asset at close to par 100%, will be compensated for any drop in the value of the asset on a credit event.

Instead of physical settlement and delivery of a reference obligation on a credit event, cash settlement became more common as less CDS users were looking for a direct cash hedge. The seller pays to the buyer

(a) Before a credit event

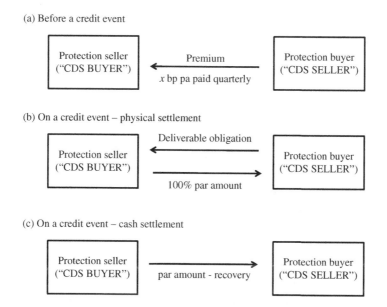

(b) On a credit event – physical settlement

(c) On a credit event – cash settlement

Figure 3.7: How a credit default swap works.

100% minus the recovery rate or final price of the relevant reference obligation. This final price is determined by a post credit event poll of a group of well-known dealers using an ISDA specified process. This process was standardised and enhanced with the ISDA 2009 Big Bang Protocol. The type of asset that can be delivered or used as reference obligation is well documented. Importantly, the standard CDS references senior unsecured debt of any major currency.

A credit event, as currently traded by the market, is actually wider in scope than a pure default or bankruptcy. Under the ISDA defined events, credit events include bankruptcy, failure to pay, restructuring, obligation default, obligation acceleration and for sovereigns, repudiation/moratorium (Appx. B.9). Bankruptcy, failure to pay and restructuring are the key credit events used in CDS. Bankruptcy and failure to pay are always pretty clear and undisputed. Restructuring is the most contentious and there is always some debate as to whether a company restructuring constitutes a credit event. The general idea is to capture attempts by the issuer into deteriorating the economic terms of the debt.

Some companies (like General Motors Acceptance Corp (GMAC) with subsidiary Rescap) are cunning and manage to "strong arm" investors into voluntarily accepting a bond tender or exchange and modify the bond terms without triggering a restructuring credit event if market conditions permit. Other shenanigans around credit events occur particularly when credit events are manufactured or avoided by creative financing. A 2018 legal case involved Blackstone's GSO Partners who persuaded homebuilder Hovnanian to default on part of its debt to trigger a credit event as part of an agreement to lend new money to struggling Hovnanian. However, at the same time GSO held a credit default swap position referencing Hovnanian that paid out on the default and the profits of which potentially contributed to the money lent to Hovnanian. This canny move caused other CDS market participants to lose money on their CDS positions. The regulators are, as always, questioning whether exploiting loopholes in CDS contracts in this way constitutes market manipulation.

The most liquid contract traded is the 5-year maturity although 3, 7 and 10 years are also fairly liquid. As with futures, market CDS contracts roll every 3 months (generally the 20th of March, June, September and December). In 2009 the Standard North American Corporates (SNAC) protocol was introduced which modified the standard CDS terms. Importantly the contractual spread became fixed at 100 bp for investment grade and 500 bp for high yield. This meant that an upfront payment is required in the CDS.

Apart from single name corporate CDS, CDS can be offered on other underlying credit assets such as loans, ABS and CDOs. Credit index products are very popular with each index containing a diversified, equally weighted basket of corporates. In Europe and Asia there are the iTraxx indices. The most popular are the iTraxx Europe containing 125 entities and the iTraxx crossover (XOVER) with 75 sub investment grade corporates. In the US the two main indices are the CDX IG (investment grade) with again 125 issuers and the CDX HY (high yield). The CDS index constituents are reviewed every 6 months and replaced with the most liquidly traded names, so that the index remains current. In addition to these indices, some sector indices and sovereign indices are available and quoted by dealers.

The most widely used model for valuation of credit default swaps is the reduced form model (Appx. B.8). In a reduced form model or catastrophe model, default is triggered by a random process and hence a sudden catastrophe. Technically, the time of default is modelled using a Poisson probability distribution that is good at describing the random occurrences of events. Thus, a credit event is mathematically described by the "first arrival time" of an event in a random Poisson process with a so-called intensity or hazard rate. The hazard rate is just the probability of default over a given period.

This modelling approach might seem somewhat unrealistic, but the simplicity is a great advantage for estimating market parameters. The model is reduced to essentially just two parameters — (i) the hazard rate or probability of default over a given period and (ii) the expected loss should a default occur. If a market standard recovery rate is used, then the credit spread is just approximately the hazard rate multiplied by 100% minus the recovery rate. Thus, the hazard rate is derivable directly from the CDS spread. In practice, valuation of CDS is slightly more complicated since we must consider the maturity term structure of credit spreads and interest rates in valuation. This requires building hazard rate curves using forward hazard rates and use of interest rate zero curves. Fortunately, the valuation of a credit default swap, not far out of the money, is fairly insensitive to the actual recovery rate assumption used.

3.4.4 *Leveraged loans*

For many years I had my eye on the juicy leveraged loan market looking for an opportunity to invest. In the early 2000s, my team became one of London's largest purchasers of CLOs (collateralised loan obligation) for collateral in structured credit and principal finance transactions but investing in the underlying leveraged loans themselves was technical and highly specialised. The secured leveraged loan world presented many key advantages over the unsecured regular bond world. The pricing was rich relative to bonds, recovery rates were higher, and you sat in a dominant controlling position at the top of the capital structure.

Moreover, the market was dominated, particularly in Europe, by syndicates of banks and they shunned outsiders in their exclusive lending club. The issuers and private equity sponsors did not relish the thought of more speculative hedge funds entering their tightly controlled market, which was essentially by invitation only. CLOs and some dedicated loan funds were allowed since they provided some liquidity and were essentially buy and hold investors with term funding (CLOs issue their own bonds and thus have their own stable capital structure).

This club-like nature of the leveraged loan market provided a great benefit. There was a stickiness to prices, and they were super stable. In fact, loan prices rarely moved from par except in the event of a great credit deterioration of the borrower. Under those circumstances the club of lenders just usually renegotiated things behind the scenes in a preferential manner to themselves, taking full advantage of the borrower's distress. Some loan indices existed but even under the direst economic macro scenarios, when other markets were having heart attacks, they barely budged. For a hedge fund they seemed ostensibly the perfect carry trade. The price would never move much, and you could just clip coupons. Plus, the disparity of economics between the loans and the bog-standard unsecured bonds meant that arbitrage opportunities abounded.

There was, however, a couple of major practical barriers to entering this market. Firstly, physically buying a loan required reams of paperwork and admin over buying a conventional liquid bond. It was as tiresome as buying a house. Secondly, no prime brokers would provide leverage and no repo market existed so cash purchases only. Who wanted to spend several weeks doing paperwork, hand over $5m cash for $5m of un-leverageable loans paying L + 200 bp? Lastly, the leverage loan club was by appointment only. You had to ingratiate yourself with the private equity sponsors, bank syndicates and trading desks and sometimes even the issuer themselves to get a piece of the action. This was the anti-thesis of an efficient electronic market.

Private equity sponsors of LBOs were particularly tricky since you had to portray you were a stable buy and hold investor and would not "flip" their deal within several minutes of being allocated. Getting on the syndicate lists for new issues was also a problem since you wanted an allocation and an invite to those initial bank presentations and access to the original deal info (which was held on a specialised electronic platform) and was for only those "worthy" enough. Strangely, after a deal was trading secondary nobody could re-find those presentations and the ephemeral representations made within.

The admin and leverage issues were solved in around 2003–2004 when several of the major investment banks created *total return swap* (TRS) platforms. You bought the loan, they did the tedious admin and warehoused for you. The banks charged an exorbitant premium but leverage was suitably high. The loan arbitrage was then playable.

The most senior loan tranches are usually *term loan* A and B/C (TL A, TL B/C). TL A is amortising and less interesting for hedge funds due to the awkward cashflow and maturity schedules. Typically, TL B/C are bullet loans with fixed maturity and trade as a combo of the B and C tranches. Essentially, all these loans are senior secured and pari-passu. A typical TL

B/C might pay LIBOR plus 150–275 bp depending on the issuer quality and the market demand on issuance.

Below these most senior tranches in the capital structure sometimes lies one or more mezzanine tranches or "mezz". These tranches have less security but offer a much higher coupon (LIBOR + 300–650 bp). Paradoxically, often these are less interesting for hedge funds to purchase since the leverage multiple that can be provided by TRS providers is lower, funding cost higher and secondary liquidity very low or nigh impossible.

Lastly, as an almost equity substitute, in some particularly aggressive LBO refinancings, zero coupon *payment in kind* (PIK) notes or other highly subordinated loans are offered. These PIK notes provide very high *internal rates of return* (IRRs) but have potentially very low recoveries on the event of a default. If they are a replacement for true equity by LBO sponsors, then any investor should look closely at ongoing alignment of interests between debt holders and true equity holders.

There are other major idiosyncrasies within the loan market which are somewhat surprising for the uninitiated. An astonishing feature is that the high yield loan market has almost universal pricing. If a company is of sufficient standing in the high yield space to bring a new loan deal, then it gets more or less the market standard pricing whatever the credit worthiness or credit rating of the borrower.

Also, when you agree to buy a house, sometimes at the last minute you can get "gazumped" as the seller changes the price on you due to high demand as other buyers step forward. Annoying, but little you can do if you want to buy the house. Something a bit similar happens in the loan market although with the added disadvantage that it is bad form to refuse to buy. If you put in your order to buy and the loan borrower feels the new issue is hot and looking over-subscribed, he can "flex" or slash the coupon at the last minute. For example, the loan might be coming at L + 250 bp, you have put in your order for $10m and at the last minute you get flexed down to L + 225 bp.

All loans are callable in the sense that they can be repaid early. Usually there is a prepayment fee on a predetermined sliding maturity scale, say initially 2% in year 1 and then 1% for year 2 etc. This means that there is effectively little upside price appreciation on loans and the economics lie mainly in the interest payments or carry. The fact that a lender can call the loan at any time is mildly annoying but there is worse which is so-called "flexing". Flexing is a repricing when you are holding the loan — a bad practice that has become even worse in the US since the start of the 2020s. The lender might feel he could get a better deal by refinancing and thus contacts the arranger and "forces" a tighter loan spread on lenders. Lenders reluctantly probably accept since they have little alternative if market conditions present few other fruitful investments. Also, they have done the credit analysis and probably suffered internal approval processes to invest in the credit.

The ratio of *covenant lite* or "cov-lite" loans have increased over the years and is also a function of tight credit spreads and excess market liquidity. In a cov-lite loan many of the covenants existing in traditional loans are reduced to the extent that they resemble bond type covenants. Nasty, not a game changer, but could unscientifically lead, in my view, to more hard defaults and lower recovery rates. Any restructuring for senior secured lenders could be delayed by softer covenants, resulting in "zombie" companies limping on before a final hard default. Official loss stats show this might be the case since post 2010 covenant lite loans have experienced an average recovery of around 50–60% and all bank loans 85–90%. However, the jury is still out since the overall defaulted cov-lite sample size is small.

An important aspect of leveraged loans which I discovered was the difference between public and private information. If you are a bond or equity holder you have visibility of the company fundamentals through publicly available information such as accounts, statements and news articles etc. However, loan holders have access to so-called private information provided to them by the company. This may include management accounts, monthly covenant tests and waivers for asset purchases/disposals etc. Loan holders have private information that is often in advance or exceeds that of bond and shareholders. The rules around use of this "inside" information are fairly strict but in my opinion, liberally interpreted by those who should know better and could benefit most from it. In principle you cannot trade public bonds and equities whilst being private. Organisations should have Chinese walls but often it is the same trader simply changing his hat from public to private and vice versa. Often, I would ring a desk at a major bank which traded loans and bonds and he would say, "sorry Rich I can't discuss that since I am private now" and I would say, "but last week you were public" and he would say, "ah but my colleague (sitting next to him) is still public so ask him" and the following week they would have changed roles. It was difficult to keep track. Bizarre, the leveraged loan market.

At the first bank meetings I attended in 2003–2004 I was among the "newbie" hedge fund managers. Everyone else in the room worked for big banks and the hedge funds were the pariahs. But amongst hedge funds we were perhaps innovators or trailblazers. The luxury of being one of the few hedge funds actively trading leveraged loans was however short lived. As the banks actively marketed their TRS platforms, a multitude of hedge fund managers joined the party. By 2007 on a major rental car LBO, I remarked that it was standing room only at the bank meeting as all the hedge funds squeezed inside the hall. The game was virtually over. The last gasp of the market before the credit crisis presented a final opportunity of flipping loans. As one of the first entrants we were given priority by bank syndicates and allocated large chunks at par of terrible cov-lite loans that were massively oversubscribed. Often 5 minutes after the allocation call, the bank would phone you back and say we have a buyer at 102 and you would flip the garbage loan to another hedge fund. This was the only bright spot in a nice cozy carry market that was being destroyed. The major downside of all the new market participants was that prices were no longer sticky. The credit crisis would provide an unprecedented amount of loan market volatility as all the TRS platforms and hedge funds were simultaneously shut down as banks panicked about their own survival.

3.5 Leverage and Financing

All hedge fund strategies require leverage. The primary reason is to achieve return on capital targets for trades. For example, if a merger arbitrage trade has 4% premium on an unleveraged basis it is not that appealing. If it can be leveraged $5\times$, then a 20% gross return on capital becomes more attractive.

All leverage arrangements have an initial margin that is posted, and a subsequent margin based on the change of mark-to-market. Importantly, it is the leverage provider that determines the mark-to-market. Although it should be objectively valued, in times of crisis and high volatility, portfolio pricing becomes more subjective and this is a nasty feature of bank leverage. As an extreme cautionary tale, I had a friend who ran an *asset backed securities* (ABS) fund with all the assets rated AAA. The average price of these assets had never changed for over a decade from par (100%) so they worked on the optimistic assumption (as did their financing bank) that they could be leveraged 50× with little risk. However, when the first rumblings of the credit crisis started in 2007, their friendly financing bank decided from one day to the next to mark the portfolio down to 98% — even though no bonds had traded in the market to justify the price move. Several hundred million of investors' money was vapourised instantaneously as the greedy financing bank seized the bonds. Unfortunately, there was little the fund manager could do in the time available to legally oppose the move.

Leverage providers also charge a financing rate based on a floating rate such as LIBOR plus a financing spread. Although it is of little consequence when trading high volatility equities, this spread is crucial in determining the profitability of tight arbitrage trades in credit and fixed income. An important job of your middle office is monitoring financing costs to ensure all those arbitrage profits are not inadvertently sucked away as financing rates change.

The second major reason for employing leverage is that it allows hedge funds to preserve cash for deployment in other trades and for margin calls. If a trade moves against you, then mark-to-market changes must be financed from your cash hoard. Preserving cash can quickly become an obsession.

Some instruments have built in leverage and do not require 3rd party leverage providers. Buying options, particularly OTM options, provides leverage since only a small premium is paid relative to the exposure gained when underlying moves into the money. Futures contracts are exchange traded and the effective leverage is provided by the exchange. There is just a tick value and an effective notional for each contract. Initial margins are small but there is subsequent mark-to-market margining. In major market crises when everything else grinds to a halt, futures and the commodity trading advisors (CTAs) that trade them enjoy continued liquidity.

The three main financing routes for a hedge fund are prime brokers (PBs), repo and TRS. The method chosen by the fund manager is dependent on the asset to be financed, leverage required and financing rate.

3.5.1 *Prime brokers*

Virtually every hedge fund has a PB and larger funds may have multiple PBs. The leading PBs are the US investment banks such as Morgan

Stanley, JP Morgan, Goldman Sachs and BofA and some European banks such as Barclays, CS, UBS and BNP. Since the Bernie Madoff scandal and the credit crisis, the leading PBs will not take on board smaller funds, so a second tier of PBs has evolved. The rule of thumb of the larger PBs used to be that if they can't "make" 250k per annum off you, they have little interest.

The top tier of PBs provide alongside leverage and financing a whole host of other services. These range from access to different sales and trading desks, in-house analysts a phone call away to business help such as capital introduction and even finding you a snazzy Mayfair office. Capital introduction ability is often promised to get you "on-board", but the scope varies considerably. Usually, it involves scheduled events and conferences or as an unpaid matchmaker between investors and funds.

Although inter-broker margins for products such as CDS are fairly standardised through clearing platforms such as ICE (Intercontinental Exchange), there is unfortunately no market standard for hedge funds. There exists a large variation in margins offered by PBs. The traditional approach is to margin and finance on an individual trade basis with clearly defined margining grids for different assets with offsets for hedges. Margins between conservative and aggressive providers can vary considerably. On a diversified portfolio basis or with offsetting risks, margins are reduced and sometimes on a bespoke basis.

Grid margining approaches have been gradually replaced by proprietary internal models that consider the entire client portfolio and the effect of off-setting trades and diversification. These are risk-simulations or similar to *value-at-risk* (VaR) approaches and provide a more holistic approach to risk. One margin number is produced for the entire portfolio. Usually, this approach yields a much lower margin than the grid approach. Prior to the credit crisis, the PBs using this more sophisticated approach managed to capture significant market share through their more aggressive margining. However, as the crisis continued, they began to question their model assumptions. As their credit officers took control, many PBs just panicked and unilaterally multiplied their supposedly sophisticated margin model output by a suitable large number plucked out of thin air.

PBs can finance portfolios on a gross or net basis. A net basis is preferable since the hedge fund pays LIBOR plus a financing spread on the net assets, which is essentially the sum of the longs and the shorts. Through careful use of different financing arrangements, for example financing long bonds and short hedge treasuries, it is possible to bring financing costs right down. This optimisation is not good for the PB since they make little money off the financing business. As with someone who always pays off their credit card early, you become a bad client.

3.5.2 *Repo market*

A second financing route is the repo market which provides very keen margin and financing rates for government and corporate bonds. As a hedge fund you establish repo facilities with different banks and negotiate rates with their repo traders. The repo buyer receives securities as collateral and the seller forward repurchases. The market standard term is overnight repo but depending on documentation there can be term or open repos.

The repo market was always seen as a stable feature of the institutional financing system but during the credit crisis, the market closed down. Corporate repos shut down first, to later be followed even by Treasury repos. This was a shock to all market participants and exposed a massive loophole in the standardised overnight repo agreements. Imagine being told from one day to the next that your repo provider was not going to finance all your bond positions? You phone round all the other houses and find they are also shutting and "apologies but will not accept any more positions". The only option left, since you do not have the cash to 100% fund your bond positions, is to sell the positions in the open market. You have gone from 1% margin on all those basis positions to 100% in a day. Funnily enough, every other hedge fund has the same problem and is selling too. Ironically, you have to sell to the same handful of banks that would not finance your positions. A nightmare situation that hopefully will never arise again.

3.5.3 *Total return swaps*

A third financing mechanism is the use of *total return swaps* (TRS). Many real and synthetic assets can be financed using OTC TRS with banks. In a TRS the asset is purchased by the hedge fund and held on the banks' balance sheet or a suitable financing vehicle. The fund pays an upfront collateral and funding leg of LIBOR plus spread and receives/pays the total return of the asset. The total return is usually comprised of carry and mark-to-market gains/losses. I have seen TRS applied to everything from portfolios of asset backed securities and novel equity indices to baskets of hedge funds.

Purchasing leveraged loans was notoriously difficult for hedge funds. Buying loans required heaps of tedious paperwork and admin and they had to be 100% cash financed. The leading banks developed around 2003–2004 TRS platforms that allowed easy leveraged loan trading. Initial margins allowed good leverage and despite high funding spreads, large return on capital (ROC) could be achieved for secured debt risk. For example, NTL (now Virgin Media) TL B loans could be margined at 5–6%. Since they paid a spread of 212 bp and financing was 45–50 bp, the ROC was over 25%. A great carry trade if prices remained stable.

3.6 Trading Across the Capital Structure

By combining equities, bonds and loans and their derivatives across the capital structure of one or more companies we can construct a huge range of relative value or arbitrage trades (Table 3.2). These range from long/short equity and long/short debt to credit curve trades, basis trades and debt versus equity. With these different trades in the "toolkit" and suitable leverage, we can also exploit numerous different event-driven and special situation trades. In the following sections, several examples of actual corporate trades and a dissection of the pros and cons of the different approaches are presented.

Table 3.2:   Types of corporate relative value and special sits trades.

Long/Short Equity	Equity vs. Equity	Relative value or special sit between different equities
Long/Short Credit	Bond vs. Bond CDS vs. CDS	Relative value or special sit between different credits or different instruments
Curve Trades	Steepers and Flatteners	Benefit from dislocated shape of credit curves
Basis Trades	Cash Bond vs. CDS	Arbitrage the negative or positive basis between cash and CDS
Loan Arbitrage	Cash Loan vs. CDS LCDS vs. CDS	Buy cash loans and hedge default risk with cheap secured or unsecured protection
Capital Structure Arbitrage	Bond or CDS vs. Equity	Trade debt against equity in relative value or special sits
Distressed Credit	Long Bond or Loan	Benefit from distressed situations and recovery plays

3.7 Capital Structure Trades

In the early 2000s, with the creation of the credit derivatives market, people started to think how to trade across the corporate capital structure. Early credit pricing models like the stochastic firm value model became more prevalent even though they proved mostly useless for calculating and trading credit spreads (Appx. B.7). These firm values models, where default occurred if the company firm value fell below a debt strike value, suggested that credit could be priced as some form of option on the equity price. Variants of the Black–Scholes model were used. For high yield names, equity value was closely linked to credit spreads and theoretical deltas could be predicted. Usually, for traders the delta of a position is its price or value sensitivity to a change in the underlying asset price. In this case the deltas would be represented as a 1% increase/decrease of the equity price leading to a delta% decrease/increase in the credit spread. In principle these could be directly tradable via liquid CDS.

This pseudo-model trading was a laudable goal but quickly became discredited in practice as theoretical models provided bad deltas for trading. The models instead became widely used in credit risk management where they could confirm the obvious — the falling share price of a leveraged company would coincide with increasing spreads and eventually possible bankruptcy. Traders themselves sensibly put the models back in the draw and derived empirical deltas from actual observed data. There were many reasons for the failure of the models but the most important one was the story behind the company and not just the correlated moves in the credit and equity. Trading debt versus equity became an art form with many subjective factors to consider.

Observation showed that companies' equity and debt prices tended to move in a quasi-stable, correlated fashion for a time until events conspired to move them to a new regime. The level of spreads had a sweet spot for these correlations of around 100–600 bp. Below this range, debt became relatively uncorrelated to equities. Above this, the company was in a volatile unpredictable region possibly leading to a terminal death spiral.

Figures 3.8 and 3.9 show some examples for Delphi (the largest US auto parts manufacturer that filed for bankruptcy in 2005) and AT&T (the telco) of equity prices and spreads and how they are negatively correlated to a certain extent through time. If we take another example, Sprint

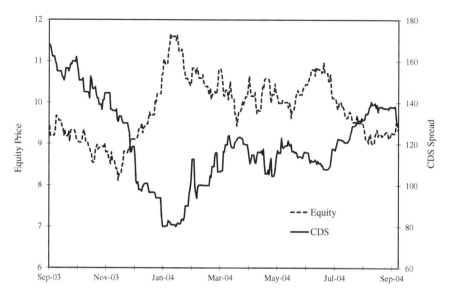

Figure 3.8: US autopart maker Delphi's equity price and 5Y CDS spread.

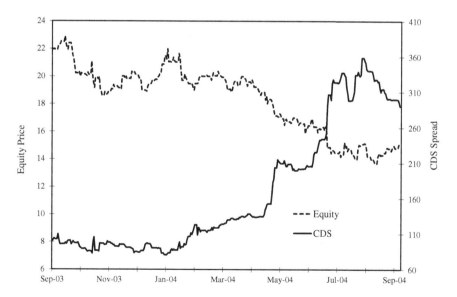

Figure 3.9: Telecom company AT&T's equity price and 5Y CDS spread.

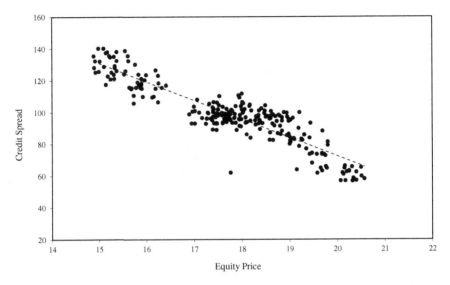

Figure 3.10:   US telecom company Sprint's 5Y CDS credit spread vs. equity price.

(another telco) and scatter plot the credit spread versus equity we can see for the period in question they follow a negatively well correlated "cloud" (Fig. 3.10). By executing trades at the extremity of the cloud we can hope to benefit from mean reversion back to the trend.

But how do you actually trade this mean reversion? Well, if for example the credit spread is too high relative to the recent line of best fit, we can sell protection via CDS and "hedge" by shorting a delta amount of equity estimated from the line of best fit. As the trade reverts, we can unwind the CDS, cover the short position and crystallise a profit.

A widely traded example was Corus, a UK steelmaker (now Tata) shown in Fig. 3.11. The credit news-flow was good, and Corus was deleveraging as planned. The equity had rallied, and the credit was visibly lagging by around 75–100 bp. By shorting a suitable low delta of Corus equity and selling €5m of 5-year credit protection at over 550 bp, around 80 bp of credit compression could be captured over the trade period of one month together with one month of carry.

3.7.1 *Execution, carry and narrative*

There were several key points to make these trades a success. Firstly, great execution was required on the CDS leg. During the "golden age" of

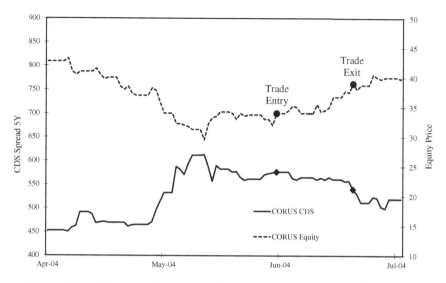

Figure 3.11: UK steelmaker Corus's debt/equity trade with entry and exit levels.

capital structure arb preceding the credit crisis (2008), it was actually possible by asking several friendly brokers and having great patience to pay virtually zero bid/offer for most liquid credits. For example, in the major liquid autos (Ford and GM), quoted spreads were 1–2 bp and by approaching several dealers it was possible to slot around $100m with little or no cost intraday.

Secondly, it was always best to have a positive carry trade by selling credit protection versus shorting equities. The reason for this (as we will detail shortly) was that things might not go as planned and positive carry was very helpful in this regard. The trade might not revert quickly enough or might go horribly wrong, and it was always beneficial to be able to have the luxury to blindly sit in the trade and let positive carry bail you out.

Capital structure trades were great in the period 2000–2005 and then the regime started to change. Flaws were gradually found in the approach, which became evident, during the rise of the LBO in 2006–2007. In the couple of years before the credit crisis, a great LBO wave started as private equity companies took advantage of tight credit spreads, buoyant equity markets and easy fund-raising conditions to buy large, listed companies. During an LBO, the equity would rise as a buyout offer was made and the credit spread ballooned out as investors correctly predicted that

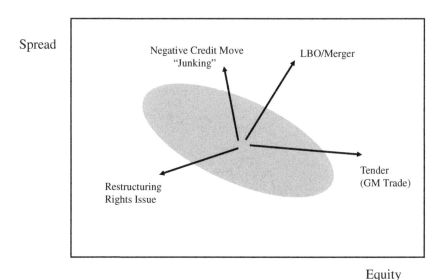

Figure 3.12:   The "flaws" of debt/equity trades.

the soon-to-be acquired target company would be re-leveraged to the eye-balls. Even a whiff of a rumoured LBO approach was enough to annihilate the nice long credit/short equity cap structure trade.

In fact, these problems were the tip of the iceberg for the simple debt/equity approach since special situations could impact the trade in numerous ways that had not been anticipated or experienced. Figure 3.12 shows a hypothetical spread versus equity chart. The perfect long debt/short equity positive carry approach was actually a beneficiary of the wave of restructuring and deleveraging in the high yield space when credit spreads tightened and would outperform equity prices. But there were other potential scenarios. LBO or leveraged mergers could increase the equity price and credit spreads. An unexpected negative credit move, such as "junking" by an agency, could cause a massive underperformance of credit. A tender, as in the infamous GM trade (below) would provoke a big jump in equities and the credit would not budge. Conditions had changed and the debt/equity landscape had become a minefield. The narrative for the trade became very important.

3.7.2 *The GM debacle*

The General Motors (GM) trade is worthy of a mention. Especially since it caused me and many in the market a great deal of pain. It was the final nail in the coffin for the standard positive carry approach. Everybody in the credit markets could see that GM's demise was inevitable. The writing was on the wall. It had high leverage, terrible sales, massive negative cashflow and cash was running short. Equity investors, as is often the case, seemed to be living in a different world from credit analysts. The equity price was very high and seemingly ignored the terrible fundamental outlook. So, in our view, it was a one-way trade. We shorted GM equity and sold credit protection on GMAC (General Motors Acceptance Corp). GMAC, the financial funding entity for all those cars, despite its high spread, was seen as a more credit worthy entity than General Motors itself and the high volume of bond issuance provided more liquid CDS. The predicted inevitability was that GM's equity would go to zero and GM would go bust within the next 12 months.

However, we did not account for a certain Kirk Kerkorian (1917–2015), an 80-something billionaire investor and one of the founders of Las Vegas who thought he could rescue GM in 2005. He tendered above market for GM's stock to double his stake to 8.8%. It rallied massively against us and we incurred a big loss. Then we realised that we were not the only ones who thought it was originally a great trade. Numerous prop desks and hedge funds had done the debt/equity trade and suddenly the trade proved over-crowded as everyone headed for the exit. The effect of everyone simultaneously cutting the trade and bailing out forced the GMAC CDS wider and more losses were incurred. Despite being down heavily in the trade we continued to believe in the fundamentals and stubbornly sat in it. It was positive carry so we wore the pain knowing that each day the carry would eat away at our loss. Eventually after 12 months of being in the hole we made a small (relative to the maximum mark-to-market loss) profit and took the trade off. It turned out that Mr Kerkorian later gave up on his equity stake and bailed out. Finally, in June 2009, GM, after racking up an eye watering loss of $81bn over 4 years, filed Chapter 11 bankruptcy. It was the biggest US manufacturing collapse in US history. You might think that in a rational world that would be the end of the GM story but in fact in 2010, GM re-emerged from bankruptcy to file at the time one of the world's largest IPOs. Today, GM's Chevy Silverado and GMC Sierra sales are beating Ford's F-Series.

3.7.3 *The Maytag short*

After the GM experience most hedge funds gave up on the cap structure arb trade but there were still opportunities if you worked hard enough.

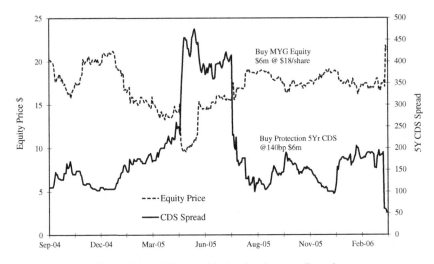

Figure 3.13:   Maytag debt/equity short credit trade.

The trade simply needed to be adapted to the specific event that might impact a company. It required a more detailed analysis of each individual company and potential catalysts to identify the optimum profile for each trade.

A good example was the Maytag (MYG) debt/equity trade based around an M&A event. Maytag was a domestic appliance manufacturer which was eventually acquired by Whirlpool (WHR) in Q2 2005 at $21 a share. The initial bid was however via an LBO from a private equity consortium. The CDS initially widened to 450 bp, the equities dipped and then moved towards $16. The second bid was announced by the more credit worthy Whirlpool for a higher $21 and the CDS tightened back towards 100 bp (Fig. 3.13).

However, considerable uncertainty existed due to anti-trust issues and credit and equity markets interpreted these problems differently. Our trade was to buy $6m MYG equity and hedge by buying $6m MYG credit protection via CDS. This was a negative carry trade, but the expectation was that a merger would be resolved within several months. The logic was as follows. If the WHR bid failed, then the LBO bid would succeed. The credit spread would widen to over 450 bp and the equity would fall slightly to $16. This would incur a very small loss. However, if the WHR deal succeeded, the MYG equity would rise to $21, and the credit would tighten to 50 bp. In the latter case there would be a large P&L gain. By Q1 2006 the WHR deal closed and a profit of over $600k was achieved.

3.8 Merger and LBO Trades

The fact that equity and credit market participants often interpret the probabilities and outcome of events differently can be exploited in many other ways. One of the problems of traditional merger arb is that after a deal is announced, the equities involved will jump, virtually instantaneously, close to their post-merger values.

Usually. the acquired company equity price jumps very close to the bid price which is usually 10–20% above the market value but can occasionally verge towards 100%. Bid premiums vary over time and in 2021, several UK companies such as Morrisons and Meggitt have incredibly seen premiums close to the upper end of this range. Sometimes, speculative rumours or inside information have been swirling around the market for some time and prior to the bid announcement the share price was already creeping upwards. Going back to Fig. 3.3, we can see for the average LBO, equity prices start to rise in the few days prior to a bid.

The acquirer, if it is a listed company, can be impacted positively or negatively by news of the acquisition depending on market conditions, whether the merger is viewed providing positive synergies (usually post-merger cost cutting) or the structure of the deal. Deals can be structured in terms of shares (of acquirer), "cash" or a mixture of both. In private equity deals there is no listed acquisition company. The private equity companies provide some cash and re-leverage the target company through debt acquisition usually via a syndicated loan.

Over the years there are some well-documented hedge funds that seem to have the exciting strategy of trading on obtaining inside information and profiting from the full jump in market value in true Gordon Gekko style. However, the reality is rather more banal. The majority of merger-based hedge funds trade the merger post-announcement and seek to profit from the much-reduced merger premiums.

Once the bid is announced, the difference between the bid or completion price and the market price becomes the new merger premium or discount. It represents the likelihood of the deal closing and the financing cost of holding the shares until the deal completes. Gradually, as the deal progresses towards completion and overcomes various obstacles the discount reduces. Low probability bids thus trade at a larger discount to the completion price. Even for "friendly" acquisitions there are many reasons deals don't close, from competition and anti-trust issues to financing problems and these can influence the probability of a deal closing.

Conversely, once a company is "in play" there is the possibility of additional higher bids from 3rd parties. Sometimes the merger discount is negative in anticipation of higher bids. Estimating which deals will close is a complex and skilled game.

Generally, the merger premium post-announcement is small at around 1–10% and thus, large positions sizes and leverage are required to achieve a good return on capital (ROC). If a deal fails to complete or breaks there will be a rapid decline in equity prices to around the pre-merger, pre-rumour price. The losses for the hedge fund can be substantial. Say for example a bid is made 20% above market, the acquired shares rise 15% to leave a merger discount of 5%. We would require 4× leverage to achieve a $4 \times 5\% = 20\%$ ROC if we ignore funding costs. If the deal breaks, the shares might tumble back down to the pre-bid price awarding the hedge fund a $4 \times 15\% = 60\%$ loss. Clearly it is risky business with high negative skew and one needs to carefully read the tea leaves. Table 3.3 shows a snapshot of a dozen European M&A trades in progress in 2021 with the current deal discount and the potential downside risk. In the buoyant market many hot deals are optimistically priced in anticipation of higher bids.

Many hedge funds have gone to the wall by badly selecting which M&A events to participate in. A high-profile example was the $1.3bn

Table 3.3:   Some European M&A deals in progress (2021).

	Bidder	Discount (%)	Downside (%)
Arrow Global	TDR	0.82	−25
CA Immobilien	Starwood	0.14	−17
Deutsche Wohnen	Vonovia	0.15	−21
Dialog Semiconductor	Renesas	0.24	−17
Gamesys Group	Bally's	1.31	−11
Euskaltel	masMovil	0.55	−12
John Laing	KKR	0.90	−21
WM Morrison	Fortress	−9.71	−36
Siltronic	Global Wafers	5.45	−18
SBanken	DNB	0.60	−26
Spire Health	Ramsay	−4.00	−23
Suez	Veolia	0.97	−27

Bailey Coates Cromwell Fund in 2005 which unfortunately had several trades go terribly wrong at the same time. Although many deals might have a high probability (>90%) of completing, this is often fully reflected in overall market pricing as many people scrutinise all news flow on the deal. Unless you have skill or an edge, the expected long-term value of the portfolio may be much smaller than you think. Despite this, some hedge funds like LTCM decided that there was a small positive risk premia for the trades and just systematically did them all. But financing for many M&A deals depends on market conditions and that is a decisive macro factor for the strategy. When the credit crisis struck, all the private equity deals evaporated.

To mitigate the break cost, various hedging strategies can be employed. Sometimes a position can be taken in the acquiring company if it has reacted to the news of the merger, which could reverse on a break or if the acquisition is in shares. This represents the idealistic and infrequent traditional view of the merger-arb trade as presented to investors.

Instead, a technique that I sometimes employed was a refinement of the debt/equity trade. Often the probability for merger success was perceived differently amongst equity and credit traders. On close investigation there were also technical questions about how deals were to be funded and how the debt of the different entities would be merged or redeemed. For example, if company A acquires company B, would company B's debt be guaranteed pari-passu with A's or subordinated or re-purchased and new debt issued? Often with two listed companies with public debt, it is possible to hedge the conventional merger-arb long/short equity trade with an opposite long/short credit trade. The reversal of the equity and credit premiums would offset each other in the event of a break. This would mitigate the downside risk if the deal breaks. Good examples of this were the prominent Lucent/Alcatel (2006) and the Sprint/Nextel (2004) deals, where significant pre-merger differences existed in the credit spreads of the companies.

3.9 Credit Curve Trades

Curve trades in interest rates and credit add an entirely new dimension of opportunities for traders. Instead of a purely directional approach, a more nuanced, partially hedged view can be taken between different maturities. Curve trading allows numerous strategies to exploit relative value, arbitrage dislocations and even target corporate or macro events.

In rates trading, most maturity points along the G20 swap curves are highly liquid, curves are smooth and macro views on future inflation and growth can be taken. With government bonds, yield curves of different maturities and liquidities exist. Yields can be slightly different for the most liquid benchmark "on-the-run" bonds and older more illiquid "off-the-run" issues. This old versus new basis is a traditional area of fixed income arbitrage and was exploited back in the day of LTCM but requires large leverage levels.

Corporate yield curves for bonds are similar to government bond yield curves with several essential differences. There may be few bonds, illiquid issues and clustered maturities leading to fragmented curves. Some corporate bonds might contain call features or other specifics that render yield calculations more subjective. Because of these issues, company credit curves are usually represented in terms of CDS spreads. Unlike bond yield curves, CDS curves are pure credit risk and do not contain an interest rate component.

The most liquid credit curves are of course the handful of credit indices like the iTraxx and CDX which contain portfolios of names. These indices cover regional variation (NA, Europe, Asia), credit grade (IG, XOVER, HY) and financial and non-financial sector variants. Liquidity is good in the major indices but the rather annoying thing for curve trading is that the underlying portfolios regularly change. Rolling into the latest contract is expensive and tiresome. The main maturities that can be traded are 3, 5, 7 and 10 years, so 3/5 and 5/10 curve trades are the most common.

Single name credit curves are arguably more interesting to trade than index curves since there are hundreds of single name credit curves that can be potentially investigated. Liquidity varies but significant idiosyncrasy exists between issuers. The major maturity dates are again 3, 5 and 10 year but often short dates trade when dealers are axed, and 7 years is also a popular maturity.

Curves can be traded in two main forms as notional weighted, or duration weighted (Appx. B.12). Notional weighted allows a directional position to be taken on spreads whilst remaining hedged against credit events. The duration weighted approach trades the change in slope or gradient of a credit curve with almost neutral exposure to parallel changes in credit spreads.

3.9.1 *Notional weighted curve trades*

In a *notional weighted curve trade*, you buy and sell the same notional for the two maturities. For example, you could sell $10m 10-year credit protection and simultaneously buy $10m 5-year credit protection on the same name. For the first 5 years (if you were ever to keep the trade on that long), you have no default exposure but just pure exposure to the credit curve. In general, since 10-year spreads are wider than 5-year, the trade is positive carry but should credit spreads move higher, the duration of the 10-year is obviously higher than 5-year and you will lose money. So, selling 10-year and buying 5-year protection is a great spread compression trade. Since no direct default risk to the name is taken, large leveraged spread positions can be assumed even to risky credits.

3.9.2 *Duration weighted curve trades*

In a *duration weighted curve trade*, the duration weighted amount of each maturity is traded. This hedging immunises the trade from parallel movements of the credit curve and allows pure relative value plays on the shape of the credit curve. The trades are categorised as "steepeners" which profit from a steepening of the credit curve and "flatteners" which as their name indicates target a curve flattening. In each case the ratio of the notionals is determined by the ratio of the "risky" durations calculated using the credit curve. The duration for each CDS is equivalent to the change in value for a 1 bp parallel move in the credit spread curve (CS01). As an example, consider a 250 bp 5-year credit spread name. If we buy a 3/5-year steepener, we might sell $10 of 3-year credit protection at 200 bp and buy $6.5m 5-year protection. This would pay off around $27k per 10 bp of steepening. It has the advantage that it is positive carry $37k per annum and also benefits from the natural steepening yield curve of 25 bp per annum. However, there is a net notional exposure of $3.5m in the occurrence of a credit event.

3.9.3 *Practical curve trades*

I am a big fan of curve trading provided you stick to a few basic principles.

The vulnerability of curve trades is execution and liquidity. Patience and opportunity are required to reduce the bid/offer close to zero for execution. Liquidity in single names can fluctuate and even dry up as people lose interest in trading them. As CDS move away from the widely quoted annual maturities, they become more difficult to execute. Ideally execution on both legs of the trade should be virtually simultaneous.

Also, the hedge ratio for duration weighted trades changes as time passes. Often a trade is held for several months or even longer. A 3/5 trade that was duration hedged gradually becomes a 2/4 trade. One can rebalance the hedge or anticipate this effect and do a partial hedge at inception of the trade, targeting a trade that is on average hedged over the anticipated holding period.

Since most credit curves have an upward concave shape it is advantageous to go with the curve. If nothing changes, steepeners will naturally roll down the curve and steepen of their own accord. For example, the 5/7 is usually flatter than the 3/5. If you trade a 5/7 steepener then over 2 years, it steepens as it evolves towards a 3/5. This is an additional form of in-built positive carry.

There may be clear reasons for dislocations in credit curves and these need to be investigated. A major reason is the maturity dates of the underlying debt. If for example a company, even if leveraged, is currently cash-flow positive and has no debt to refinance for 6 years, then the credit risk is reasonably low up to 5 years and then considerably larger between 5 and 6 years. This should be reflected in the term structure and the credit forward rates.

Trading credit curves can lead to large, unexpected exposure from corporate events including releveraging, refinancings and restructurings. Before blindly entering a seemingly blindingly obvious relative value curve trade the future fundamentals and scenarios need exploring. The positive angle is that curves provide unique exposure to certain events.

3.9.4 *HCA curve steepener*

As an example, consider the HCA curve steepener that we traded in 2005–2006. HCA is an operator of hospitals in the US. During the 2005–2007 LBO craze it was flagged as a stable releveraging candidate due to its stable earnings and good credit metrics. In late 2005 we bought a 5/7 steepener by selling $13m 5-year credit protection and buying $10m 7-year credit protection. At the time, HCA 5 year was around 150 bp and the 5/7 18 bp. The 5/7 region was very flat relative to the 3/5 section of the curve so the trade benefited from positive carry and positive roll. We considered it to be an option on a potential LBO event that unusually paid us premium. The trade was jump-to-default negative $3m notional but we viewed an HCA default as a remote possibility. In July 2007 the sale was

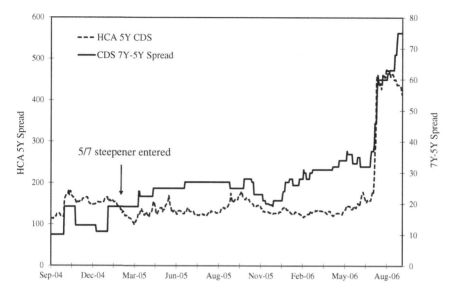

Figure 3.14: HCA 5Y CDS level and 5/7 curve steepener during an LBO.

agreed to a private equity consortium. The leverage post LBO was predicted to rise to an unhealthy 6.6× debt/EBITDA ratio. On announcement of the deal the LBO credit spread widened to 460 bp and the credit curve steepened to 75 bp (Fig. 3.14). The profit realised was in excess of $450k. After this LBO, HCA performed a successful IPO in 2011, deleveraged as a public company and now, in 2021, there is talk of it becoming an LBO target once more.

3.9.5 *UPC curve flattener*

Flatteners might seem to be the underdog of curve trades but sometimes curves get so steep that reversion to a more reasonable mean is highly likely and they can even become positive carry. Also, flatteners have the benefit that they are jump-to-default positive so they can be used to hedge other credit exposures. An example of this was the UPC flattener trade.

UPC holding is one of the largest cable network and broadband providers in western Europe. The company was well leveraged but had stable cashflow. At the time of the trade in 2006, leverage was 4.0× through the bank debt and 5.1× through the unsecured bonds. We had separately

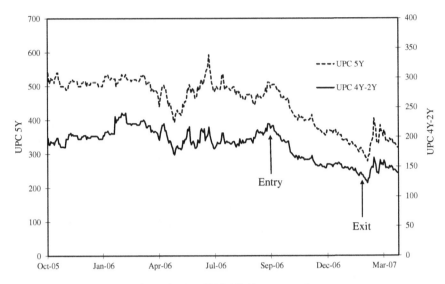

Figure 3.15:   UPC 2/4 flattener trade.

acquired a long position of €13m UPC J1/K1 loans. The CDS credit curve was extremely steep for short maturities and close to 200 bp for 2/4s (Fig. 3.15). We positioned a 2/4 flattener by buying €17m 2-year protection and selling €10m 4-year protection. The trade jumped to default positive by €7m on unsecured debt and was more than sufficient to hedge the UPC loan exposure. The flattener was also positive carry since the 2-year level was so tight relative to the 4-year. Additionally, we could also benefit from the default hedged positive carry of the loans. Over six months the 2/4-year level flattened to below 150 bp.

3.10 Loan Arbitrage

Leverage loans trade in a different market, with a distinct mindset, to most credit traders who focus on bonds and CDS. It is a more specialised market which is traditionally led by bank syndicates who have a larger influence on pricing and issuance terms. A company issuing leverage loans will usually negotiate with the bank lenders, who will often retain the majority of the loans after primary issuance.

Other traditional participants in the loan market are CLO managers which have term funding for illiquid loans in their structure. However, for most investors there were many administrative and funding difficulties for purchasing loans relative to the well-developed market of bonds. In the

2000s, hedge funds entered the clubby world of corporate loans though the development of the *total return swap* (TRS) for loans. Market making of loans by brokers became more widespread.

Despite these new players, the spread and pricing of the secured loan market always seemed generous relative to the unsecured bond market. In some sense, the spread ratio between loans and bonds should theoretically be a function of the relative ratios of the expected loss between the secured and unsecured. However, this is just based on simple models and statistics of averages. In practice, for an individual company before the secured loan takes a real credit loss, the bond holders must face a near total or complete wipe-out.

This difference in pricing leads to the possibility of arbitraging loans versus bonds and CDS on the basis of recovery rate assumptions. Since one is naturally long the cash loan, the trade consists of buying a smaller amount of CDS protection to hedge in the event of default. In general, this is not a very good hedge against mark-to-market changes since the loan is much stickier than the CDS. There is no meaningful dynamic delta except on an extreme event. For this reason, most people would question the value of buying unsecured protection on a secured loan and prefer to run the loan risk naked.

3.10.1 *INEOS loan arbitrage*

Around 2005 the *loan credit default swap* (LCDS) market appeared. An LCDS would reference the secured loan rather the unsecured bonds on a credit event. Perhaps the leader at the time was Morgan Stanley, and my fund was one of the first funds to trade LCDS and become an active participant. Post credit crisis, this single name market declined in volume and never recovered to its previously predicted potential. However, LCDS provided a cleaner way of arbitraging loans and bonds synthetically without all the messy financing and TRS.

An example trade was the INEOS loan arbitrage trade. INEOS was the third largest chemical company globally but had a highly leveraged capital structure. The company had €8.4bn of debt with an adjusted EBITDA of €2.0bn. The loans benefited from first priority security over the assets and were only 2.8× leveraged through the term loan A, B/C and base facility (Table 3.4). The recovery rate on the €2.4bn of bonds at 4.2× leverage would be expected to be very low relative to the loans in the event of a default. In most cases there would be a leverage covenant breach in favour of the loan holders well before a hard default. This would

Table 3.4:   INEOS capital structure (c2006).

			Nominal Euro (mm)	Debt/Adj EBITDA**
Loans	TL A	E+225 '12	1,476	
	TL B/C	E+275 '14	3,534	
	Base Facility/ Securitisation		1,169	
			6,232	**2.8x**
2nd Lien		E+375 '15	400	**3.0x**
Bonds		E 7.875% '16	2,368	**4.2x**
			8,469	

**Assuming Adj EBITA = 2,009 mm.

Table 3.5:   INEOS loan arbitrage trade PL on a credit event.

	PL on Credit Event		
Bond Recovery	Loan Recovery		
	80%	90%	100%
60%	−3,000,000	−500,000	2,000,000
50%	−2,500,000	—	2,500,000
40%	−2,000,000	500,000	3,000,000
30%	−1,500,000	1,000,000	3,500,000
20%	−1,000,000	1,500,000	4,000,000
10%	−500,000	2,000,000	4,500,000
0%	—	2,500,000	5,000,000

enable a restructuring to the detriment of equity and bond holders before the loans would be impacted.

The arbitrage trade was to sell 1-year and 2-year INEOS protection on senior secured loans (€10m 1-year and €15m 2-year) via LCDS and buy smaller amount of unsecured CDS protection as a hedge (€3m 1-year and €2m 2-year). This provided a highly positive carry trade which jumped to default positive under most realistic scenarios. Table 3.5 shows the P&L

under various bond and loan recovery rate permutations, assuming a credit event occurred. The most probable range of outcomes would be 90–100% recovery on the loans and 0–60% on the bonds, all of which generate a positive P&L. In practice, a covenant breach as mentioned would provide 100% recovery for the loans and a lower recovery for the bonds. This would generate several million of windfall profits. Subsequently no default occurred and approximately €500k of positive carry was generated over two years for negligible credit risk.

3.11 Basis Trades

Basis trades are the classic bond/CDS arbitrage trades. They are essentially very simple. You buy the cash bond and buy credit protection on the bond using CDS. Usually there is an attempt to match the maturities of the bond and the CDS as closely as possible. Additionally, if the bond is fixed rate, an interest rate hedge is required via shorting Treasuries or an interest rate swap. The carry on the basis trade is the bond spread minus the CDS premium adjusted by any financing and rate hedging costs. In practice, this is approximately equal to the effective asset swap spread of the bond minus the CDS premium which is the quoted basis. Usually, it works best in terms of buying the bond and buying protection but there are occasional cases when the reverse is viable and one can short the bond and sell protection. Basis trades are popular with bank prop desks since they can often achieve "LIBOR minus" funding. For hedge funds, the funding and leverage are crucial elements in the economics and each basis trade must be carefully evaluated.

Often basis trades are offered by brokers with the CDS and bond "sold" together at certain basis level. Generally, they have a bond on their books they want to sell. Offering the entire package to a client facilitates this. However, unless the broker is well "axed" in both bond and CDS, I have always found there is less value in pre-packed basis trades than hunting out your own. By keeping an eye on cash markets and securing a keen level on the CDS, the basis can be improved dramatically.

Often there are technical reasons why a basis is large and this leaves a measurable arbitrage. For example, the basis on Xerox '09s was a very large basis for a short maturity bond in 2005, particularly in Euros. The only reason I could find to explain the abnormally large basis of 40–50 bp when most other bonds at the time were around 20 bp, was that the bond issue was widely distributed and small clips of $1–2m were buyable at any particular time. Amassing a large enough position to make the trade worthwhile required much patience. In particular, it required running a small unhedged inventory until the CDS could be executed, which was in a generally larger $5m clip size.

Also, the maturity of many bonds cannot be exactly matched by the market standard CDS available. Often an under hedging is required so that the bond has a slightly longer maturity than the CDS. If held to maturity this can leave an unhedged bond position for several months. From a default perspective since the unhedged period is small, this possesses little risk as probability of default is proportional to the spread times the short time period. Arguably, there are circumstances, especially when a company's debt maturities are clustered round certain key dates, that the default probability is magnified at these dates.

Many high yield bonds contain issuer call features after a certain number of years at a defined price level above 100%. Basis trades on callables are difficult since the CDS contract's maturity cannot be easily determined. Most people hedge to the first call date which usually provides high effective basis levels. If interest rates fall or the credit improves through deleveraging, then the probability of the bond being called is high since the issuer can replace with cheaper debt. If, however, credit quality falls the bond might not be called and one is left with an almost naked bond position.

3.11.1 *Supervalue basis trade*

An example of a basis trade is the Supervalue (SVU) trade. Supervalue is a US retailer that was leveraged through the $12bn mega purchase of Albertsons. The short end of the CDS curve was artificially tight versus cash due to short dated sellers of credit protection. Limited price visibility existed in the short end of the curve for market makers. The trade was to buy $15m SUV 8.5% 05/10 bonds, buy protection $15m to 03/10 using CDS and sell $15.9m Treasuries 4 5/8% 11/09 as an interest rate hedge. There was a slight mismatch, as with most basis trades, between the bonds and the hedge which would leave two months of credit exposure if held to maturity. The basis versus the CDS swaps curve was approximately 35 bp and 65 bp versus Treasuries after funding (Fig. 3.16). This provided a credit and interest rate hedged trade with positive carry that could be held until maturity. Even better, the margin for this hedged trade could be

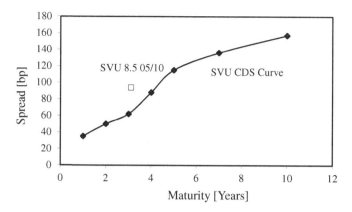

Figure 3.16:   Supervalue basis trade and CDS curve.

aggressively provided by our PB at around 1–2% so theoretically the annual rate of return was approximately 40%. What a great trade you might think?

Well, unexpectedly the credit crisis temporarily flushed out all the "freebie" basis trades. An unforeseen by-product of the crisis was that the interbank repo market that was used to finance bonds shut down and PBs changed margin rates and climbed in their bunkers. The theoretical basis jumped to an incredible 200–300 bp resulting in large mark-to-market losses for basis portfolios. In reality, you could neither trade the CDS nor the cash bonds since dealers stopped making markets in CDS. Nobody was open to finance bonds as the entire credit markets ground to a halt. Everybody was forced to unload those positive carry (previously risk-free) basis trades at a massive loss. Now everybody knows where the true risk lies in basis trades and really expensive term funding is required to weather a credit crisis storm.

3.12 Portfolio Construction

Building a portfolio of trades allows a manager to increase returns whilst controlling risk through position sizing and diversification. In discretionary trading, each trade is hand-curated. When a new trade is added to the portfolio its risk must be considered both on a stand-alone basis and in terms of its impact on the existing portfolio. On a stand-alone basis a trade may have fundamental position size limitations dictated by liquidity,

Pre-Trade Analysis   **Portfolio Managers**

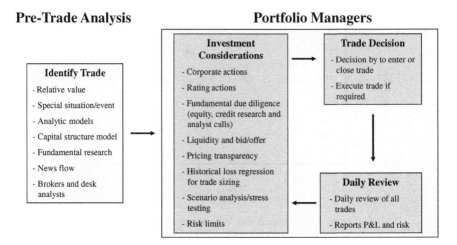

Figure 3.17:   Discretionary trade life cycle.

available leverage and funding and the predicted distribution of future returns.

Figure 3.17 outlines the typical life cycle of a trade from a portfolio manager's perspective. The original conception for trade is derived by continually monitoring the markets together with a phase of detailed analysis to identify opportunities. These opportunities may be based on relative value or special situations with the aid of analytical models and fundamental research. Often many spreadsheets with proprietary add-ins will be used to scan the markets for potential trades using various indicators, ranging from price-based factors such as curve slope, basis and relative spreads to fundamental metrics such as company leverage and projected EBITDAs. Although most of the data in these, sometimes huge, spreadsheets will use live links from various APIs, some must be manually maintained from other unstructured data sources such as company reports.

Ideas can be obviously generated from news flow and conversations with brokers and analysts. Often the importance of broker trade ideas is dramatically overstated. As a general rule of thumb, if you know the desk analysts (that support a bank's own traders) they can prove more insightful than sell-side analysts. Desk analysts rely on trading profits for their bonuses and have "skin in the game". However, these are a rare breed. Usually as a hedge fund you deal with the sell-side, in particular, sales-people who garner information from their internal traders (who have an obvious self-interest of talking-up their own trading books). I used to keep a list over many years of all the "must do" ideas generated by the over dozen investment banks I dealt with and diligently tracked their reliability and predictions. The outcome was very mixed and my conclusion was that none provided an even moderately sustained "edge". There was however, one salesman from a major Swiss bank that unwittingly provided ideas that were 100% uniformly bad over several years. He was a consistent contra-indicator on when not to buy or sell a particular credit position, presumably since at that particular time his trading desk was attempting to execute the reverse trade in market moving size.

Once a potential trade has been identified it must be screened by the portfolio manager for a range of practical investment considerations that might impact its risk profile and profitability. These include upcoming corporate and ratings actions and a further dive into fundamental company due diligence. The liquidity of the trade and pricing transparency must be considered for execution. Risk analysis is then performed, including historical analysis for trade sizing alongside scenario analysis and stress testing. Lastly, the trade must fit within the constraints of both individual trade and portfolio risk limits.

If a decision is taken to execute the trade, then a review of the trade is undertaken every day and a decision is made whether to continue with the trade or adjust the notional size. The screening process in Fig. 3.17 becomes essentially iterative. Each trade has a target profit. In general if the fundamentals and original rationale of the trade are maintained, the trade is continued until this target profit is attained.

3.12.1 *Liquidity considerations*

Often bond issues in high yield have finite sizes in the range $50–1bn. If an issue is say $200m it would be unwise to trade, as a rule of thumb, more that 5–10% of the issue size or $10–20m. Beyond this amount the notion of "market" becomes slightly meaningless especially if you wish to rapidly exit the trade. I did have an old friend who, while working on a prop desk, ended up buying 1/3 of an issue and then discovering that two other guys he knew owned the rest. Although they effectively controlled the issue and its pricing, they all had to give each other the heads up before trading a significant amount — an unavoidable gentleman's cartel that should make regulators wince.

Liquidity is not limited to credit. Equities, particularly small cap and distressed names can have surprisingly low liquidity. Whilst shorting the equity US autoparts makers, which appeared highly liquid in the credit space, I discovered that it would unfortunately take days to extricate myself from the corresponding equities with little market impact. The VWAP (volume weighted average price) required seemed endless.

Liquidity is also not a constant variable. At times of crisis, liquidity evaporates totally and this is hard to quantify from a risk management perspective. The impact on prices can be unimaginable. For example, pre-credit crisis I would have felt comfortable describing all of the loans in my portfolio as good quality and the most liquid. Anything considered less than high quality was sold in 2005–2006 as we considered that market leverage was heading out of control. However, before the crisis hit, the last major new issue was the Prosieben LBO loan. It was massive at €7.2bn with poor spreads and weakish covenants. We politely declined but were strong-armed by the Lehman head of syndicate into participating. We agreed to a modest purchase since despite the bad economics, we envisaged a future IPO for the media company. In the event, the deal launched well but pretty much the next day the credit crisis started. We still had a position of high coupon mezzanine tranche that we had purchased. During the liquidity maelstrom it traded down from 100% to an amazing 1% mark-to-market. Yes, that's a virtually instantaneous decline of 99%. The technical reason was that due to market volatility, TRS providers raised initial margins and this caused a few forced sellers who were under margin pressure. However, there were no buyers at all since everyone who could buy was already long and TRS providers were not accepting new loans. The banks that wrote the deal were also still full to the gunnels so there was no price support or buyers. As the loan declined in value, the required margins increased. More sellers who had badly managed their cash appeared and the price declined further in a vicious spiral of deleveraging. All it took was a stressed sale in the secondary market of €1m of ProSieben loan to reprice the mark-to-market of the entire €7.2bn loan issue for all other holders. When it reached a bargain basement price of 1%, I even thought of buying some for my personal account without leverage but none of my retail brokers could figure out how to buy a loan (as even they struggled with bonds). After the crisis the mezz tranche climbed back and redeemed par (100%). ProSieben even later did an IPO as originally planned.

Academics would say that there is a liquidity premium for investing in illiquid or less liquid assets. However, in practice any premium that one could assign is hard to quantify and time varying. We can on a day-to-day basis look at the average liquidity and costs, including the effects of market impact and slippage, but this does not represent the true downside risk of liquidity. Loss of liquidity can occur under exceptional circumstances as "black swan" style events. Characterising, as a time average premium, is an unrealistic proposition and severely underestimates the risk. Even the most liquid assets, such as S&P 500 futures in the *flash crash* (2010), can experience dramatic liquidity events as market makers pull in their horns.

3.12.2 *Funding constraints*

Funding and leverage are also major considerations for position sizing. I have always been amazed that at most financial institutions I have worked at, traders have little idea of their funding rate, cost of capital and target return on capital. For a hedge fund, capital is a scarce resource and must be deployed with care. Trades are funded either by the repo market or prime brokers ideally using net funding. If a hedge such as shorting treasuries is required, this must be accounted for in the overall profitability. If after leverage and financing costs the target return on capital is low, then the trade is probably not worthy of consideration. What might be profitable at a bank prop desk with sub-LIBOR funding might not be appropriate for a hedge fund. Finally, it may be that the return on capital is sufficient but that the size risk limits provided by PBs constrain the profitability of the trade.

3.12.3 *Profit targets*

The most important factor determining the trade sizing is the potential P&L of the trade. Supermodel Linda Evangelista famously remarked "I don't get out of bed for less than $10,000 a day". Obviously for your average hedge fund trader to get out of bed the trade must make much more. There must be a decent target return for the effort involved in contemplating, analysing, executing and living with the trade. However, most rational traders are equally interested in the possible downside risk.

Surprisingly, most experienced hedge fund managers are highly risk adverse and obsessed by worst case outcomes.

Historical simulation is a good starting point for establishing downside risk. From this we can start to ask many questions. If we had put the trade on at different points in history, what are the typical distributions of returns and the different loss percentiles? What constitutes an average loss and the 90%, 95% and 100% tail losses? The maximum loss that you could have experienced is what focuses the mind. Based on the historic analysis, what is a reasonable target return before you would take profits and how long would we expect this to take? If we had executed the trade in the past how much losses must we typically wear until this target profit is reached? This in my view is crucial. In my experience "Sod's Law" prevails and a loss must usually be worn before a target profit is reached. This analysis is particularly true for mean reverting trades for which timing trade entry can be very difficult before any weak reversion effect kicks in.

Historical simulation, although useful, is often erroneous for any form of event driven trade. As discussed, many hedge fund trades are event driven in that a catalyst or event has already occurred or is expected to occur. Frequently, these events have not been witnessed in the existing historical dataset for a particular company so over-reliance on a company-specific dataset is dangerous. In such cases we must seek comparisons with other similar datasets. For example, if company A is unleveraged but will be releveraged on an LBO then we should look to another previously LBO'ed company B to see what effect an LBO could have on company A's credit spreads. Many of these events are based on the current market environment so we must carefully adapt historical observations. Another example, if company C indulges in an equity rights issue historically, we might expect a fall in the share price. However another similar company D might have just performed a rights issue and its effect was seen as beneficial in shoring up the company's balance sheet, leading to a subsequent rise in share price. Thus, estimating the different return scenarios for trades should not just be based purely on analytical data analysis but also involve a strong dose of skill and common sense.

3.12.4 *Mind the skew*

The conventional academic approaches to modelling the return from trades often rely heavily on normally distributed returns for simplicity. Although this simplicity is often a great convenience, when representing complex trades it can prove extremely dangerous. Many catalyst-driven trades have return distributions that are significantly non-normal. The mathematical convenience of manipulating normal distributions often leads to overlooking the risks embedded in an individual trade.

It is common to consider the skew of trades as a first order correction to the ideology of normal distributions. Whilst variance measures the width of a distribution, skew measures the asymmetry. Statistically, the mean of a distribution is the first moment, the variance the second moment and the skew the third moment. The fourth moment called kurtosis measures the tail risk of a distribution but in practice, traders just bundle everything together that is non-normal and call it "skew".

The skew is very important for both traders and investors alike but often provides an unhealthy divergence of interests. All too frequently, hedge fund trades are trades that effectively "sell" options and receive premium in disguise. These are negative skew trades, and they are often not entirely visible to investors until things go wrong. This usually occurs when the analogous option "strike" of the trade is hit, and large losses are incurred. Apart from the obvious selling out-of-the-money (OTM) options on equities, more cynically we can include many trades that reap "carry" with high probability like leveraged merger trades. Most merger trades pay premium but if they "break" there is high downside risk. In some sense even buying short-dated bonds or selling CDS are similar. Since carry is paid, there is minimal everyday market volatility due to short durations but if the company has issues, there can be big declines in bond prices or even default losses.

One day in the back of a cab our marketer was moaning that it would be easier to sell our fund if we had straight line performance. She later showed me charts of several of the funds that investors she knew were interested in. It turned out later one of these funds was Bernie Madoff's $65bn Ponzi scheme. However, outside direct fraud, whenever I see a hedge fund with high Sharpe ratio and straight line performance exhibiting no volatility then, in my opinion, they are either (i) not marking their book correctly, (ii) fast trading or most likely (iii) selling loads of negative skew options. Fact is one can go many years with great performance and success raising money by selling negative skew pseudo-options.

Beyond simple skew we must also consider that many trades, due to their event driven nature, can shift between different, almost discrete pricing states. This implies multimodal probability distributions for possible returns. The HCA curve trade described previously has two distinct

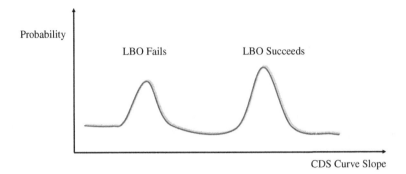

Figure 3.18:   Multi-modal distribution for HCA curve trade.

states (i) no LBO with flat curve or (ii) LBO with steep curve. Each state has its own volatility and the trade cannot be described in terms of skew (Fig. 3.18). Instead, a deeper understanding of the rationale of the trade is required to comprehend the risks involved.

3.13 Risk Management

Beyond identifying and executing alpha generating trades, the second most important role of a portfolio manager is risk management. Quantitative risk management evolved with the introduction of value-at-risk (VaR) models but after numerous financial debacles the limitations of such approaches are now well-known by risk managers. VaR is usually supplemented with scenario analysis and stress testing and more ad-hoc techniques appropriate for discretionary trading.

3.13.1 *VaR models*

The benchmark risk management methodology used these days in financial institutions is *value-at-risk* (VaR). VaR was pioneered by JP Morgan as *RiskMetrics* way back in 1994 and became widely adopted and insitutionalised. I first programmed up a VaR model for a Japanese bank in 1995 and at the time it was seen as very high tech. Usually a delta VaR approach is taken, which is sufficient for portfolios that are linear and do not contain too many options. If options are included a more complete modelling of portfolio "greeks" such as gamma and vega is required.

The delta approach for equities is well established. Volatilities are estimated for each equity and multiplied by the appropriate equity weights (Appx B.14). A correlation matrix is used to evaluate the portfolio volatility and hence the VaR. Correlations are notoriously unstable so although they can be estimated from historic data, it is often preferable to fix more stable values using a defined methodology. For example, for equities within an industrial sector or group we use a fixed correlation, and we vary the correlation between sectors. Using a simple tiered rule such as this based on hierarchies, the job of populating a correlation matrix can be pretty painless.

For credit and interest rates there are term structures that must be included in the VaR framework. The easiest way is to compute the CS01 for the credit spread for each instrument and then multiplying by a credit spread volatility. If we wish to incorporate curve risk, then a CS01 approach must be used, which is bucketed for several maturities along the curve and a correlation applied between buckets. A similar approach can be applied for interest rate curves by calculating the relevant DV01s. Incorporating into the basic VaR framework is a bit tricky and estimating the correlation matrix requires additional assumptions.

Once the risk-adjusted position vectors and correlation matrix have been estimated, the VaR calculation can proceed. If deltas are used, then a simple closed form can be applied. For more complex VaR, a Monte Carlo simulation can be used. We can also use a historical VaR simulation where we can simulate the portfolio performance using actual historical data. This technique has the advantage that actual historic correlations and volatilities are used but the disadvantage that the full "phase" space of market possibilities is not explored.

3.13.2 *Stress testing and scenario analysis*

Usually, VaR is supplemented with other more subjective techniques such as stress testing and scenario analysis. There is considerable overlap between the two techniques, but both are required for a robust risk management framework.

Stress testing is where shocks are applied to various markets and the effect on the portfolio mark-to-market is calculated. For example, a ±1% move in equities, a ±1% move in rates or a ±1% move in credit spreads. Different size moves can be evaluated including extreme moves.

Simultaneous stress of multiple parameters can be considered. Basic stress tests usually assume that changes are instantaneous "shocks". These moves can be characterised as a number of standard deviations of volatility of the risk factor.

A problem arises however when we wish to ask the question: what is our effective exposure to the movement of the S&P 500 equity index? Essentially, we can frame the question in two ways (i) our direct equity exposure to movements in the S&P 500 and (ii) how much everything else in our portfolio moves if the S&P moves. For (i) alone we could adopt several routes such as summing the volatility adjusted deltas and rescaling to the volatility of the S&P. This however assumes that all equities move in a correlated manner albeit with different volatilities. An alternative is to use a beta-based regression approach where we estimate the effective beta of each equity to the S&P and tally up the beta weighted positions. A better method which in some sense captures (i) and (ii) is to insert the S&P as a separate instrument into the VaR machinery, estimate the correlations and calculate a conditional VaR based on the movement of the S&P 500.

Thus, in more sophisticated approaches, the exposure of the portfolio to a number of underlying driving risk factors can be generated. These can include macro factors and other markets. For example, the impact of changing oil prices can be examined by estimating the correlation of the portfolio value to moves in historic oil prices for stress testing.

Scenario analysis usually concerns construction of specific "what-if" scenarios that have already occurred historically or might pan out in future markets. Construction of scenarios is arguably more realistic than stress testing. Historical scenarios might include the dot-com crash, Gulf war, Russian crisis and Lehman default etc. in which there was market turmoil or shocks. The relevant short market time series is used to estimate the effect on the current portfolio if it had experienced the historical event. Possible hypothetical future scenarios that have never been witnessed or observed for a very-long time, can also be constructed. For example, a stagflation nightmare of rising inflation, rising bond yields and low growth over a sustained period is a topical scenario many people are currently evaluating in 2021.

Based on VaR and scenario analysis we can establish and monitor various hard and soft limits. These usually include notional net and gross exposures, maximum exposure to risk factors and maximum loss on credit events. We can also apply limits to bucketed risk by sector, asset class and geography. Using the VaR machinery we can apply risk-adjusted limits that include volatilities and covariances. These are often called covariance or CoVaR limits. As we shall discuss in systematic trading in Chapter 4, an iterative process can be applied to optimise risk within various constraints but for discretionary trading, this is less relevant.

3.13.3 *Real portfolio risk*

A key problem with real hedge fund portfolios is that the above techniques are only suitable for highly diversified, well-behaved portfolios. Real portfolios have multiple trades based around rationales and catalysts. This is in addition to the observation that most gaussian quantitative VaR type methodologies are highly inappropriate for portfolios with strongly skewed returns and multimodal return distributions. These real portfolios are, by definition, based on idiosyncratic trades that have been selected for their perceived out-performance and asymmetric risk and return.

For one of my biggest investors, I was legally required to provide a daily VaR estimate. I constructed a complex VaR model with many bells and whistles capable of including equities, bonds, CDS, loans, rates, and fx. However, reconciling against the real daily P&L moves was very hard. Although in the very long term it might have been slightly statistically credible, over the short and medium term it struggled with the numerous special situation and relative value trades in the portfolio. Mean reversion trades were particularly difficult to model. Eventually we required a different sub model for each trade type which led to a fundamentally different and more holistic risk approach.

Knowing the individual risk characteristics of each trade allows comprehension of the true tail risk in an entire portfolio. Risk models all struggle with quantifying extreme tail risk and the illusion of portfolio diversification is all too real. Under extreme events, the low probability tails across different trades can all add up in an unexpected fashion as their correlations tend to +1 or −1 values. To mitigate this risk, an understanding of the strategy drivers helps but the cost of eliminating these low frequency risks is often prohibitive and a drag on portfolio performance. Typical approaches often include static approaches like buying deeply OTM options such as low-cost credit protection for several bp that might balloon out on a crisis. Buying cheap CDS protection on banks, monolines and AAA subprime worked a treat in the credit crisis but the negative carry is often dissuasive in stable markets. Dynamic approaches that use fast volatility indicators to buy volatility protection can also be employed, although their statistical validity is limited by the small number of historical financial crashes and every evolving crisis possesses its own peculiarities.

3.14 The Old School Approach

The objective of this Chapter was to provide an overview of the "old school" discretionary quantitative trading. One where trading decisions are highly subjective, based on sketchy data and human intuition. That is not to denigrate the discretionary approach but to emphasise the fact that although it is quantitative, it is not formally rule-based and can never clearly be systematised. The catalysts for reach individual trade are different and depend on the context and market conditions. The examples in the Chapter show that such discretionary investment decisions use comprehension and understanding to form an opinion on complex corporate events. Many of these events are idiosyncratic and to diversify and spread risk, the more idiosyncratic the trade, the better. Each trade must be analysed from various perspectives, from technical and fundamental aspects to execution and liquidity risk. Discretionary traders must study the news flow on numerous companies and the narrative of each company's fundamentals. Although equities are electronically traded, only 25% of high yield bonds and less than 2% of loans are traded in this way. The discretionary trader must deal with opinionated sell-side brokers and analysts daily but remain faithful to their own convictions. Importantly, the individuality of different trade types and situations renders a uniform risk management framework problematic. Each trader must "know their book" rather than rely on a simplistic VaR framework.

In the next chapters I shall outline a different hedge fund approach — that of computer-based trading from systematic to newer AI methods. Systematic trading in many ways, is the anti-thesis of discretionary trading. It is based on statistics and scientifically repeatable observations to construct trading rules or strategies. The trading environment of a systematic hedge fund is impersonal and more akin to a library than a trading floor. Rather than having people yelling at each other, you can hear a pin drop. Strategy development requires mathematical algorithms and extensive historical data to back-test and verify strategies for liquid markets. In contrast, discretionary traders are forward looking and operate in a world of incomplete data and subjective human comprehension of events, which renders any scientific approach impossible.

Chapter 4

Systematic Profits

4.1 Systematic Investing

Systematic investing has rapidly grown in recent years and almost represents a third of hedge fund assets. Rather than relying entirely on human discretion, systematic investing uses computer-based strategies to make trading decisions. Removal of humans from the investment process reduces the effect of human emotions and biases, and replaces them with a more scientifically rigorous, statistically based approach. Systematic strategies are based on algorithms which are developed on the basis of historical data to make predictions about future market movements. In general, these predictions are relatively weak but when combined with disciplined automated risk control, they can produce consistent returns under many different market conditions. Systematic algorithms are by definition "backward" looking since they only have access to historical data and thus, they are unable to predict "unexpected" future events. Instead, they rely on exploiting small, regular statistical effects and market inefficiencies that human traders are ill-suited to. Computers can assiduously follow repetitive trades with close to even odds, that human traders quickly find mind-numbing and tedious. Systematic trading systems are often completely automated in their investment decisions, trade execution and workflow, requiring little human intervention.

4.2 The Main Types of Systematic Hedge Funds

The two main types of systematic hedge funds are *commodity trading advisors* (CTAs) and *long/short equity* funds (L/S equity). Within the CTA category we can include systematic *global macro* strategies and so-called *managed futures*. Many global macro strategies are currently traded by the major CTAs. Other types of systematic funds can exist, for example, long only *risk parity* but these can be generally derived from strategies employed by CTAs and L/S equity funds. In this Chapter we will primarily focus on systematic CTAs and will detail L/S equity approaches later in Chapter 5.

Historically, the correlations between the two major systematic styles of CTA/macro and L/S equity are close to zero. However, the correlations between discretionary and systematic styles of both are above 0.5, which indicates that similar strategies and indicators are used by both discretionary and systematic managers. Particularly, for L/S equity strategies where the discretionary/systematic correlations can approach 0.8, it is likely that many of the quantitative factors and anomalies that human traders adopt have been replicated by machines.

Importantly, systematic trading differs from so-called *high frequency trading* (HFT) which seeks to exploit ultra-high speeds and preferential access to exchanges. HFT systems do not generally make a prediction of market direction like longer term systematic investors. Instead, they anticipate order flow, trade before slower market participants and are often controversially paid to provide liquidity.

4.2.1 *Commodity trading advisors*

CTAs follow directional strategies across multiple asset classes which can include equity indices, bonds, currencies and commodities. Typically, they employ *trend-following* strategies and employ exchange traded futures contracts and fx forwards. The largest CTAs with assets under management (AUM) over $20bn, like Man AHL Diversified and Winton, trade over 500 global markets and have supplemented their core trend-following with additional algorithms. They attain high diversification across markets and strategies. Figure 4.1 shows the typical sector diversification with around 20–30% each split across equities, fx, rates and commodities.

In the last decade the larger CTA managers have diversified away from futures trend-following to seek better performance. Some CTAs like

METALS: Copper, Gold, Silver, Nickel ...
ENERGY: Brent, Henry Hub, Heating Oil, Nat Gas ...
AGS: Corn, Wheat, Soybean, Coffee, Sugar, Cattle ...

G10: AUD, GBP, EUR, CAD,JPY ...
EM: HKD, INR, PHP, TWD, BRL, MXN, CZK, HUF, RUB ...
CROSSES: GBPEUR, CADEUR ...

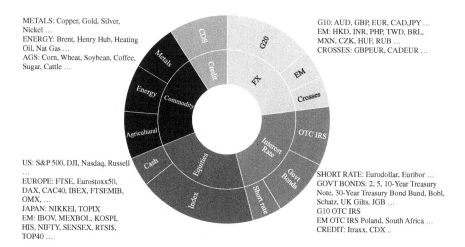

US: S&P 500, DJI, Nasdaq, Russell
...
EUROPE: FTSE, Eurostoxx50, DAX, CAC40, IBEX, FTSEMIB, OMX, ...
JAPAN: NIKKEI, TOPIX
EM: IBOV, MEXBOL, KOSPI, HIS, NIFTY, SENSEX, RTSI$, TOP40 ...

SHORT RATE: Eurodollar, Euribor ...
GOVT BONDS: 2, 5, 10-Year Treasury Note, 30-Year Treasury Bond Bund, Bobl, Schatz, UK Gilts, JGB ...
G10 OTC IRS
EM OTC IRS Poland, South Africa ...
CREDIT: Itraxx, CDX ..

Figure 4.1:   CTA diversification across futures and OTC markets.

AHL Dimension specialise in non-trend strategies such as reversion, timing and cross-sectional algorithms. Others like AHL Evolution focus on newer, less liquid markets such as OTC interest rate swaps (IRS), credit default swaps (CDS), newer markets and volatility/option products. However, beyond a certain size of AUM, capacity constraints dictate that slow trend following of liquid futures is the dominant strategy.

The most successful CTAs have been around for over 25 years. This is a long time in the world of hedge funds. The major benefit of investing in CTAs are the high risk-adjusted returns (returns relative to risk taken) which exceed most other investments. The handful of largest, most successful CTAs have achieved long term Sharpe ratios of around 1.0, exceeding other asset classes including equities and bonds (Appx. B.13).

Often, to seduce investors, plots are shown of the Sharpe ratios of various asset classes versus CTAs. More often than not these plots involve suitably optimistic CTA indices. Instead, it is perhaps a bit more interesting to ignore such indices with all their selection problems and survivor biases and dig beneath the surface to look at real hedge funds. I decided to look at a slightly larger CTA universe from a well-known, reliable monthly hedge fund report. The results are shown in Fig. 4.2. The top 40 funds had an average AUM of $1.2bn and an average Sharpe ratio of 0.58 since inception (an average return of around 7% per annum with a volatility of 13%). The AUM is probably on the low side since many of

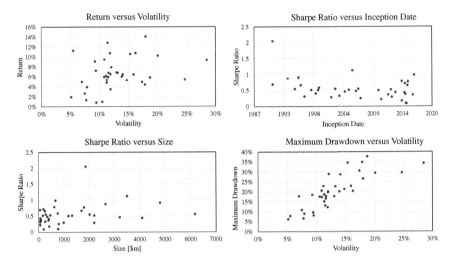

Figure 4.2:   Historic performance of leading CTA funds.

the larger CTA programs only report their leading public fund although they usually have numerous other investment vehicles, such as managed accounts. Here for ease of calculation, I have assumed that the effective Sharpe ratio is return divided by volatility. Only one exceptional fund possessed a Sharpe ratio more than 1.5 and that is surprisingly since the early 1990s. Thus, we can probably conclude that a successful CTA should have a long-term Sharpe ratio above 0.5 and in practice, above 1.0 is extremely rare. In hedge fund terms, CTAs target high volatilities mainly in the range 10–15%. The maximum observed drawdowns scale almost linearly with the volatility with the average maximum drawdown of −20%.

The secondary attractive reasons for investing in CTAs are (i) the low correlation to equities and bonds and (ii) the high liquidity for investors. The correlation with equity and bond indices is surprisingly low. A historical calculation shows that the average long-term correlation value of CTAs versus equities is −0.02 and to bonds 0.05 (Table 4.1). This low correlation means that it is highly diversifying for investors (who are generally long equities in their portfolios) to invest a proportion of their assets in CTAs. During periods of market crisis, such as the 2002 dot-com bubble and the 2008 credit crisis, CTAs have achieved very high returns. This was largely due to being positioned long government bonds prior to

Table 4.1: Long-term correlation of CTAs versus bonds and US equities.

	CTA	Bonds	Equities
CTA	1.0	0.05	−0.02
Bonds	0.05	1.0	0.20
Equities	−0.02	0.20	1.0

sell-offs. Often this negative correlation with risk assets in a crisis is termed CTA "crisis alpha". In crisis months, most hedge fund strategies experienced negative returns, whereas CTAs posted positive returns with average returns of around 2%. Statistically speaking, CTA returns demonstrate positive skew of 0.5–1.0 relative to the negative skew of −0.8 of equities which, as we know, can experience large swift sell-offs in crises.

Finally, the high liquidity of CTAs is due to the liquid nature of their underlying futures contracts. Unlike most hedge funds during the credit crisis, futures and hence CTAs remained liquid and did not "gate" investors. Managed accounts for CTAs are often used by institutional investors with 1–2 days liquidity.

The dominant strategy of CTAs is directional trend-following or *momentum*. Some academics call this *time series momentum*. A CTA builds positions in the direction of the sustained trend in each particular market. Due to this directional nature the gross leverage (longs plus shorts) of CTAs is relatively small when compared with arbitrage and relative value hedge funds. Typically, they are not more than 1.5 × leveraged in equities and commodities but can be several times this in bonds due to their lower volatility. This directional leverage allows high returns and high volatilities to be achieved. As we have seen from Fig. 4.2, positions are commonly dynamically risk-scaled to target volatilities of typically 10–15%. The larger CTAs use similar trend-following technology and are fairly highly correlated (Fig. 4.3). Although they follow trends at different speeds, the average trend speed and market allocations are broadly similar across these funds, leading to similar performance.

CTAs experience many drawdowns and in fact spend most of their time in drawdown. Drawdowns can be painful and last several years. This is due to the positive skew of momentum strategies. Trend-following makes out-size returns when a strong trend appears and slowly

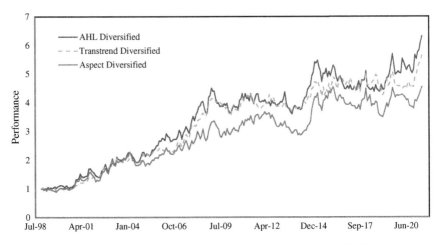

Figure 4.3:   The European "titan" CTAs are highly correlated.

"bleeds" money in range bound or trendless markets. Typically, drawdowns equivalent to the CTA's volatility target occur every couple of years with maximum historical drawdowns in backtesting of 1.5–2× the volatility target.

4.2.2 *L/S equity*

L/S equity funds trade "cash" equities both long and short. Unlike CTAs, they are "hedged" funds which seek to reduce their overall directional market exposure. If the market rises (falls) they will make a profit (loss) on the long positions and a loss (profit) on the short positions. Thus L/S equity funds seek to exploit differences or relative inefficiencies between equities to find alpha uncorrelated with movements in the major equity indices. L/S equity funds will often trade a potential universe of several thousand equities and be long and short hundreds at a time to achieve diversification.

Because any pricing inefficiencies between the long and short positions are small, leverage must be employed to achieve meaningful returns. Typically, a L/S *market neutral* equity fund will be 1.0–3.0 × long and 1.0–3.0 × short with very low net leverage. This provides a gross leverage of 2.0–6.0 × investor capital. Some L/S equity funds claim to be "notional neutral" when they have zero net leverage. However, this can be some-what misleading for investors since a fund can be notional neutral without being truly "market neutral" and thus insensitive to overall market move-ments. It is common to seek performance in bullish markets by sometimes gaming equity beta and skewing the portfolio to be longer more volatile stocks relative to the shorts. This can lead to a surprise for investors if market conditions change. Indeed, if we look at generic L/S equity hedge fund indices, they include so many funds that are not true market neutral but are exposed to "risk-on" assets, that they exhibit a long term 60–80% correlation to the S&P 500 and even 50–70% to global bonds. These dis-appointing levels of decorrelation indicate investors must look carefully at a fund's portfolio if they wish true uncorrelated returns. In a world run by relentless Quantitative Easing (QE) liquidity it is all too easy for frus-trated managers to give up on their shorts.

L/S equity funds employ many relative value strategies over different time scales. Short term "statistical" arbitrage, exploiting dispersion and mean reversion between equities (buy the recent poor performers and sell the out-performers), might have position holding periods of several days. More fundamental value and factor-based strategies might have time-scales of several weeks or months. The biggest pricing anomalies are available in mid and small cap equities which are more volume con-strained and expensive to trade.

Many of the most successful L/S Equity players like Renaissance Technologies (RenTech) and D.E. Shaw have been around for over 20 years. RenTech is arguably the World's most successful hedge fund with its Medallion fund returning more than 35% annualised over a 20-year span. But despite these famed successes there have been several major shake-outs of the computer driven L/S equity space. Prior to 2007 the "bread and butter" mean reversion strategy had experienced decreasing returns as the strategy became more crowded. A big "quant quake" occurred in 2007 when many funds simultaneously liquidated the same stocks. Major market neutral funds saw drawdowns of up to −30% which caused many large funds, including Goldman's Global Alpha fund, to close down.

A recurrent problem with L/S equity is that knowledge diffusion and cross-firm recruiting means that the largest US funds now use similar technology and strategies with reduced returns. In recent years there has been an increase in so-called factor strategies, and this is the focus of the next chapter.

4.3 Overview of a Typical CTA Trading System

It is interesting to consider a birds-eye view of a typical CTA trading system that might be used by a large systematic investment manager (Fig. 4.4). Many markets are traded and these have associated market data time series (prices, volumes, …), and non-market or alternative data. This alternative data might include traditional fundamental data (economic, inventory, …) and newer alternative sources (news, social media, …).

The relevant time series are input into a range of strategies which are based around general strategy concepts (momentum, reversion, carry, fundamental, …). Some of these concepts may be purely based on prices while others may require intermediate signals generated from manipulating specific data (GDP indicator, inflation and news sentiment, …).

The signals for each market are combined with strategy weights assigned to the specific market (Appx. C.1). Some strategies are inappropriate for certain markets, for example, a carry strategy is less appropriate for equities than fx. The applied strategy weights are dictated by several considerations including historical performance in the individual market (Sharpe ratio, drawdowns, …), length of live trading and backtesting history.

The individual market signals are combined together in a portfolio construction process to optimise predicted portfolio risk-adjusted returns

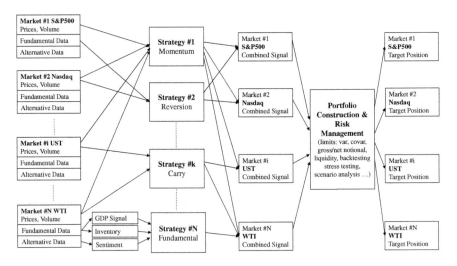

Figure 4.4:   Hypothetical multi-strategy CTA combining strategy signals.

within various risk constraints and budgets. Usually, this process involves a combination of backtesting results and a *value-at-risk* (VaR) style methodology that uses historical correlations between markets. Prudent risk limits are commonly imposed on VaR, market covariance, gross/net notional, gross/net risk adjusted notional and liquidity. These are supplemented with key information from scenario analysis and stress testing. Often from the initially proposed target positions, an iterative process takes place as positions are gradually trimmed or expanded within the applied risk constraints, while optimising the risk adjusted returns to attain the portfolio target volatility. On the basis of this rigorous portfolio construction, the individual target positions are calculated for each market.

4.4 Systematic Strategy Types

The majority of systematic strategies are based on equations or simple algorithms. Contrary to popular belief, many strategies are in fact so simple they can be written on the back of a beer mat. The algorithms exploit well defined statistical relationships and effects in markets. It is important for a scientific approach that these effects are stable and persistent through time and if possible, universal across similar markets. We can classify the mainstream "traditional" systematic strategies into several types depending on their underlying algorithms (Fig. 4.5). The major strategies are *momentum, carry* and *value* and virtually all CTAs use a blend of these core algorithms. These time series strategies are also possible in cross-sectional form where markets are ranked and simultaneous long and short positions are held. Reversion strategies are often used to complement momentum in some markets like index equities that have high reversionary properties on certain timescales. Beyond these major strategies, there are a host of minor technologies ranging from market timing and fundamentally based to technical analysis and volatility derived.

4.4.1 *Momentum*

The main CTA strategy is trend-following or momentum, due to its simplicity, long-term success and extremely high capacity. By diversifying across numerous markets, CTAs can manage assets in excess of $10bn using momentum strategies, without being materially impacted by trading costs.

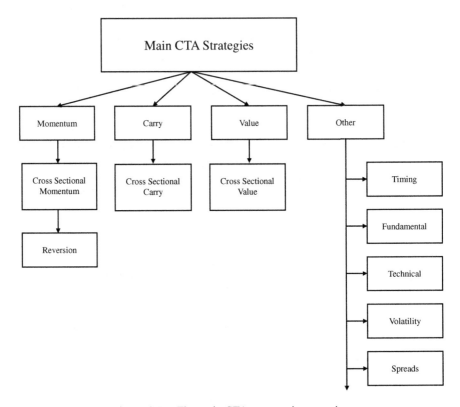

Figure 4.5:   The main CTA systematic strategies.

Using a simple mathematical equation based on historical prices we can build a momentum signal. The simplest signal approach used by many CTAs is a combination of two moving averages but other methods such as the kernel technique exist (Appx. C.4). Using this momentum signal we can buy the underlying market if the trend is positive and sell or short the market if the trend is negative. The size of the trading position is determined by the magnitude of the momentum signal. This process requires normalisation of the signal and often risk-scaling based on the relative volatility of the underlying market.

Trend-following or momentum can be applied to all types of market from equities to commodities. Although the momentum effect might be quite small over the long term in each market (for example, a long-term Sharpe ratio of 0.2–0.5) by combining many uncorrelated markets, a CTA can in practice achieve a respectable Sharpe ratio towards 1.0.

Table 4.2: Long-term Sharpe ratios of momentum, carry and value.

	Momentum	Carry	Value
Equities	0.4	0.2	−0.1
Rates	0.8	0.8	0.5
FX	0.7	0.6	0.3
Commodities	0.5	0.6	0.2
Combo	1.0	1.3	0.3

The long-term momentum performance of different sectors varies from being lowest in equities and highest in interest rates and fx (Table 4.2). The higher momentum performance of rates and fx is arguably due to the higher carry in these markets which is slightly captured when applying slow trend signals to back-adjusted time series.

Momentum has relatively few parameters to be specified but the main one is the speed of the momentum signal. Usually this is determined by fitting to historical data while taking into account the turnover and transaction costs of the underlying market. For example, copper which is expensive to trade will use a slower trend signal than government bonds which have much lower transaction costs. In general, a large CTA will use a combination of trend signals operating at different speeds for each market.

Momentum strategies are generally positive skew making large returns during occasional trending periods. The Achilles heel of trend-following is trendless or range-bound markets where the strategy slowly loses money. Also, in very quick sell-offs or market reversals trend-followers can be slow to adapt and can quickly lose money before they de-gear, reduce risk and change direction. Although fast momentum might have kicked in to follow the new trend, the slower momentum signals will often still dominate. This is probably the case during the 2020 covid crisis where most CTAs running slower momentum failed to capitalise on the significant decline in equities. Luckily, the extreme diversification of CTAs across asset classes often provides protection in major risk-off events. By often being both long equities and government bonds, the flight to safety effect of government bonds hedges the equity losses.

An example of trend following strategy for the Euro currency is presented in Fig. 4.6. The market price is shown (top) and below, the raw

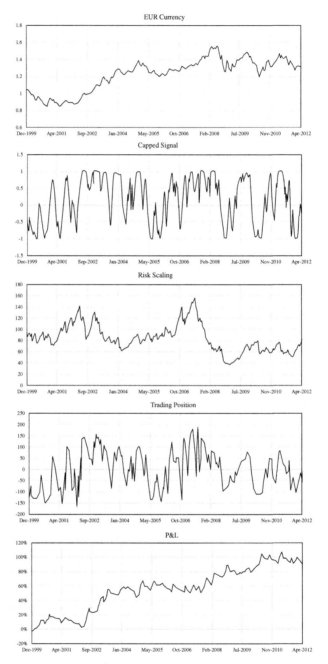

Figure 4.6:   Momentum strategy for EUR Currency showing market price (top), capped signal, risk scaling, trading position and P&L (bottom).

capped signal generated by the strategy. A volatility risk-scaling factor is applied (middle) and the final position is shown. At the bottom is the simulated cumulative P&L for constant trading notional which clearly shows the high returns obtained from capturing trends and the decay of P&L in trendless markets. Importantly, it is the combination of the momentum signal with the risk-scaling that results in long-term stable returns.

In recent years, momentum in liquid futures markets has struggled for long periods of time. Although large CTAs did not really decline in value, they have struggled to find alpha and remained range bound until the strong gains in commodity prices in 2020–2021. Various not entirely satisfactory explanations have been offered for this stagnation in performance, including the effects of high frequency trading, arguments that CTAs are now too big relative to the underlying futures markets, the decline in G7 interest rates and government influence in markets via QE. In an attempt to boost performance, CTAs, such as AHL Evolution, have moved into trend-following OTC interest rate swaps and CDS indices (Appx. C.8). Both these asset classes have proved more profitable than traditional liquid futures (Fig. 4.7). Other profitable markets CTAs have explored for momentum are newer, less liquid futures markets such as electricity futures and so-called "frontier" markets like Chinese futures.

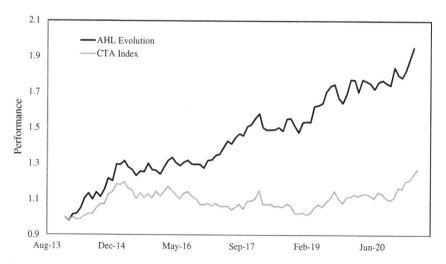

Figure 4.7: Traditional CTAs have recently struggled while specialised OTC funds like Man Group's AHL Evolution have prospered.

4.4.2 *Reversion*

The opposite of trend following is so-called "reversion". Mean reversion strategies seek to exploit reversals of the market back to an average level. The definition is less well defined than trend strategies and varies between managers. Strategies seek to find a recent pattern of reversion and exploit the reversion hoping it will continue. For example, reversion might be selling a market on a sudden upwards "spike", selling and buying at the extremities of a range or "buying the dip" on a sell-off against the main trend. Perhaps the simplest reversion methodology is combining a fast-moving average on the price with a much slower moving average. However, reversion trades can be dangerous if a market does not revert and simply moves to a new level or establishes a trend in the opposite direction. "Buying the dip" was in recent years the winning trade in equity markets although the sudden VIX crash (2018) and the massive coronavirus drawdown in March 2020 were enough to test the nerves of leveraged dip buyers.

4.4.3 *Carry*

Carry is the profit made simply by holding an asset. For example, in the simplest form of carry the holder of bond receives interest in the form of a coupon. Carry in all its multitude of forms is undoubtedly the largest form of hedge fund "alpha" and is largely misunderstood by investors. Investors often think they are getting alpha but in fact they are receiving hidden carry.

Carry exists in most asset classes and many forms — dividends in equities, coupons in bonds, interest on deposits in foreign currencies etc. Even in futures where there are no physical interest payments, the slope of the futures curve for different maturities has an embedded carry. If higher maturity futures contracts have a lower value than the nearby front contracts then on average they will rise in value as they near maturity.

One of the most successful long term carry strategies is fx carry. Having worked in derivatives and the imaginary world of efficient markets, I was actually very surprised how effective fx carry trades are, especially when diversified across currencies in risk-adjusted portfolio. In the theoretical no-arbitrage world there should be no free lunch by investing unhedged in higher yielding foreign currencies. Theory says foreign currency devaluation should eat away all the positive carry. However, in reality the strategy has a long-term Sharpe ratio of close to 0.6 (Table 4.2). A caveat to fx carry is that, if you naively invest without the correct risk management framework, the strategy exhibits high skew when the USD suddenly strengthens.

Many systematic strategies can be based around carry and using carry as a trading signal. A simple CTA carry strategy is to buy and sell futures on the basis of the slope of the futures curve (Appx. C.5). In fx carry trades the *interest rate differentials* (IRD) between the two currencies are also used as carry signals. Carry signals are particularly effective in emerging market currencies where IRDs are large, and bonds and swaps where coupons are paid. Combined across asset classes, carry has a high long-term Sharpe ratio ~1.3 with low correlation to momentum (Table 4.4).

4.4.4 *Value*

Value signals are based on whether a particular market is over or under-valued based on price and fundamental information. The methodologies for deriving a value signal for different markets are highly subjective. Examples might include shorting the Australian Dollar based on *purchasing power parity* (PPP) or buying equities due to dividend yields (Appx. C.6). Since fundamental value data is often rather slow moving, value signals are usually much slower than momentum signals and react less to market conditions.

Using simple definitions for value, the long-term Sharpe ratio achieved is around 0.3, which is much lower than for both momentum and carry (Table 4.3). However, the value correlation is slightly negative which means that although it is a weak signal, it is additive to momentum and carry portfolios (Table 4.4).

4.4.5 *Cross-sectional*

The key strategies of momentum, carry and value can be used on a relative value or cross-sectional basis. For example, cross-sectional momentum involves the ranking of markets by momentum and buying the strongest trending markets and shorting those with the weakest trends. Similarly, cross-sectional carry requires ranking of the carry signal across various assets and going long for those with the highest carry signal while

Table 4.3: Long-term Sharpe ratios of cross-sectional momentum, carry and value.

	Momentum	Carry	Value
Equities	0.0	0.3	0.4
Rates	−0.3	0.8	0.6
FX	0.7	0.7	0.4
Commodities	0.5	0.8	0.1
Combo	0.4	1.3	0.8

shorting those with the lowest. Statistical arbitrage is also a form of cross-sectional strategy although it plays on reversion rather than momentum.

It turns out that the behaviour of momentum and value in cross-section is quite different from in time series (Table 4.3). Momentum is a strong signal in time series and a much weaker one in cross-section. This is primarily due to the negative Sharpe ratio of rates in cross-sectional momentum. However, whereas value only attained a Sharpe ratio of 0.3 in time series, it is a much stronger 0.8 in cross-section. This illustrates the merits of considering both time series and cross-section aspects in portfolio construction.

4.4.6 *Timing*

The simplest equity timing signal is "sell in May and go away" or flatten an equity position over the summer. Surprisingly, this out-performs the major equity indices over a very long period of time since most positive returns lie outside the summer period. There are many variants of this idea — the "Halloween" effect, weekend/holiday effect, month-end etc. and some have more statistical support than others. Also, the anomaly is not limited to equities since timing and seasonal effects appear in currencies and strongly in commodities. Unfortunately, the vast majority of these have been published in the academic literature and this probably decreased their effectiveness. For example, one of my favourites was the high Sharpe ratio month-end effect (buy equities 2–3 days before end of month and sell at the start of the new month) which existed for decades but surprisingly completely disappeared or even reversed shortly after its publication in around 2011 (Fig. 4.8). This may however be a coincidence and caused by massive QE but I continue to have my doubts.

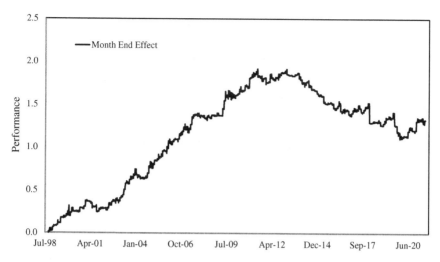

Figure 4.8: The Month End effect "reversed" suspiciously after being widely published.

4.4.7 *Fundamental*

Fundamental macro strategies can also be based on non-price data such as traditional econometric time series and newer alternative data sources. Often these signals are linear multi-factor econometric models which incorporate economic factors such as GDP, inflation, employment etc. (Appx. C.3). Typically, models use linear regression of market price changes versus the level or change (derivative) of the econometric time series.

Often, since econometric data has a publication lag, extrapolation or forecasting methods are used. In recent years there has been a move towards *nowcasting* techniques, to reduce signal lag using extensive up-to-date surveys. Additionally, the rise in computing power and "big data" over the last 5–10 years has led to increased use of alternative datasets in fundamental signal generation. *Alternative data* loosely describes non-price data, so can, depending on your definition, still encompass the more old-fashioned traditional, fundamental data. However, the modern alternative data may include news articles, social media, consumer transaction data, expert views, geolocation data and even satellite and weather data. The data has the potential to provide new uncorrelated signals to combine with other price-based strategies. The alt data field is expanding quickly and is discussed in Chapter 8.

Using fundamental data for directional prediction of macro markets is a difficult quest that should not be underestimated. There are few markets and the trades are mainly directional in nature. The economy is always evolving and the scope for error is very large. Using fundamental signals on a stand-alone basis, excluding any price-based signals to limit market risk is somewhat dangerous. Some of the most disastrous trades I have ever witnessed are fully systematic econometric-based strategies which have ploughed on ignoring the market and "assuming" they were right based on the fundamentals (which Mr Market was temporarily ignoring).

4.4.8 *Technical analysis*

Technical analysis or the study of market patterns has been around for a very long time and has a huge literature and following amongst both discretionary and systematic traders. It includes many theories and indicators, for example Bollinger bands, RSI, pendants etc. Interestingly, when rigorous science and backtesting is applied to these indicators, virtually all of them fail and consequently most are not used by mainstream hedge funds. I have a well-known and much used technical analysis book on my desk. Once, a couple of my former colleagues were assigned the job of testing as many of the strategies and theories contained within its around 1000 pages. Surprisingly over 95% of the technical strategies detailed failed miserably. Those that did were fairly simple and involved the concepts of support, resistance, ranges and breakouts.

One cannot automatically dismiss technical analysis and rule it out as hokum and bad science. There is a clearly academically established 52-week rule in equities. Often one observes that markets like to reach round numbers. For example, it is curious why the equity market in 2007 hit the same value it did in the dot-com peak of 2000. One of my first jobs in finance was as a junior USD swaps trader and my successful boss was fervent believer in technical analysis. Technical analysis is rooted in human behaviour and markets are complex systems based on this behaviour. The scientific process of systematic trading is reliant on statistics and it may be that the ephemeral effect of technical patterns eludes the scientific methodology. If there are too few observations, we can never formulate a proper theory.

4.4.9 *Volatility*

Numerous quantitative funds trade options and hence volatility. Options are available on most futures contracts, fx and large cap cash equities. Selling options is the classic "negative skew" trade which leads to regular small profits and the occasional large loss or blow-up. Many smaller CTAs with high Sharpe ratios or "straight line" performance are, in reality, selling options.

Volatility can also be traded directly using VIX futures or OTC variance swaps. Volatility generally declined since 2008, which led to the dominant hedge fund trade of selling volatility, which culminated in the February 2018 VIX crash. Although short lived, this sell-off created a sudden spike in volatility. Several ETFs which shorted volatility had their capital wiped out and hedge funds were burned. Litigation over the VelocityShares Inverse VIX ETF or XIV is still ongoing in 2021 (Fig. 4.9).

Volatility can be exploited in many other strategies and it is worth noting a few, well researched examples. Volatility trading versus CDS is possible for capital structure arbitrage or as a macro strategy within the stochastic firm value framework (Appx. B.7). Implied volatility can be used as a directional indicator for equities by considering the skew and

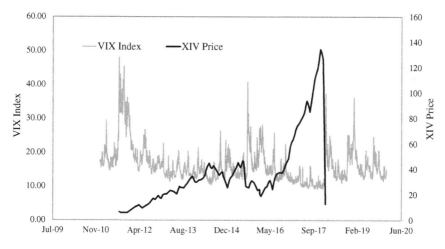

Figure 4.9: The XIV or VelocityShares Daily Inverse VIX blew-up during the VIX crash (2018).

decay of option vol surfaces. The bullish *volatility risk premium* (VRP) signal, which compares realised and implied volatility has been widely documented (Appx. D.8). Trend-following the back-adjusted VIX futures time series has quite a successful track record. Also, term structure inversion of VIX futures is often touted as a good risk-off signal and together with buying vol can be used in various "tail protection" strategies.

4.4.10 *Spread trading*

Spread trading is a well-known futures trading strategy. By trading long and short futures of different maturities, we can hedge directional futures risk and instead trade spreads or changes in the slope of the futures curve (Appx. C.8). The spread can be readily traded as a momentum strategy or using reversion. This provides a different and diversifying strategy for CTAs and is often used in energy and other commodity markets. However, for the larger CTAs, spread trading generally only represents a small allocation relative to the other strategies. This is because to obtain a reasonable level of volatility for the strategy, even though the net leverage is close to zero, the gross leverage (longs plus shorts) is very high. This can be problematic since liquidity and execution in the different maturity contracts becomes a constraint and the potential for large, unexpected gap moves or regime changes can lead to infrequent large losses. Spread trading is usually a negative skew and high kurtosis strategy as many unfortunate hedge funds have experienced. In 2006, $9.5bn Amaranth Advisors blew-up on natural gas spread trading primarily due to a huge long winter, short non-winter strategy that went spectacularly wrong. In September 2006, various estimates placed their natural gas spread trade losses at $3.3–4.0bn as spreads moved suddenly against them. It probably did not help that Amaranth represented over 50% of NYMEX open interest in many gas futures contracts leading to severe liquidity and financing problems.

Spread trading can also be applied to other coupled or linked assets beyond futures. For example, in the reversion of dual-listed equities (same cash equity listed on two different exchanges), different share classes or even different maturities on interest rate curves using swaps. Reversion trades often have high probability of success but to exploit the small reversion profits, as with futures spread trading, large gross leverage is required. If the reversion "breaks" then large losses can occur. These trades have high negative skew in that they make small money most of the time but infrequently incur large losses.

4.5 Multi-Market Diversification

Once a strategy is developed it can often be deployed across several markets to increase diversification and risk-adjusted returns. Although momentum is relatively weak in each individual market (Sharpe ratio 0.2–0.5), by adding many markets together we can achieve persistent Sharpe ratios around 1.0 (Table 4.2). Individual markets might have strong trending periods with good performance, then for a certain period have no strong trends and slowly lose money for years. These strong trending periods are virtually impossible to predict so it is difficult to decide how to allocate to each market.

The simplest allocation method is "1/N" whereby we allocate an equivalent amount of risk capital to each of the N markets over the long term. Dynamic allocation over-lays, involving correlation between markets and other techniques, almost always disappoint in practice and fail to beat the ignorance of "1/N". Thus, common sense allocation techniques are thus generally employed by the portfolio manager. A widely used but simplistic method is to allocate a certain risk budget to each sector (equities, rates, fx, commodities) and then within each sector allocate to subsectors and geography to maximise diversification or the effective "N". For a CTA a typical risk allocation might be 25% equities, 25% fx, 25% rates and 25% commodities with commodities split equally between AGS, energy and metals (Fig. 4.1).

The ultimate market diversifier is the highly successful long only *risk parity* (RP) strategy pioneered by AQR and Bridgewater. In risk parity the objective is to be long risk assets but immunise the portfolio against large drawdowns in an inexpensive way. Although a long equity portfolio can be hedged using options, this is impractically expensive. Instead, by diversifying across asset classes in a risk adjusted framework, the risk portfolio can be partially hedged. For most of the last couple of decades, bonds have been negatively correlated to equities and that has provided a hedge against risk-off events. Similarly, commodities are intended to provide an inflation hedge. Gold and JPY are also included to provide risk-off hedges. Despite the idiosyncratic risks involved, they may in the future displace bonds if yields continue to remain low. Since the credit crisis

(2008), low bond yields and volatilities require significantly larger bond notionals, on a risk-adjusted basis, to effectively "hedge" the higher volatility equities in a risk parity portfolio. Many prudent investors view this excessive bond leverage as an accident waiting to happen.

4.6 Multi-Strategy Diversification

Often, we will have developed many strategies and these can be combined into a "multi-strategy" portfolio for further diversification. The ubiquitous momentum, carry and value strategies have strong independent Sharpe ratios and low correlations (Table 4.4). The correlations between momentum and carry are 25% and value is even slightly negatively correlated. Combining these strategies across many markets provides a theoretical Sharpe ratio of over 1.5 (Fig. 4.10).

Table 4.4:   Long-term average correlations between momentum, carry and value.

	Momentum	Carry	Value
Momentum	1.0	0.25	−0.10
Carry	0.25	1.0	−0.02
Value	−0.10	−0.02	1.0

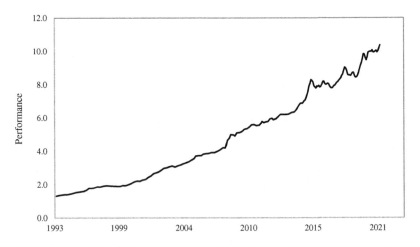

Figure 4.10:   Combining momentum, value and carry with OTC instruments.

A very large multi-strategy CTA might have some 40–50 strategies with some specialised for individual sectors. For example, we might have timing and reversion strategies on equities, relative value and seasonality in commodities and relative value spread trading in energies.

Usually, strategies are combined by a linear superposition of strategy signals. The normalised signals are added up after applying an allocation weighting to each signal (Appx. C.1). Once the market weights have been decided within each strategy, the strategy weights are used to provide a target portfolio. To this we must apply our risk-management framework for final portfolio construction. Risk constraints are impacted in an iterative process of changing market and strategy weights to maximise the risk-adjusted returns for a given portfolio target volatility.

Although we might possess quantitative methodologies to combine strategies, their practical results are often disappointing. All too frequently, assigning allocation weights to strategies becomes an "art-form" left to the portfolio manager rather than a strict science. We can use mathematical techniques using portfolio optimisation, correlations, Kelly criterion (by Sharpe ratio), recent performance etc. but in general these are less important than confidence in a strategy derived from testing and live performance. When real money is at stake, portfolio managers prefer a momentum model with 25+ years of actual battle experience than a new glossy strategy just developed by a junior quant with limited live testing. The spectre of over-fitting always looms in the back of a portfolio manager's mind.

4.7 Practical Aspects of Systematic Trading

Developing an automated trading system that integrates the systematic strategies with the fund's brokers and administrators is a complex task. Most importantly the system must be real-time, highly fault tolerant and extremely reliable, usually running 24 hours a day with little or no human intervention. Some funds might prefer to have human traders as part of the execution process, particularly for OTC instruments, but most systematic funds use algorithms for execution. A schematic for an integrated trading system is shown in Fig. 4.11. In essence, the entire trading system must perform the following tasks.

The system is built upon a historical database that is updated periodically (intraday) with latest market prices and other non-price data. Strategies then can be run periodically intraday to determine target positions in individual markets. This can be part of the strategy to increase

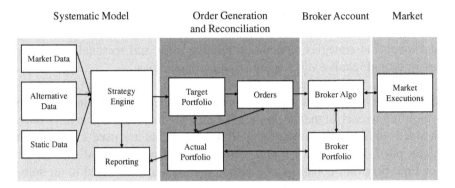

Figure 4.11:   The systematic trading process.

trading speed or to increase capacity via interlacing. Large potential changes to positions must be buffered and spread over time to reduce market impact and this effect must be accommodated in any backtesting or performance simulation.

The current positions are compared with the latest target positions to determine the next trade to execute. This requires an internal tally of trades performed and a broker query. Some major brokers are notoriously bad at intraday reconciliations and there must be much reliance on the internal manager's tally of trades that are actually executed.

The necessary orders are directed to the broker via an API. The orders will use a proprietary algorithm or broker algo (e.g., Iceberg, VWAP) to place trades and achieve optimum execution. Orders are typically market or limit orders. The correct execution of trades is monitored, cancelled and amended as necessary.

There is a post-trade reconciliation with the broker and if possible, this is performed intraday. The end-of-day position is calculated and the trade reconciliation is carried out with the broker and the fund administrator. The system must have the ability to automatically detect and allow easy manual queries of mismatched trades.

Lastly, the trading system must produce intraday risk and P&L reports. The reports should be emailed to various connected parties as required (senior management, investor etc.). The P&L tracking error should be monitored versus the theoretical strategy to determine slippage at regular intervals and any deviations must be explored.

The automation of as many of the tasks as possible is desirable. However, achieving this requires a long period of human supervision and oversight. Many occasional errors (such as broker APIs failing, data failures etc.) are only visible sporadically during live testing. Gradually, an automated self-checking process can be developed to diagnose and warn against various systems failures.

4.8 Strategy Development

The detailed strategy development process for an institutional systematic hedge fund consists of several key stages: strategy conception, research, implementation, backtesting, research report, peer review by experienced colleagues, acceptance and finally live-testing using proprietary capital (Fig. 4.12). Often it is an iterative process which can take several months, especially if a strategy is referred for further research during the internal peer review. In a large firm, the majority of strategies fail the process and are never used to manage client money.

4.8.1 *Strategy conception*

For most researchers, the strategy conception is the most important stage and points the direction for the project. Ideally a strategy should be based

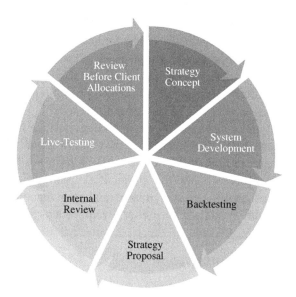

Figure 4.12: Typical systematic strategy development process.

on academic literature, a plausible idea or effect rooted in common sense and market experience. A strategy is most credible if it is simple, robust, applies across a wide range of markets and has few internal parameters or variables to be specified.

4.8.2 *System development*

The strategy is defined as series of equations and programmed up as an algorithm by researchers. Python/C#/C++/R/Mathlab are all common languages used. The strategy will access databases of static, historical and live data and will run intraday either continuously or at pre-defined times to provide predictive trading signals. These signals are converted into the number of contracts that will be traded in each market. Usually, when accepted for live-testing, the strategy software will be later integrated with execution, portfolio and risk management and middle/back-office systems.

4.8.3 *Backtesting*

The crucial part of the research process is backtesting to discover the historical performance of the strategy. The price history together with other relevant historical and static data is contained within a database. Historical data is split into non-overlapping training ("in-sample") and test ("out-of-sample") datasets. Sometimes several test datasets will be formed and withheld until further long in the development process as a final check. The training data is used to estimate the various parameters used in the model. Various fitting and error minimisation algorithms can be used to achieve this. Often t-tests and other statistical significance tests will be applied to the results.

Simple strategies, such as momentum strategies, have few parameters and do not require much data to fit. Complex multi-factor strategies may require many years of data and in some cases, it may not be statistically possible to correctly estimate the parameters with great confidence. Typically, greater than 10–15 years of historical daily data will be used for backtesting. Intraday models will of course require less data.

4.8.4 *Performance evaluation*

Evaluating performance of a strategy requires various metrics to allow comparison with other strategies. The essential metrics are return, volatility (standard deviation of returns), Sharpe ratio, drawdowns and correlation with different assets and strategies. These can be calculated for a given time period or on a rolling window basis. Other more detailed metrics exist (e.g., time to recover from drawdown, skew, Sortino ratio...) but these are essentially second order metrics.

Particularly interesting for strategies is behaviour under times of stress. A strategy should be tested in bull and bear markets, under different volatility conditions and regime changes. No strategy is perfect and all thrive or fail under various stress conditions. For example, diversified trend-following worked well during a slow-motion train wreck like 2002 and 2008 where the bear market lasted many months but failed miserably in the 2018 VIX crash where a very fast sell-off, after a period of low volatility, led to over-leveraged long equity positions. As with discretionary trading a series of stress tests and scenarios must be applied.

4.8.5 *Internal review*

For all hedge funds before live-testing there will be an internal research review to evaluate any new strategy or any material changes to existing strategies. This is often a peer review process involving neutral or unbiased colleagues with sufficient knowledge and expertise to evaluate the strategy. Any deficiencies or inadequate research will lead to a requirement for further research or a refusal to implement the strategy in live-testing. Usually after live-testing there is a mandatory additional review before allocating and managing client monies.

4.8.6 *Live-testing*

Before allocating client monies to a strategy, a period of live-testing is usually conducted. Although notionals used might be small relative to the eventual sums deployed, the live-test serves to resolve any observable problems in the actual trade process, for example, live order execution and reconciliation. Generally, due to weak Sharpe ratios of most systematic trading strategies, the live-testing cannot easily verify the performance of the strategy with statistical rigor. This would require several years of live-testing which is not possible in a commercial environment.

4.9 Key Issues with Developing Trading Strategies

Even if the correct development process is followed, there are many practical issues that must be considered when successfully implementing a systematic strategy. These range from potential over-fitting of model parameters and stability under regime changes, to transaction cost modelling and effective risk scaling. The effect of human discipline and the temptation to tamper with models is often overlooked, but is a key factor in strategy success.

4.9.1 *Over-fitting and feedback*

A serious problem in systematic trading is "over-fitting". If a systematic strategy contains several unknown parameters, these are estimated by varying them to find the best fit to the historical training data ("in-sample" data). The strategy can then be applied to unseen test data ("out-of-sample" data) to evaluate its performance. A strategy that is over-fitted has enough parameters that it can fit the training data with a deceptively high precision, but completely fails to fit the test data or more importantly, underperforms expectations with "live" data. Thus, the performance of the great new model often tends to be illusory.

This effect can be somewhat mitigated by (i) having ample data for training and test, (ii) splitting the data into multiple test datasets and (iii) having a simple strategy that cannot be over-fitted. However, financial data is often limited and finite and occasionally research programs suffer from "feedback" (Fig. 4.13). If a strategy works well in training and not

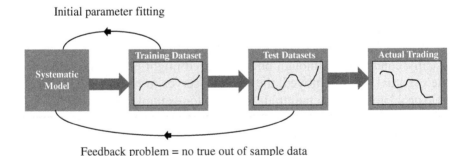

Figure 4.13:   Feedback in the research process results in no true out-of-sample data and over-fitting.

in test, there is a tendency to "tweak" the underlying model to make it perform both well in training and test. If this is done often enough by enough researchers in the team then very quickly there is no true out-of-sample data that can be used to validate the strategy. Some of the largest hedge funds I know have so many quant researchers constantly optimising strategies and allocations that their internal overall program has Sharpe ratios of 4–5 but achieves less than 1.0 in practice.

4.9.2 *Regime change*

Systematic strategies are by their definition backward looking and vulnerable to black swan style events. A regular criticism levelled against systematic trading is it is like driving while looking through the rear view mirror. If a particular market event does not appear in the historical dataset, then it can be difficult to predict how a strategy will behave. All strategies are conceived and tested on incomplete knowledge. Every new financial crisis is somewhat different from the previous ones. The 2007 quant quake, the 2008 credit crisis, 2018 VIX crash and 2020 covid crisis were all very different in origin and character.

Also, often a financial crisis or major event can precipitate a regime change in financial markets. These can often change the low-level dynamics of markets across different time-scales which can disrupt model performance for long periods of time. If a market becomes truly random then all of our long-term statistical effects will disappear. For example, markets can be trendless for long periods of time. Volatility regimes can also influence strategies in different ways. Moderate volatility can be beneficial for some models but high volatility is often associated with unpredictability and chaos. The dot-com bull market of 2002 was very different from the declining volatility bull market in equities and bonds triggered by quantitative easing (QE) in the post 2008 world.

Regime changes can also occur for other more subtle reasons. The phenomenal increase in computing power per \$ has impacted systematic funds in several ways. Since 2010 the rise in HFT has led to a change in micro-structure and arguably a false impression of liquidity in the markets. HFT effectively makes money by anticipating order-flow and trading before slower traders. Slow moving trend funds have high autocorrelation between trades. Their next trade is highly likely to be in the same direction as the previous one. I suspect this has become an unquantifiable "dripping tap" or drag on the returns for many slower CTAs.

In addition, with widespread technology, much more money has poured into systematic hedge funds leading to crowded strategies and a decay of profitability of well-known strategies. One academic paper claimed that once an effect or strategy was published its profitability decayed by 50%. I would go further and claim that for many niche strategies, virtually all profitability is destroyed. Figure 4.14 shows a typical, if somewhat cynical, life cycle for a strategy. The unknown proprietary strategy exhibits a high Sharpe ratio, then someone for the public good (and arguably to increase their academic publication rate) "discovers" and publishes the anomaly or effect upon which the strategy is based. At first, a few people copy the strategy which provides a small increase in Sharpe ratio as momentum boosts the effect and arbitrages close more efficiently. Then, as everyone else piles in, the effect disappears and the Sharpe ratio decreases rapidly as overcrowding occurs. As everyone, disillusioned, abandons the strategy there are liquidations and the Sharpe ratio even turns negative as everyone runs for the exit and burns their models. Eventually it becomes unpopular and recovers to a much lower equilibrium Sharpe ratio, as another initially great strategy bites the dust. This removal of "low lying fruit" has created a competitive arms race amongst hedge funds to find new strategies based on new instruments such as OTC markets and on the latest advanced technologies such as machine learning and alternative data.

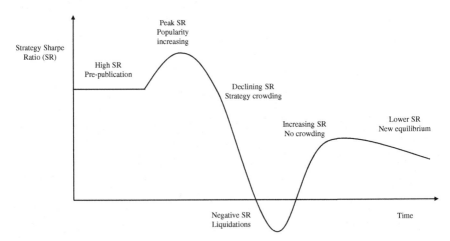

Figure 4.14:   Strategy publication and over-crowding may cause a reduction in realised performance.

4.9.3 *Transaction cost modelling*

The backtesting for the systematic strategy provides an estimate of the theoretical gross returns and risk profile. However, to reflect reality we need to include the effects of trading costs, financing and execution slippage. Trading costs paid to brokers and exchanges are known costs and simple to include.

Execution slippage is the hardest to model and is dependent on market liquidity and size of trades. Slippage is the amount the actual execution price varies disadvantageously from the theoretical execution level. Market impact is an important component of slippage, and is the amount the market moves adversely against the strategy during execution due to liquidity effects and other market participants anticipating order flow. Academically, it is widely accepted that the market impact of trades scales with the market volatility and a factor based on the trade size relative to the market volume over the period traded (often called the p-rate). However, execution models can only be tested by practical market experience and empirically with trades of different sizes under various market conditions (Appx. C.9).

Often it is possible to design a great theoretical strategy with a very high Sharpe ratio but once slippage and costs are correctly represented the Sharpe ratio is much reduced. This is often the case for faster strategies that look great on paper but are overwhelmed by unexpected trading costs when live trading, producing a small loss day after day. Estimating the critical size or "capacity" of a strategy before transaction costs materially deteriorate performance, is a critical calculation in systematic trading that requires experience and skill.

Figure 4.15 shows the typical market impact costs for liquid futures contracts, the E-mini S&P (ES) and the slightly less liquid Nasdaq (NQ). These numbers may seem small but for fast daily trading they soon add up. If for example, we trade $100m ES in and out a day every day of the year, this is around 5% drag on our performance per annum. This cost barrier is the reason large funds are constrained to trade slow. Typically, we might expect from a large CTA with slow momentum rebalancing on a daily basis, costs of 0.5–1 bp for equity indices and bonds and up to 3–4 bp for markets like copper. More illiquid commodity markets must thus be traded at slower momentum speeds to reduce turnover and slippage.

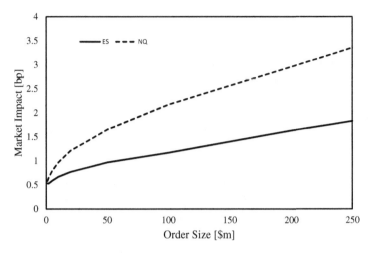

Figure 4.15:   Typical market impact costs for S&P 500 (ES) and Nasdaq (NQ) futures.

4.9.4 *Risk-scaling*

Risk-scaling is used by the major CTAs to improve long-term, risk adjusted returns. The position size on each market is rescaled inversely to the volatility of the underlying market (Appx. C.1). In this way, the risk attributed to each market can be placed on a common footing and we can combine different assets in portfolios on a risk-weighted basis. Thus, we can have, say a 10% target volatility and assign 25% of the risk budget to each of equities, fx, rates and commodities where the notional amounts of each asset class will differ significantly. Bonds, due to their low volatility, will have a much higher notional contribution than high volatility equities. As the volatility of each market changes, its notional will be dynamically reweighted to reflect the same risk contribution. Overall, it is a very neat and widely used concept.

Historically, risk-scaling increases the long-term Sharpe ratio of long only portfolios and trend-following by around 10–20%. However, risk-scaling works best in periods of market crisis by controlling risk, stabilising volatility and reducing drawdowns. If sharp falls are experienced in markets, then the volatility increases and the market position size is reduced. This de-gearing effect seems to work well across most markets. However, the main sectors that benefit are equities and corporate credit and this is arguably due to a leverage effect. If equities and bonds fall, their volatility increases as the individual corporate capital structures become more leveraged and riskier.

It is, however, not all plain sailing with risk-scaling. Under certain circumstances it can lead to undesirable results. A worst-case scenario is a large sudden move against the well-established, existing trend, enough time for the strategy to deleverage due to the increased volatility and then unexpectedly the market reverses back towards the trend. Under these circumstances a loss has been "locked-in" with no net change in the underlying market. As risk-scaling and "buying the dip" strategies have become widespread in the past decade, this scenario seems to have become unfortunately more frequently observed.

4.9.5 *Human discipline*

Although in the introduction to this chapter I suggested that systematic trading removes human emotion and bias from the investing process, nothing could be further from the practical truth. Human discipline is paramount to a successful systematic strategy.

The systematic models are the fruit of a long research process. In periods of poor performance there is a large temptation to change parameters or add improvements. These quick fixes and questionable enhancements are extremely bad practice. In all likelihood your original system only has practically a Sharpe ratio of less than 1.0. Although this sounds great, it can take years to statistically verify a Sharpe ratio such as this. Trend-following for example, can remain in drawdown for years. Unless you believe the original research was genuinely flawed in some respect, it is better to "strap oneself to the mast" and weather any storms. Instead of tampering and perhaps deteriorating the performance further, patience is necessary. In practice, the only time you should ever make sudden changes to a system is when the operation of the underlying market is disrupted and will markedly deviate from the historical training data. A good example of this is excluding say, the Swiss Franc when you know there is government intervention or excluding an equity which is subject to a hard special situation.

I find traders of a discretionary background struggle with the robot-like discipline required for systematic trading. They are prone to second guess the system and gasp in wonder at the all too many daft decisions the system makes. The computer, like an emotionless poker bot, plays the odds. It can persist in making wrong decisions for a very long time since it "believes", correctly or not, that long term statistics will prevail. Discretionary traders have their own world view and this is often at odds with a systematic strategy. For them, leaving the computer 100% in command is pure torment. Unfortunately, they are all too ready to override the system and ruin the small bias to the dice rolls that systematic trading involves.

Investors are even more impatient. Often, they review hedge fund performances on a quarterly or even a monthly basis. It is simply impossible to determine the final outcome or success of a systematic trading system on such short time scales. Unfortunately, this behaviour is a recipe for disappointment and it is rooted in a misunderstanding of statistics. In the original presentation, they saw 15–20 years of profits chugging ever higher but this is different from what they physically experience. The difference is timescale. Myopic investors need to get their magnifying glasses out and see that historically, the strategy actually went sideways for ages and did indeed have drawdowns. Investing in a 10% volatility strategy and not being able to persist through 10–15% drawdowns is not a viable allocation methodology.

4.10 Good versus Bad Strategies

Finally, it is interesting to consider what makes a good systematic strategy versus a bad strategy from both a theoretical and practical point of view (Fig. 4.16). This helps with the selection and design of strategies and the interpretation of results.

Good strategies are simple in concept with relatively few internal parameters making them intuitive and intrinsically "believable". "Simple is better" or some variant of "Occam's razor" applies when constructing a good strategy.

Good strategies must provide enough historic trades in the available dataset to provide "decent" statistics and be amenable to statistical tests. Too few trades and strategies cannot be accepted on a statistical basis. For example, a very slow seasonal trade with 10 trades over 10 years and a winning ratio of 6 in 10 trades is less statistically credible than a faster reversion strategy with 1000 trades of which 550–600 are "winners".

The flip-side to the above argument is that strategies with a smaller number of trades or turnover are preferred over faster strategies. Slower, low turnover strategies are more predictable in the nature of their

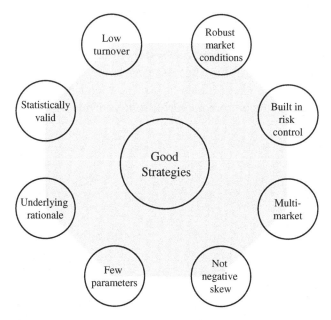

Figure 4.16:   The key attributes of a "good" systematic strategy.

potential costs and slippage and have much larger capacity. Slow trend trading can manage in excess of $10bn whereas fast intraday strategies might have less than $50m capacity before trading costs impact their performance.

Good strategies are robust under different market conditions with stable volatility and consistent drawdowns. They must have performed well during major crises and key dates that most strategies have been known to fail on. Drawdowns are inevitable and can be regular but recoveries must be fairly swift. Ideally many historical drawdowns must be visible and they must all be in a bounded range with no major anomalies. Typically, 1–2 × the annual volatility target is good.

Good strategies must have "built in" risk-control to reduce losses when things go wrong. Trend-following is good in this regard. If the trend changes, the strategy slowly adapts to the new trend. If there is a sudden increase in volatility, the strategy reduces its position size and there is no "stop loss" level. Hard stop losses are avoided by major funds since they can produce chaotic uncontrolled liquidations at the worst moment. Rules-based controlled exits are preferred.

Lastly, strategy skew is a major consideration and neutral or positive skew is preferable in the long term. Negative skew trades (i.e., selling options) might appeal optically to investors in the short term but positive skew trades (i.e., trend-following) out-perform eventually with no nasty "blow-ups". Positive skew trades, however, spend much time in draw-down and require much more patience from your investors.

Chapter 5

The Factor Game

5.1 Equity Factor Investing

As the efficient market hypothesis (EMH) finally lost its grip on the academic community, the research focus drifted towards studying other significant factors that influenced equity returns. Equity returns were found not only to be correlated to the overall market but to other factors such as company size and fundamental valuation. This led to the rise of so-called "factor investing" that was widely adopted by many systematic L/S equity hedge funds. As knowledge and acceptance of the factors spread, factor investing has become part of the mainstream with long-only ETFs and smart beta indices evolving to incorporate the most common factors.

5.1.1 *The capital asset pricing model*

Way back in 1952, Harry Markowitz at the University of Chicago published his seminal work entitled *Portfolio Selection*. His concepts of diversification leading to reduction of risk and the trade-offs between changing portfolio return and risk were groundbreaking. He developed the "efficient frontier" which described the boundary of portfolios for the highest expected return for each level of risk or volatility (Appx. A.1). Founded in the concept of efficient markets and random walks they led to the development in the early 1960s of the *capital asset pricing model* (CAPM).

In the CAPM the expected return on an asset can be represented as a linear equation. The well-known *beta* for the asset is the factor of proportionality or sensitivity of the asset returns to the expected excess market returns (Appx. D.1). The excess market returns are usually defined as the return of the asset above the so-called risk-free rate. In a sufficiently diversified portfolio, the specific risk of each equity is assumed to be diversified away and the portfolio returns are driven by the overall systemic market movements related by the aggregate of the portfolio betas (Appx. D.2).

CAPM is essentially a one factor model since one random variable (the excess market return) multiplied by the beta, is supposedly adequate to describe movements of a diversified portfolio. The success of CAPM was remarkable but unfortunately, academic work suggested CAPM could only explain around 2/3 of the differences in diversified portfolio returns. This discrepancy required the inclusion of other additional factors to close the gap between theory and practice (Appx. D.3).

5.1.2 *The Fama–French three-factor model*

Eugene Fama, again from the Chicago School of Economics, is viewed by many as one of the key founders of the efficient market ideology. His Ph.D. thesis was based on stock prices being unpredictable random walks. He also demonstrated that in real markets, extreme market moves were more common than expected, resulting in return probability distributions possessing fat tails.

Despite his affiliation to the dogma of efficient markets, it is surprising that in later years he started to question the foundations of the CAPM model. The list of anomalies or deviations from the CAPM were starting to pile up and could no longer be ignored. Together with Kenneth French, he added two further factors to CAPM to try and explain the observed variation of real equity portfolios from the existing framework.

The two factors they added in 1993 were (i) the market size of a company and (ii) fundamental company valuation. The market size factor was termed the SMB (Small market cap Minus Big) factor, which accounted for the observed effect that companies with small market capitalisation outperformed, on average, large capitalisation companies. The second valuation factor or HML factor was based on High book-to-market ratio Minus Low (Appx. D.4). This introduced the long known empirical effect that relatively "cheap" companies outperform expensive companies and became known as the Value factor. Book-to-market (BtM) ratio is the measure they used but other formulations of representing company relative value are possible.

The combination of these three factors — market beta, relative market capitalisation and relative market valuation allowed the explanatory power of the factor-based model to reach 90% of diversified portfolio returns. This was pretty impressive but it was just the start of the factor game.

5.1.3 *The Carhart four-factor model*

As the academic community accepted the inevitable demise of the efficient market hypothesis and the pure CAPM, the factor floodgates opened. Many effects that quant traders had known for years were "rediscovered" by academics knowing that their careers would now still survive if they published against the efficient market orthodoxy.

An example was the Carhart four-factor model (1997) which introduced cross-sectional momentum as a fourth factor (Appx. D.5). The monthly momentum factor was calculated as the "equal-weight average of firms with the highest 30% eleven-month returns lagged one month minus the equal-weight average of firms with the lowest 30% eleven-month returns lagged one month. The portfolios include all NYSE, Amex, and Nasdaq stocks and are re-formed monthly". Thus, for a chosen universe of equities the average 12-month returns are calculated, with the latest month removed. The equities are ranked and the top 30% became long trades while the bottom 30% are shorts.

The reason that the most recent month is excluded is common amongst academic analyses. It is rather unusual, but is an attempt to exclude the observed effect of short-term reversion observed in many equities. In 1990 a couple of academic papers dissuaded the academic community from including short-term momentum. Bruce Lehman's paper *Fad, Martingdales and Market Efficiency* showed that portfolios of positive returns in one week were on average losers in the next week and vice versa. The paper by Narasimham Jegadeesh boldly entitled *Evidence of Predictable Behavior of Security Returns* demonstrated that from 1934–1989 the winners/losers in one month have returns of −1.4%/+1.1% in the next month. Also, momentum relative to the market seems to become a reversal effect over very long-time scales. Thus, momentum factors focus on timescales called "intermediate momentum" in the

6–12 month range. In practice, any real trading system usually accounts for these effects by having a superposition of momenta of different speeds and not quite as simplistic as the Cahart model with the brutal exclusion of the last month.

Many academics dislike momentum as a factor since it is not fundamentally or economically based. It is an irrational irritation and cannot be simply explained. Many unprovable pseudo arguments have been proposed, from slow diffusion of news over time and underestimating earnings surprises to complex investor behaviour such as observing 52-week high/lows, herding, delusion of crowds or the phenomenon of not wanting to miss out (I am feeling that with the skyrocketing bitcoin cryptocurrency today). However, whatever the rational explanation for momentum is, it is a ubiquitous first order effect that every trader has experienced and cannot be overlooked.

5.1.4 *A flood of factors*

The expansion of the search for factors has reached crazy proportions. Over 500 academic factors have been published in the literature. Many of these factors are of dubious quality and are highly correlated with one another. Even on Bloomberg "Factors to Watch" (FTW) screen, there are, for say in the STOXX 600 index, 190 factors available with the top dozen or so being (dispersion, dividends, growth, leverage, momentum, profitability, revisions, size, sentiment, surprises, share buybacks, technicals and value). Many of the factors are weighted averages of several underlying metrics. For example the value factor is a weighted sum of book-to-price, cashflow/market cap, net income/market cap, EBITA/EV, earnings/price and sales/EV. Many of these composite factors and secondary factors have their merits. However, to enter the pantheon of great factors there are several requirements in my opinion.

Now we could just blast the market data with Principal Component Analysis (PCA) and extract the major market moving eigenvalues (Appx. D.10). However, this quickly becomes a data fitting exercise and provides no understanding or rationale to the extracted factors. Instead, the factors need to be intuitive and derived from common sense and not an unexplainable random data fitting. In addition, factors need to be universal and globally applicable to different financial markets, unless there is a convincing reason for them to be specific to certain markets. To be desirable, factors need to be of sufficiently low turnover and hence trading costs, that they can be invested in without all your theoretical gross profits being eaten away.

Lastly, and perhaps most importantly, they should be consistent through time and durable. Although some factors have proven testable for almost 100 years, perhaps even this is insufficient to allow us to assume stationarity and existential persistence of factors. The best we can reasonably ask is that through time, we would expect a long-term risk-adjusted return without too many extensive drawdowns. It may be that there are periods when the factor declines to work but these should be explainable and hopefully decorrelated to the other major factors such that a composite portfolio of factors is still viable over the long term. Another aspect that one should carefully consider is whether the academic publication and universal knowledge of a factor will deteriorate or even destroy its performance.

Perhaps, for the major factors such as size and value, their academic publication is less of a problem than we might otherwise think. Their Sharpe ratios are weak and they have prolonged periods of terrible performance which can last years. Most investors lack patience and are all too ready to abandon such strategies (especially when they are in a bull market for equities). Most hedge funds are measured on their month-by-month returns by investors and thus badly performing strategies will be rapidly deallocated. In my opinion, the major factors will survive the onslaught of smart beta overcrowding and periods of mediocre performance and remain long-term viable for the very patient investor.

5.2 Review of the Big 5 Factors

Thus, if we apply our filter to the rapidly expanding universe of factors, we find that we dramatically reduce the number of factors for practical long/short equity investing. We are left with the big 5 — market beta, size, value, momentum and quality. As with a Venn diagram, many alternative factors can be formed by the intersection of these pure factors. Indeed, these main factors are subjected to numerous nuances and mathematical definitions. For example, a growth factor is essentially a subset of quality and for most people, value definitions include factors that reside in quality.

The convention in the academic factor community is to assume dollar neutral or notional neutral portfolios. That is to say, the notional of all the longs is the same as the shorts and the same dollar allocation is given to each equity in the portfolio. To correspond to the broad literature on the subject this is the approach adopted in this Chapter. However, in practice hedge fund portfolio managers have the investment option to be market neutral which can be achieved by being beta neutral or volatility weighted neutral. In the case of market neutral portfolios, the generic factor results are very similar to notional neutral but the market and size factors are obviously significantly modified.

5.2.1 *The market beta factor*

The most blindingly obvious factor is the market beta. Just being long high beta equities and short low beta and diversifying out the specific risk is in fact one of the strongest factors. As everyone knows, market indices go up over time. Shorting markets (except for short periods of time in crises) is a losing game. If you have ever tried running a long/short equity portfolio over a long period of time, it is very difficult in the last few decades to make money from your short portfolio. The long-term Sharpe ratio over around 70 years for the market factor is 0.4 (Table 5.1). The skew is negative (−0.6) which indicates that there are long periods of positive performance and sudden sell-offs. This is a characteristic of what we experience by being long in equity markets. The maximum drawdown of −55% is surprisingly like most of the other main factors.

5.2.2 *The size factor*

The size factor was essentially the first factor to be added to the CAPM model. The academic reasoning was sound and relatively uncontroversial.

Table 5.1: Long-term US long/short equity factor performance (last 70 years).

	Shape Ratio	Skew	Max Drawdown (%)
Market	0.4	−0.6	−55
Value	0.2	0.8	−50
Size	0.2	0.6	−54
Momentum	0.6	−1.5	−58
Quality	0.5	0.2	−30

Small companies are simply riskier and in an efficient market, we should be paid more to hold them. Generally, small companies are more susceptible to economic problems, more uncertain in their profitability and cashflows, vulnerable to squeezes in capital and importantly (in my experience) less liquid to trade. Historically, small cap stocks are more volatile due to all these effects.

Table 5.1 shows that the Sharpe ratio is weak (0.2) but the skew is positive (0.6). The positive skew might be because small companies outperform in periods of economic expansion or perhaps a lottery effect. If small companies are perceived as having large growth potential by investors they can be viewed as positive skew lottery ticket style investments. Some studies have shown that screening small companies to discern the higher quality ones (conditioning using the quality factor below) can lead to higher returns from the size factor.

5.2.3 *The value factor*

The grandfathers of value investing were Graham and Dodd, who published *Security Analysis* in 1934. They distinguished between pure speculation and investing which, in their view, was distinguished by detailed fundamental analysis. In *The Intelligent Investor* (1949), Graham recommended that for passive investors who invest for the long term, they should seek a "margin of safety" by buying companies at prices below their intrinsic value. Apparently, his best value investment was buying a major stake in the insurer GEICO for $712k in 1948 and it later reached an amazing $400m in 1972.

Warren Buffet, the legendary value investor, is well-known as a keen disciple of Graham and strangely, his company Berkshire Hathaway later acquired GEICO. Buffet loves the free float of insurers for acquiring other investments. I used to work for AAA rated General Re that was acquired by Buffet. Unfortunately, since Buffet believes "derivatives are financial weapons of mass destruction" and definitely not great long-term value, he quickly closed down the financial products arm manufacturing long dated exotic derivatives where I worked. Viewed the later demise of AIG Financial Products during the credit crisis, this was probably a prescient call.

Thus, the value effect was well documented for over 50 years before it was qualified by the academic community to be of sufficient standing to break into the CAPM club and to be a worthy factor along-side market beta. The dislike of academics mainly stemmed from the fact that they could not explain where the value effect came from. Surely if markets are efficient then there should be no value in value stocks, as everything should be fairly priced. Was the effect a risk-based effect or an investor behavioural effect? For example, are value stocks more distressed, troubled companies and hence riskier to justify their discount? Or do value companies (as opposed to growth companies), since they often pay dividends, have a higher sensitivity to interest rates? On the behavioural side, arguments have been proposed, such as the fact that humans prefer lottery ticket style growth stocks over dull, unexciting value stocks that have been moving sideways for years. The reverse argument is that many value stocks often have a nasty back story and known concerns surrounding them. This makes them scary and investors often feel wise avoiding them … but if the clouds clear then sometimes they can out-perform.

Graham's original methodology for value was buying a portfolio of stocks with a price-to-earnings ratio below 10 and a debt-to-equity below 50%. He provided an exit strategy as well — by selling stocks if they had risen 50% or if not, sell them anyways after a 2-year holding period. Over the last 50 years, the simple strategy has performed remarkably well on the S&P 500 although sometimes when the market is highly valued, it is impossible to find any stocks meeting the criteria. It is interesting to note that Graham's methodology combines value (the P/E ratio) and a small measure of quality (the debt/equity ratio).

The academic value factor is traditionally calculated as book-to-market (BtM) value. The book value is the common shareholders equity and is technically taken as the accounting value from the balance sheet. This is effectively assets minus liabilities adjusted for intangibles, preference shares etc. The market value is simply the market capitalisation. The value factor is robust to other similar value metrics. Over the long term for a large set of definitions, the value factor has achieved a modest Sharpe ratio of 0.2.

In 2006 Joel Greenblatt published the great book *The Little Book that Beats the Market* and his "Magic Formula" (Appx. D.7). The book was ostensibly about long only-value investing but his value formula includes aspects such as *return on capital* (ROC) which overlap somewhat with the quality factor. Interestingly, Greenblatt observed that he found it difficult to consciously beat his formula and manual intervention significantly decreased the long-term performance. The reason he surmised for this was that value formula picked many risky, beaten down stocks which he disliked due to various well-known issues. If he was too clever and decided to exclude them, it was sometimes the case that they would turn out to be the big winners that would boost portfolio performance. This effect probably explains the strong positive skew of the value strategy.

5.2.4 *The momentum factor*

The momentum factor as we noted with the Carhart four-factor model is a highly persistent and pervasive alpha strategy. Simply ranking stocks on the basis of their recent historic returns and going long/short those with the highest/lowest returns is performance wise, a strategy that exceeds the other fundamental factors (Table 5.1). This form of momentum is known as cross-sectional momentum and has slightly different characteristics than the time series momentum or trend following we discussed for CTAs. Time series momentum involves trading the trend on individual markets or assets and not trading the trend of each market versus another. In fact, trading time series momentum on individual equities does not perform that well in general.

A criticism of cross-sectional momentum is that turnover is much higher than for many of the other factors. In implementing momentum and any other faster factor strategies we must be careful to model and monitor trading costs including slippage. However, the higher turnover provides a key benefit in that the portfolio adapts more quickly to market regimes and equity fads and fashions than many of the other slower factors. In a value strategy the same equities can remain beaten down and cheap for years before they see any movement and the portfolio can stagnate. This can be frustrating. Instead, momentum portfolios are always rotating and changing to adapt to the next favoured theme.

A disadvantage of momentum portfolios is the occasional brutal sell-offs. Time series momentum used by CTAs is nicely positive skew. In contrast, cross-sectional momentum has the highest factor skew at −1.5. The recent November 2020 momentum crash was a case of point. During the coronavirus rally, the success of the Pfizer vaccine was announced and all the covid losers such as airlines, retail and hospitality suddenly rallied. The covid winners such as tech, online retail and take-away providers declined. Some shares, like Rolls-Royce making aircraft engines, despite unsustainably burning through their capital bases, rallied over 60% in a day. The move in the momentum factor relative to value was extreme to say the least. I liked the following quote on Bloomberg: *A quant shock that "never could happen" hits Wall Street models*. It was calculated that under the theoretical assumption of a normal distribution, the "crash of the momentum factor on this day should occur only once in −5, 944, 505, 312,

905, 660, 000, 000, 000, 000, 000, 000, 000, 000, 000, 000, 000, 000, 000, 000, 000, 000, 000, 000, 000, 000, 000 days". So much for using momentum factors and assuming normal distributions.

To improve the momentum concept, various conditioning methods are often applied. For example, conditioning the raw signal for smoothness of momentum, volatility, seasonality etc. Also, momentum itself can be used to condition other factors. However, many other effects and factors can overlap with momentum and this produces higher correlation between factors quickly. The fact that the factors are raw, under-fitted and vaguely orthogonal is a great thing that one should be wary of meddling with. For example, combining the negative correlation of momentum and value in portfolios is already a good diversifier and arguably a better way of increasing portfolio risk-adjusted returns than by fine tuning the definition of each factor or cross-factor conditioning.

5.2.5 *The quality factor*

It may seem likely that more profitable and higher quality companies should outperform over the long-term. As we mentioned, Graham even included a quality leverage factor in his original value formula and considered profitability in his investing process. However, it took till 2006 for Fama and French to rigorously demonstrate that firms with higher profitability have higher future returns. In 2013, Robert Novy-Marx published *The Other Side of Value: The Gross Profitability Premium* and showed that the ratio of gross profits to assets was as powerful a predictor of returns as the common BtM value metric.

Novy-Marx further showed that the most profitable firms are usually fast expanding growth firms. Surprisingly, even if companies have higher valuations their future returns will be higher. This provides a link between profits, growth and valuations. If a stock seems bad on the basis of a value factor, the fact that it is highly profitable and fast growing means it can still be worth buying. The fact that gross profitability is of better predictive value than net profits or earnings is unsurprising from my point of view. Fast growing companies re-invest for growth and often have high return on capital. Importantly, as Amazon proved with its endless growth phase, it is not a requirement to have any profits.

Often this profitability factor is encompassed within an overall quality factor. This quality factor includes other sensible metrics to discriminate high quality companies from the crowd. The quality factor is called QMJ (Quality minus Junk) (Appx. D.6). A high-quality company might have high earnings, low leverage, high asset turnover, low earnings volatility, a good balance sheet etc. and not just profitability. Using a standard definition of quality, the long-term Sharpe ratio is 0.5 (Table 5.1), low positive skew (0.2) and the smallest drawdown of all the factors at around −30%. A further unexpected benefit is that quality is a strong crisis diversifier possessing a negative correlation (around −0.5) to corrections in the S&P500. All things considered, quality is perhaps the most powerful factor.

5.3 Investing with Factors

It is interesting to consider what drives the individual factors and under what conditions they thrive or suffer. Since the 2008 credit crisis there has been extensive QE and very low rates. Equity markets have strongly rallied, leading to strong market factor returns. However, all the other US equity factors with the exception of quality have experienced lackluster performance (Table 5.2).

Typically, momentum performs best in positive inflation and growth scenarios. In 2008, momentum exhibited its worst drawdown of −58% with a huge momentum crash that bottomed in September 2009 and has only achieved a Sharpe ratio of 0.1 since the credit crisis. Value in contrast is a defensive factor and historically performs best when inflation and growth expectations are falling. In the aftermath of the dot-com crash, it rallied +27% and with the covid crisis +11%. However, in the anemic interest rate world of QE when everyone was focused on tech stocks, value produced a negative performance with a −0.2 Sharpe ratio. The quality factor actually had increased performance since the credit crisis with 0.6 Sharpe ratio versus the long term of 0.5. Quality over the long term has prospered when inflation is rising and growth expectations are falling whilst providing downside protection during periods of market volatility.

Table 5.2: US factor performance long term (LT) and since credit crisis (CC).

	Share Ratio LT	Share Ratio CC
Market	0.4	0.4
Value	0.2	−0.2
Size	0.2	0.0
Momentum	0.6	0.1
Quality	0.5	0.6

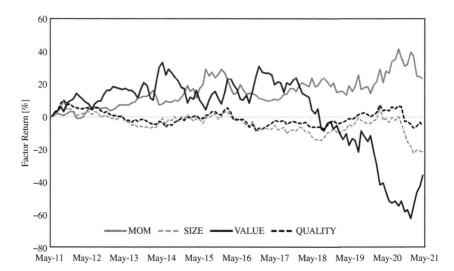

Figure 5.1:   Recent US equity factor returns.

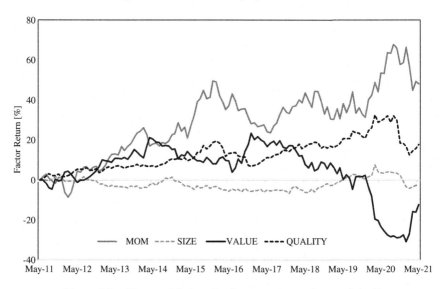

Figure 5.2:   Recent global equity factor returns … less exploited?

In the last few years in the US, equities momentum has fought back (Fig. 5.1) and has been the leading factor. Value has declined significantly since 2017–2018 and only slightly rebounded in 2020–2021 with the news of the Pfizer vaccine success. For global equities both momentum and quality have performed positively and significantly better than the US (Fig. 5.2). The outperformance of global quality is difficult to explain and is possibly due to the lower growth expectations and less bullish markets during the period outside the US. Anecdotally, I find that factor returns are generally better sustained in recent years in Europe and Asia as many factor returns have dwindled in the US. If I design a model for US equities and instead plug in European equities, generally a higher performance is exhibited. This may possibly be due to less funds exploiting factor models in Europe relative to the US.

5.4 A Reversion Factor?

In passing, we can consider the inverse of momentum or reversion. As mentioned, the academic factor studies ignore the most recent month of momentum due its pesky reversion tendencies. For many years this reversion effect was the bread and butter of so-called statistical arbitrage hedge funds. The core strategy was deceptively simple. By selling recent winners and buying recent losers, traders could profit from reversion back to the mean (Appx. D.9). Profits for such strategies were exceptional for many years but the alpha for the most part, particularly in US markets, has dried up somewhat (Fig. 5.3). This is probably a result of the diffusion of knowledge of algorithms, technology and the improvements in electronic execution. Adding to the decline in alpha is probably the numerous

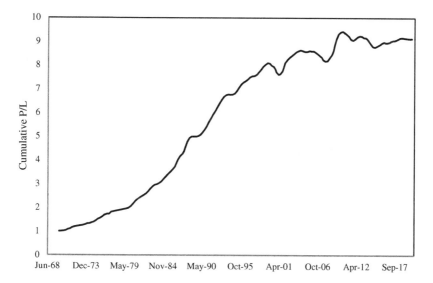

Figure 5.3:   The returns of classic statistical arbitrage have diminished in the 2000s.

academic publications of the effect. To currently capitalise on reversion effects, the traditional reversion signal must be coupled or conditioned with other factors such as those derived from alternative data discussed in Chapter 8.

5.5 The Blunderbuss Approach

The blunderbuss fires pellets indiscriminately in all directions with the hope that some hit their target. A similar approach is possible in factor discovery. For example, an alternative approach to factors is the Worldquant methodology. You either love it or loath it. In 2015, Zura Kakushadze published *101 Formulaic Alphas* providing 101 formulae (mainly involving price and volume) for alpha signals. These signals were seemingly not engineered on the basis of an intuitive approach but instead most likely by a formula generator that provided equations such as "(−1 *rank(((stddev(abs((close − open)), 5) + (close − open)) + correlation (close, open,10))))". The paper was swiftly followed up by an analysis of over 4000 alphas of a similar vein. Many of the factors presented were technically driven and thus more suited to shorter holding periods than the main quant factors we have discussed.

Now, most academics and systematic traders would decry such an approach as irresponsible, massive data mining and that if given enough mathematical attempts of varied complexity, it should be possible to generate any number of illusional so-called alpha signals. After all, how many monkeys does it take to write Hamlet? However, Worldquant has been highly successful so perhaps there is more to the method than meets the eye. Perhaps by combining an enormous amount of obscure, weak alpha signals (many of which will be somewhat correlated) a more highly persistent alpha signal can be created? Who cares if some alpha signals are fleeting or ephemeral if you have so many? By 2017 Worldquant reportedly had 4m alphas, managed $5bn and apparently has never had a down year.

5.6 The Evolution of Factors

As we have discussed, the performance of several key factors such as momentum, value and size have decreased noticeably since the credit crisis. Whether this is due to the influence of QE or the more widespread use of factors in investing is debatable. The factors are now widely documented and used in many active strategies including long only smart beta products. The quality factor has thrived both before and after the crisis with a Sharpe ratio of 0.5–0.6 but this is arguably a more contemporary factor that has only more recently been published (2013). Also, European markets, which are less exploited, seem to have retained their factor performance relative to the widely mined US equities. If factors become more widespread, are they destined to go extinct like the woolly mammoth as the academics hunt them all down? What is the future of factors now that computers and market data are widely available? In 2020–2021 the status quo is a quasi-existential quant crisis for managers using the major factors. The unpalatable alternative of looking for low-capacity idiosyncratic single equity opportunities is much harder, especially for machines.

However, it is perhaps too early to be pessimistic on the disappearance of factor alpha. There are good fundamental reasons underpinning the main factors that suggest they will be viable in the long term. As we have mentioned, investing in factors requires great patience and long-term analysis suggests there are extended fallow periods leading to alpha famine. If the key factor markets are overcrowded now and underperform, eventually "lightweight" investors will become disappointed and be driven out, leading to eventual alpha recovery. The alpha factors essentially become markets in their own right with bullish and bearish periods.

Another important concept is the evolution of factors. What might have been applicable as a factor definition in history might have been replaced (as with covid) by a new "variant". Take for example the old fusty definition of value as the price-to-book ratio. Since before the credit crisis, value stocks have massively disappointed as tech stocks have soared. Unfortunately, the innovation and intangible benefit of new business processes of tech companies is not reflected in their value factors due to ancient accounting practices. Amazon, Alphabet, eBay, Netflix etc. have all created novel business processes, which are often high value quasi monopolies that did not exist two decades ago. Arguably, the nature of the old value factor has changed over the last couple of decades and the definition should evolve as well. Measuring such innovation and intangible benefits is however tricky. If as a proxy, data such as cashflow were included in the value factor then we quickly converge towards a hybrid of the value factor and the better performing quality factor. Thus, perhaps the artificial boundaries between the factors are eroding and we must in future consider elements of reported company performance with higher granularity.

Chapter 6

AI Again

6.1 AI Revisited

A geeky programming friend of mine came round for Sunday lunch the other day. He noticed an impressive looking book on the side. "Ah, a new book on neural nets. You getting into the latest thing?" The tome looked very authoritative with numerous contributing academics extolling the latest benefits of neural networks to the world of finance and investing. I laughed and told him to look inside the cover. "What, published in 1990?" I said, "Yep, almost 30 years ago everybody was doing almost exactly the same thing". "To no great success … again", I added, to dampen his enthusiasm on a wet weekend afternoon.

Almost 30 years ago there was a flurry of interest in using *artificial neural networks* (ANNs) for predicting financial markets. Desktop computers, limited in processing power with DOS or buggy versions of Windows allowed people to experiment with neural nets. Although processing power was low and memories small, operating systems were less bloated. By using complied C++, surprisingly powerful neural nets could be built. One of my first bosses in a Japanese bank was a pioneer and had constructed, as a hobby, an ANN fx trading system in his garage. Over the next few years with mediocre results, disappointment set in and most people abandoned the neural net field. The hype and speculative frenzy died out as people realised applying neural nets to finance was a far harder problem than expected.

In the last decade, there has been an AI renaissance and neural nets have been "rediscovered". This has been driven by the rise of the internet, so-called "big data" and computing power. Although early, ambitious attempts to build "general" AI failed, behind the scenes academics have created a field called *machine learning* (ML). ML encapsulates many algorithmic techniques, including neural nets, for learning and classifying large datasets. Outside finance there is a burgeoning world of applied ML algorithms from self-driving cars to personalised movie suggestions.

6.2 Classifying Cats and Dogs

The recent advances made in machine learning caught most people's attention when the *dogs* vs. *cats* prediction problem was solved. Since the major use (at least in my family) of the internet is watching cute pictures of cats and dogs, it became a well publicised media sensation.

The original dogs vs. cats data set was originally used as one of those super annoying CAPTCHAs (Completely Automated Public Turing test to tell Computers and Humans Apart) that appear when you log into certain websites to distinguish you from a robot. In a 2007 Microsoft paper, *Asirra* (Animal Species Image Recognition for Restricting Access) was introduced as a semi-secure methodology. It made the bold and nonsensical claim:

"We present Asirra, a CAPTCHA that asks users to identify cats out of a set of 12 photographs of both cats and dogs. Asirra is easy for users; user studies indicate it can be solved by humans 99.6% of the time in under 30 seconds. Barring a major advance in machine vision, we expect computers will have no better than a 1/54,000 chance of solving it".

But so much for the 1 in 54,000 security, since in the same year, as a result of a Kaggle competition, a paper was published that stated "we describe a classifier which is 82.7% accurate in telling apart the images of cats and dogs used in Asirra. This classifier is a combination of support-vector machine classifiers trained on colour and texture features extracted from images". The competition was finally won by Pierre Sermanet who achieved an incredible 98.9% classification accuracy using convolutional neural networks.

Beyond cats and dogs, recent well-advertised ML triumphs included the work of Google's DeepMind in playing video games and learning Go to an expert standard. These advances in pattern recognition and beating humans at well-known games created a buzz in financial circles. Investors once again returned to imagining AI based computers could beat human traders. Most of the media ignored the fact that systematic computer-based trading had already existed for over 25 years in one form or the other. But AI was more exciting since it evoked computers acting like brains and employed more complex learning algorithms. If we could crack the cat vs. dog problem, surely financial markets were next? However, as we shall see, the financial market prediction problem is a lot more complex than classifying cats and dogs.

6.3 Machine Learning for Hedge Funds

With the rapid increases of computing power over the last few years, machine learning techniques have become available to hedge funds. Rather than using closed form equations or simple algorithms, as in traditional systematic trading, ML allows a computer to directly extract trading rules from data using statistics. ML can "slice and dice" data to classify into different categories or use regression to extract values from datasets. ML techniques use a learning or training process in which they try to extract investment rules before applying to test data and then finally live data. As time passes and more data is ingested by the system, the ML algorithm can adapt, modify and learn new rules.

Unfortunately, as with the rapid development of any new technical field, there is much gobbledygook written about ML. There has been such an explosion of terminology and jargon that even die-hard systematic quants struggle to comprehend the real concepts and potential pitfalls behind ML. Luckily, most of the techniques obscured by the jargon are merely a reinvention and relabelling of algorithms known for decades by statisticians and scientists (who were successfully analysing data well before the ML crowd turned up). The difference in recent years is arguably the size of datasets and availability of increasingly cheap computer resources. What I could achieve in fitting particle physics data from the CERN LEP collider on a Cray supercomputer back in the 1980s, you can now easily achieve on low cost rented cloud servers. The entire field of data analysis has become more accessible. These days, previously boring statisticians have been "replaced" in job adverts with cooler sounding "data scientists".

Although ML is a very powerful technique for extracting trading rules from data, there exists several caveats which we shall explore. As in all

ML applications, there are several existential challenges ranging from insufficient quantity of data for training and sampling bias to irrelevant features and data fitting. Arguably, the principal problem with ML techniques is the large amounts of training data they require and the consequent "over-fitting" when applied to the limited datasets available in financial markets.

6.4 The Growth and Death of AI Funds

In an attempt by investors to distinguish machine learning based funds from traditional rule-based systematic funds, an "AI Fund" category has been created in the last few years. Funds in this category are included based on the (i) extent they use ML techniques, (ii) ability to adapt to market conditions, (iii) integration of diverse data sources and (iv) lack of human intervention in the investment process. The category makes no distinction between the underlying strategies or markets traded.

An AI index was created by Eurekahedge, a leading investor database of hedge funds. It contained 27 hedge funds that were subjectively deemed to be predominately AI based. The performance of the index was very strong from the end of 2009. Its long-term Sharpe ratio is around 1.7–1.8 with an annualised return of 12.4%. The only losing year was in 2018 where it returned –4.3%. A major criticism levelled at the index is that many of its constituents are considered by many informed investors to not be fully AI based but use AI methods for a small proportion of their overall investment strategies. Also, the index performance looks great on the surface, but I noticed that the original 27 funds are down to 12 the last time I looked. This is suggestive that it is harder than it looks to get AI investing to work and perhaps "winners" dominate in the index performance.

6.5 Von Neumann's Elephant

A physicist's view on the "over-fitting" problem was provided by John von Neumann (1903–1957). For me, trained as a physicist, it epitomises the problems faced by financial AI techniques and to a lesser degree, all systematic trading. Von Neumann was probably one of the 20th century's greatest physicists and he contributed significantly to many fields including quantum mechanics, game theory, the foundations of mathematics,

Figure 6.1:   John von Neuman (right), with Robert Oppenheimer (left) in 1952, was a genius on practically everything, from quantum mechanics and game theory to H-bombs and over-fitting.

Source: Wikimedia Commons, public domain.

numerical analysis, linear programming and even self-replicating machines (Fig. 6.1). Speculative self-replicating von Neumann probes have become almost science fiction fact as they rapidly colonise the Galaxy by cannibalising asteroids and planets to reproduce.

von Neuman was one of the key members of the Manhattan project to build the atomic bomb and later the H-bomb. As a vehement anti-communist, he proposed, on the basis of pure logic and his game theory, to bomb the Russian's before they attained the technology. In 1950 he was quoted as saying "If you say why not bomb [the Soviets] tomorrow, I say, why not today? If you say today at five o'clock, I say why not one o'clock?" Fortunately, the application of pure mathematics to global H-bomb diplomacy was ignored. However, what always interested me was his famous quote on over-fitting of data concerning an elephant.

"With four parameters I can fit an elephant, and with five I can make him wiggle his trunk".

In other words, you can hypothetically describe a complex shape such as an elephant with only four variables and add even more complexity with adding just a fifth variable. The fitting power rises very rapidly with just a few variables. Thus, in the average machine learning algorithm with an extensive range of variables or internal parameters, there lies an inextricable problem. We can fit almost anything perfectly, even complex time series. However, the ability to arbitrarily fit history with no insight or explainability provides no ability to predict the future. If we can fit an elephant today, what use is it when the next animal is a lion?

Traditional systematic trading suffers from this problem but to a lesser degree. Systematic trading strategies, at least if a half decent research process is pursued, are based on insight and rationale. They attempt to elucidate simple repetitive statistical patterns. Machine learning however, if unconstrained, can lead to dangerous irrational delusions of predictive ability.

6.6 One Financial History

Data mining using machine learning is a powerful tool for classifying and categorising data. Given a large number of internal parameters, the ability of ML to fit training (in-sample) datasets is unrivalled. For many applications this provides good out-of-sample classification. As discussed with our cats vs. dogs, ML algorithms can be brilliant.

For a time series we can forget fitting a trivial simple moving average (1 parameter) or momentum (2 parameters) since with machine learning we can provide a super fit to the in-sample data. But the question is does this provide any predictive capability for financial markets? Sadly, the answer is usually no.

The reason for this is that for the cats vs. dogs classifier there are of course millions of cats and dogs in the world for training, in-sample and also out-of-sample verification. The data is literally virtually unlimited. In contrast we have only one financial history. However you design or set up the ML algorithm, this one finite history is an intractable barrier to successful market prediction. We do not have multiple parallel universes on which to refine and test our algorithm.

Our financial history is both unique and very short. The one history encapsulates all the different causal events that have occurred along its path. For example, at a macro level in Chapter 2, I illustrated the fact that successive central bank interventions have responded to financial crises but often "kicked the can down the road" to establish the next financial crisis. The downward sloping road of bond yields for the last decades is not the result of a random walk of markets. It is a structural macro effect.

At a micro level of an individual corporate a similar story exists, since for each company there is a specific narrative. Causality abounds. Unlike Newtonian physics, for financial markets time is not reversible. The causal events only make sense when you press "play" in one direction.

Some people try to build synthetic or randomised data series for models but, although this is perhaps a useful methodology in other fields, it is in my opinion largely inapplicable for financial markets. Although, we could build a multi-market simulation using volatilities and correlations, as in a VaR risk simulation, the underlying assumption is that markets are essentially random. The reason that systematic trading works is that on certain timescales there are weak, repetitive features that are not random. An alternative is to cut the real market time series up into chunks and rearrange to form a new time series, but this destroys the underlying causal framework beneath the markets. The reordered time set is also not (as in real life) ergodic, in the sense that it does not explore the total "phase" space of market possibilities that could have occurred in different worlds. It is difficult to see how synthetic datasets can be applied in a sensible way for building strategies.

Supplementing market data with alternative datasets, which we shall discuss in detail in Chapter 8, can also be used for increasing the amount of data available for ML techniques. But again, one should be wary of the one financial history problem. Big data does not necessarily improve ML techniques, since however many extra data points are added the problem essential reduces to a single data vector for each time point. There may be several market data points we wish to predict, plus any number of complementary alternative data sets but there remains only one time dimension.

To compound the lack of available time series data, any detected strategies will require detection of very weak signals. As we have seen from systematic trading, financial markets are very close to random. Achieving neutralish skew trading algorithms with much greater than 55% long term accuracy is very hard. Any potential patterns that could be elucidated from history by ML are therefore weak ones which require large amounts of data to have statistical confidence in. Beating the signal to noise problem is difficult. In fact, it is all too easy to find fleeting patterns in the noise.

Lastly, any use of ML techniques should ideally discover something new. Many obvious persistent statistical market effects have already been data mined by the numerous armies of quant researchers and systematic traders. When you plug in your carefully crafted ML model it should come as no surprise that the major effect you "discover" is the ubiquitous momentum strategy. This and a handful of first order effects are unfortunately nothing new. Many of our results will be highly correlated to existing systematic strategies. With machine learning we should thus be trying to reveal second order patterns or weaker linkages between well-known strategies.

6.7 Machine Learning Techniques

Machine learning extracts rules and inferences directly from data. Rather than assuming a relationship between observed variables, ML uses the data itself to derive empirical relationships (Appx. E.1). The simplest ML technique is in fact the linear regression formula we learn at school. By fitting a line through the datapoints of two series using a least-squares fitting, we can fit a gradient and an intercept for a linear equation. If later we are given a new data from one of the series, we can make a prediction using the linear equation of what the corresponding value will be for the second variable (Appx. E.2).

Although this linear example may seem trivial it is the essence of ML. By using an in-sample data set we can fit or train the model. Then we can use the fitted model to provide out-of-sample predictions. This type of machine learning, where we calculate a value, is called regression. However, the second major type of ML output is called classification, where we can sort the data into different categories.

The linear case has essentially two fitting factors — the gradient and intercept. However, we can imagine the case where very complex functions are fitted through multi-dimensional data or as boundaries. These functions can require many variables and the ML algorithms are termed parametric. Non-parametric AI techniques do not use a specific function but instead interpolation between known datapoints to provide regression or classification.

The ML training process can be unsupervised, where the algorithm is presented with raw data and has no preconceived notion on what might be useful. It can also be supervised learning, where a human provides clues or "features" of what might be important in the dataset. Supervised or semi-supervised learning seems to work best with the limited datasets available in finance. For example, in a simple 2D problem we might consider (i) price returns over the last month and (ii) volatility to be the relevant features for predicting future price changes. We are asking

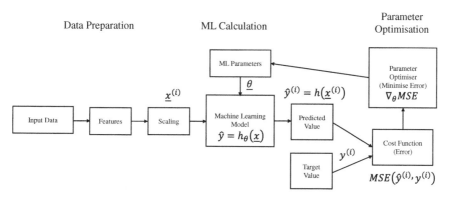

Figure 6.2: The ML process requires a minimisation of the error between predicted and target values in training to optimise the model parameters.

specifically confined questions of the data. An ML algorithm then might discover rules like "high past returns and low volatility provide high future returns".

A generic ML process is shown in Fig. 6.2. We can consider the actual ML algorithm at the heart of the process to be nonspecific and interchangeable. Once suitable features have been selected for a problem, they need to be normalised or scaled using a technique such as min-max standardisation or Z-scores. Normalisation places features on an equal footing when feature weights and ML parameters are initially assigned during the training process. The training data is prepared as a vector of features for each date in the sample. For each date a target value is given, which might be the market return over a desired time period. The ML algorithm analyses the data and compares the predicted output with the target value for each date. A performance measure must be used to determine how well the ML algorithm fits the training data. Usually this is a cost function such as the *mean square error* (MSE). Through an iterative process (typically gradient descent) the ML model parameters are varied until the error is reduced and the best fit is achieved. Once the model parameters have been optimised the ML algo is said to be "trained". The next step is to use the model on unseen (out-of-sample) data and then make predictions on live data.

6.7.1 *Algorithmic indifference?*

There now exist many ML techniques (kNN, SVM, decision trees, ANN ...) and they use different methods of varying complexity to fit the training data. Some models are parametric and use fitting functions or kernels like SVM to describe classification boundaries. Consequently, depending on the application some techniques are perhaps better suited to particular situations than others. Curiously however, in the naïve absence of any idea what ML algo to use, it might not make any difference which model you actually select. In 1997 there was an interesting idea published by Wolperts called the NFL (No Free Lunch) theorem which stated that if you have no *a priori* knowledge of a statistical problem, there is no reason to prefer any ML algo over another.

Taking this idea further, given a benchmark ML problem with lots of data, many ML techniques achieve broadly similar results. A classic benchmark problem is recognising written handwriting using the MNIST dataset. It contains 60,000 labelled samples with 28×28 pixel arrays. Lots of different ML classification techniques can achieve around 1–3% error rate for the problem. In 2001 Banko and Brill of Microsoft demonstrated that given enough data, different ML algos performed identically well on complex problems. Apparently to crack your problem, perhaps it is not worth fixating on the latest ML algo with the latest gizmos. However, the problem lies in the small print "given enough data". In financial market problems the data is severely limited and thus ML algo selection and the data features chosen are, as we shall demonstrate, of critical importance.

To illustrate how we can apply ML to develop trading strategies I shall outline two diverse techniques. The first technique is the well-known neural net which, although useful in many other applications, proves particularly slippery when applied to financial market prediction. It inspires people since it approximates to the wiring of a brain but in essence it is the archetypical black box model. The second is the often-overlooked k-nearest neighbours (kNN) which is probably the simplest and most transparent ML technique. This algorithm is a personal favourite since it is robust and you have a clear indication of what it is up to if you are prepared to look under the hood. Being able to easily investigate why the algorithm makes particular decisions addresses the issue of explainability.

6.8 Artificial Neural Networks

If we were to write a brief history of neural networks, it would currently run as three distinct waves of research interest and progress. In between these waves, interest in the technology effectively died out. Often these waves are referred to as the AI summers and winters.

Wave 1 covered the 1950–1960s and started when Frank Rosenblatt built electrical *perceptrons* with weighted connections which attempted to model neurons. Amazingly, they were built as physical electrical machines. In 1969 Marvin Minsky published his famous book *Perceptrons* that detailed a litany of significant problems, including the inability to map to a XOR logic gate and other linear decision boundaries. This neatly killed off interest in neural networks and thus ended wave 1.

Wave 2 started in the 1980s when in 1982 John Hopfield noticed similarities between the brain and so-called "spin glasses" which led to the Hopfield model. A major technical issue in implementing neural net applications was how to calibrate them in training but in 1986, new backpropagation or "backprop" techniques developed by David Rumelhart remedied the problem. Multilayer perceptrons were developed for speech recognition applications. Unfortunately, excitement petered out as training and calibration problems were encountered.

Wave 3 is where we are now in 2021. In the 2000s neural nets became fashionable again with the rise of the internet, big data and increased computing power. The success of deep neural nets and techniques such as reinforcement learning have created breakthroughs from computer vision to the discovery of protein structures. AI enthusiasts would now claim the eternal summer of AI is now upon us and the winters of disappointment are banished forever.

6.8.1 *From perceptrons to neural nets*

The simplest element of a neural net is the perceptron (Fig. 6.3) modelled on neurons in brain cells. In a neuron, the build-up of electrical charge from dendrites above a certain threshold triggers an action potential down the axon. In the perceptron, this threshold is represented as a mathematical step function or better a smooth function. Once the weighted sum of the perceptron inputs exceeds a threshold, an output signal is given (Appx. E.3). Overall, it seems a pretty good analogy of a real biological neuron.

By combining many perceptrons in linked layers we can form a neural network. A *deep neural net* has several layers of connections between the input and the output layer. These are called hidden layers (Fig. 6.4). Each connection has a unique weight and each node an activation function.

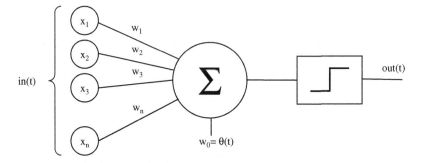

Figure 6.3:   Schematic Perceptron where inputs are weighted, summed and triggered an output above a threshold value.

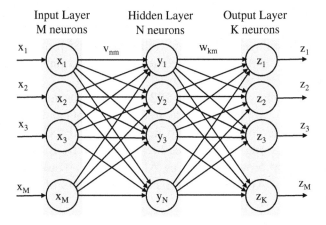

Figure 6.4:   A neural net with one hidden layer. Each connection has a unique weight and each node an activation function.

In a sense, the connections can "remember" rules as ways of combining input signals. Once the net structure (nodes and layers) is decided, the model effectively resides in all the weights of all the connections. The number of weights can quickly rise to a large number of variables for even a simple net. The one hidden layer example already requires $M \times N + N \times K$ variables to be fitted.

6.8.2 *Training neural nets*

To train a neural net we forward propagate each sample training signal through the net and calculate an "error" or cost function for batches of samples. Then we use "back-propagation" backwards through the net changing connection weights to minimise the error function. Using the perceptron learning rule the weights are reinforced for the connections that give the correct predictions (Appx. E.3).

These back-propagation techniques use gradient descent techniques for optimisation. The fitting space is a multi-dimensional landscape increasing with the number of connections. In this process it is easy to get trapped in local rather than global minima and hence find the "wrong" solution. This method requires big data sets, batching and randomisation of weights etc. to aid convergence. There exist many fancy techniques for increasing convergence rate but appropriateness depends on the underlying dataset.

For prediction in financial markets, it is preferable to use semi-supervised learning with input "features" rather than just solely raw data. Some features are integrated variables resulting from a calculation over a time window e.g., trend, volatility etc. This is called semi-supervised learning. The net is trained on a time series to optimise profit or an associated risk-adjusted return such as Sharpe ratio.

6.8.3 *Over-fitting markets*

A major issue for neural nets is the possibility of over-fitting. In late 2017 I volunteered to give a talk on the issue. A talk rather optimistically entitled *Deep Learning for Market Prediction — the S&P 500*. My presentation of the direct application of neural nets to over-fitting single markets outlined my disappointment with the technology. Predicting macro equity indices, which are highly random like the S&P 500, is a notoriously difficult challenge but illustrates the issues involved well.

As an example, for S&P 500 futures we can apply a neural net with five price and volume features and two hidden layers (5,5) for a one day ahead prediction. The neural net provides amazing fitting to training data with a Sharpe ratio close to 4 (Fig. 6.5). However, the test period is comparatively rather disappointing (Sharpe ratio ~0.6) so the Sharpe ratio test/train ~15% (Fig. 6.6). Unfortunately, the common finding is that the out-of-sample result is always much lower than the test. This demonstrates the unrivalled over-fitting capabilities of neural nets. In retrospect, what do you expect with so many model "degrees of freedom"? A similar over-fitting story exists for many other markets examined. Although we may pick different features, the test/train Sharpe ratio lies for most markets in the range 10–30%.

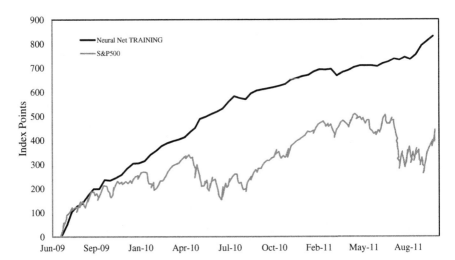

Figure 6.5:   The neural net provides an amazing fit to training data with a high Sharpe ratio.

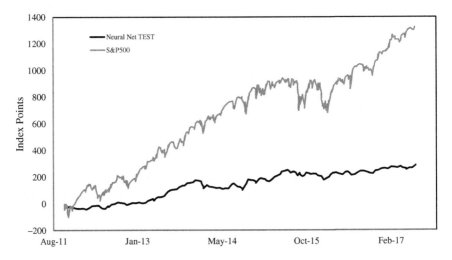

Figure 6.6:   The neural net test data has a disappointingly low Sharpe ratio.

The above examples used a static training period of 3 years and a test period of 6 years, but the general result does not depend too much on the window size. In ML it is common to use a rolling window approach to incorporate the latest data in learning. Repeating the above experiments,

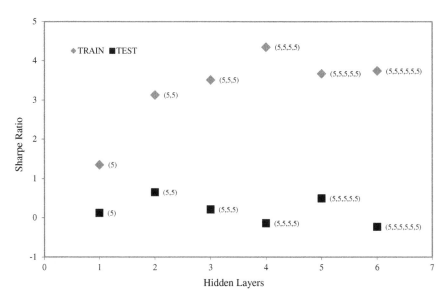

Figure 6.7: Adding more layers/nodes increases over-fitting to training data for GBP.

we can incorporate a rolling window for training of say 1 year for "walk forward" backtesting. In this way we discard old data and refocus on more recent data. This provides an increased measure of adaptability. The results are generally weak with Sharpe ratio 0.4–0.6 per market and are highly unstable. More research shows that the neural net is highly dependent on training window size, since it must have enough data to train and capture relevant examples of market behaviour to avoid severe instability.

Several other observations are worth noting. Adding more neural net layers or nodes increases over-fitting to the training data. Beyond a couple of layers, the model is too complex to specify with the limited data and has even weaker predictability in test. The Sharpe ratio fluctuates and is unstable. Typical results are shown for GBP currency in Fig. 6.7. Also, some features may have increased predictive power (e.g., day of week, intraday returns, …) but increasing the number of features also allows higher over-fitting of training data with a finite training dataset. Adding features slightly increases test performance but adding more meaningless or correlated features eventually decreases performance (Fig. 6.8).

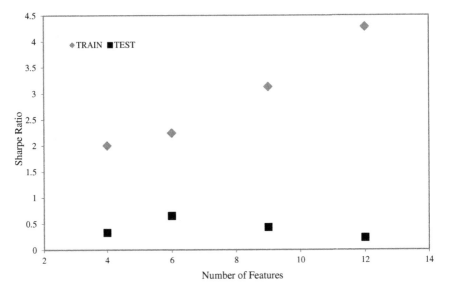

Figure 6.8:   Adding certain features initially improves predictive power but gradually increases over-fitting for GBP.

6.8.4 *Routes to success*

Thus, although neural nets are successful in many applications, their naïve application to financial market prediction proves to be highly challenging. They are limited in market prediction by lack of data, regime changes in markets and high noise to signal relative to other applications. The out-of-sample performance is often disappointing. Many of the issues with neural nets are inherent in any ML technique that has numerous internal fitting parameters.

The question naturally arises — what routes to success can be pursued to improve the performance of neural nets? Solutions include better features/supervision, more data and possibly better net configurations.

Neural nets are an inherently unsupervised ML technique but by using features rather than raw price data, we constrain training and boost the out-of-sample performance to a certain degree. Although we might include a large set of data features, in practice it is preferable to carefully chose a smaller set of relevant features. If we use "good" features that have sensible concepts they provide a certain explanatory power. Although this might provide an overlap with systematic trading methodologies, the neural nets still provide a non-linear way of combining features and signals. Ideally the features should be lowly correlated or orthogonal. In certain circumstances it is worth checking to see if any of the features correspond to eigenvalues in a traditional PCA (Principal Components Analysis) or well-known signals. To avoid over-fitting there exists a technique of regularisation which essentially artificially reduces the degrees of freedom of the model. Regularisation combined with a small feature set can attempt to mitigate over-fitting problems but at the cost of dumbing down the model. However, as a cautionary tale, I once had a colleague who was forced by his peers to simplify his ML currency algorithm to such an extent that all the interesting effects were removed and all that was left was a rediscovery of first order momentum — at least it was not over-fitted.

More data could include faster trading, combining multiple markets and adding uncorrelated data sets. By moving to faster trading including intraday trading, we expand the amount of data available for training and testing. But if we move to intraday trading, accurate execution and cost modelling become essential. Combining multiple markets with weak out-of-sample Sharpe ratios also allows creation of higher Sharpe ratio portfolios. ML strategies, if you remove the first order trend component, often have lowish correlation to CTAs thus are diversifying if added to existing systematic strategies. Also, applying ML to L/S equity portfolios has potential as we shall discuss in the next section. Although the equities are correlated, excluding the principal market beta effectively provides hundreds of underlying time series for machine learning.

Lastly, including uncorrelated non-price data sets such as news, sentiment and other alternative data can increase performance but as previously mentioned, we should remain wary of the one history problem. Although we can increase the size of the dataset, the way we use the data can arguably make a difference. Many people claim walk-forward training is better than traditional backtesting but essentially, they are equivalent and suffer from similar issues. Batching and randomisation of data are also useful in ML applications but in time series analysis of market data, preserving causality and the order of time is crucial.

Often it is argued that better neural net configurations are possible for time series data. It may be true that the basic multilayer sandwich neural net is ill adapted to financial time series. There exists a new generation of neural nets called *recurrent neural nets* (RNN) with internal states specifically designed for time series. However, in my rudimentary studies these seem to offer little benefits. Traditional neural nets which include some historical time series artifacts, either through some lagged inputs or integrated features, seem to achieve similar results to RNN.

6.9 The Simplest ML Technique — kNN

Moving away from neural nets, it is interesting to study the most basic ML technique kNN. KNN existed, in my opinion, well before many of the other ML techniques appeared. Apparently, it was first developed by Evelyn Fix in 1951. I remember programming up a variant of nearest neighbours on a BBC micro-computer in the 1980s. Although kNN is poo-pooed by ML afficionados as being too simple, I would argue that simplicity is its strength. It is not black box and extremely robust — you know where you stand with plain old kNN.

KNN is the simplest of all machine learning techniques. It has no fitting function and is non-parametric for classification or regression. Instead, it employs "lazy learning" using a local approximation for decision boundaries. We can visualise the datapoints as being fixed in a multidimensional hypercube where the axes are the data variables or features. The training examples are vectors that describe points in this multidimensional feature space (Appx. E.4).

The example in Fig. 6.9 is based on two categories (square or triangle). For $K = 3$ neighbours we would classify the new example (circle) as

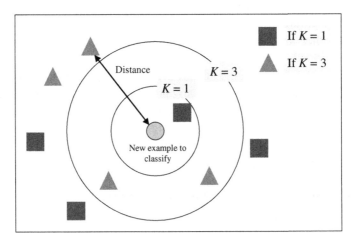

Figure 6.9: Using kNN to classify a new sample into one of two classes (squares or triangles).

a triangle, since within the training distance there are 2 triangles versus 1 square. For regression, the output is the weighted sum over the values of the kNN of the object being assigned in the feature space. Weights can be uniform (1/K) or Euclidean with distance from object (Appx. E.4). Unlike most ML techniques you can thus visually interpret the results (not a black box).

6.9.1 *Applying kNN to L/S equities*

As an example, we shall consider applying the kNN approach to L/S large cap equities contained in the S&P 500 index. By applying ML to a large diverse pool of equities in a long/short strategy, we attempt to mitigate the lack of training data. By remaining market neutral, we reduce the issue of macro market moves and focus the ML on idiosyncratic movements of individual equities. In this manner we can try to reduce the one history problem particularly during periods when market dispersion is high.

For our strategy we chose various historical features as inputs. Some features are integrated variables e.g., momentum that are algorithmically computed from the raw data. In general, the individual features might provide weakly profitable signals, but our goal is to use kNN to combine them in a non-linear fashion. The output is the average historical risk-adjusted return of kNN and we use this to construct a prediction.

In practice, we select just six features (momentum, reversion, volume, volatility, news score and sentiment) and run kNN daily on all the 500 equities in the portfolio (Fig. 6.10). One of the problems with kNN is the "curse of dimensionality" as with a finite amount of data, the

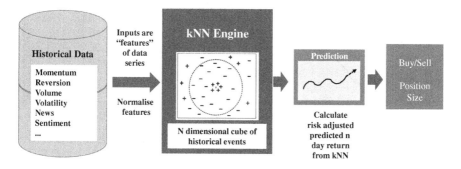

Figure 6.10: Using kNN for L/S equity portfolios.

effectiveness declines as the number of dimensions increases. Mathematically, this means that the number of neighbours becomes very sparse. We can sometimes reduce the number of dimensions by compressing several related features into each dimension or using a statistical technique like *principal components analysis* (PCA).

It is customary in ML to apply a "walk forward" training technique to allow learning from newer data. Starting with no knowledge, we add historical features to database as we roll forward in time. To make more recent data more relevant, we weight data in the training set towards the last 5 years using all equities. Using kNN, we rank the predicted risk-adjusted returns, buy the highest quintile and sell the lowest predicted quintile so are always market neutral (to first approximation). The results are shown in Fig. 6.11, a long-term Sharpe ratio of around 1.5 with stable volatility.

There are several advantages of this approach over the neural net method we used earlier. Firstly, by considering 500 equities we have much more data to analyse for model training relative to a unique time series of a single equity index. Secondly, by adopting a market neutral approach we are neutralising larger macro market moves and focusing on the

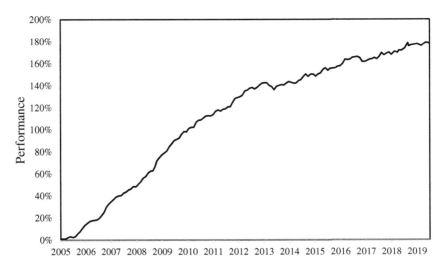

Figure 6.11: Non-compounded performance of market neutral L/S equity using kNN technique and walk-forward testing.

idiosyncratic movement between equities. Lastly, by picking features that already potentially have alpha we are using kNN to discover non-linear relationships between them rather than a simple linear superposition.

6.10 Comparison with Traditional Systematic Investing

It is interesting to compare traditional algorithmic or systematic trading to machine learning based strategies. There are many similarities and overlaps but several notable differences (Table 6.1).

6.10.1 *Strategy conception*

Systematic trading strategies are based on an *a priori* concept, idea or effect that is hypothesised by humans. Pure data mining is seen as a scientifically bad approach and the systematic concept is often based on a well-thought-out fundamental effect that is scientifically investigated. This process is deemed to reduce the probability of over-fitting and arriving at spurious causal linkages.

In machine learning, particularly when unsupervised, the rules are automatically generated by the trading strategy. Constraints can be applied (for example trading speed, costs and performance characteristics) but the ML algorithm is given a free hand. In more supervised ML the computer is directed to which specific features to explore.

Table 6.1:   Systematic versus machine learning strategies.

Algorithmic/Traditional Systematic	Machine Learning
• *A priori* concept/idea/effect for trading strategy (from humans).	• Machine Learning generates rules for trading strategy.
• Signals combined as linear combination.	• Signals can be non-linear.
• Underlying equation/algorithm.	• ML "discovers" algorithm.
• Not adaptive to market regime.	• Adaptive (slowly).
• Intuitive, understandable, maybe simple.	• Often lacks transparency (black box).

6.10.2 *Signal combination*

Trading signals are usually combined in a linear manner in systematic trading. The generic approach is signal normalisation and linear superposition through a series of weighting factors.

The process of signal combination in machine learning is embedded within the algorithm. This leads to non-linear combination of signals that can provide additional potential sources of alpha relative to systematic trading.

6.10.3 *The strategy algorithm*

For systematic trading there exists an underlying, often relatively simple algorithm for a strategy. This can be easily written down as a mathematical equation and usually encoded in a few lines.

With ML there is no distinct equation, and the "algorithm" is "discovered" from the learning data. Usually, since we are using an off-the-shelf ML technique provided in say a 3rd party Python library, it is more precise to say that the entire internal algorithm itself is a fusion of the ML technique plus all the fitting weights that have been ascribed during the learning process.

6.10.4 *Market adaptation*

Systematic trading strategies do not adjust their algorithms to different market regimes. Their internal parameters are generally fixed unless a human decision is made to manually refit the model. A guiding principle for good practice is that model parameters should be stable through time and human intervention should be kept to a minimum.

ML strategies change their parameters as more data is digested. Initially parameters will be fixed using the initial learning data but as time passes, more data is added and used to refit model parameters. The speed at which the model "adapts" to new market conditions is dependent on the weight applied to newly acquired data relative to the older historical data. Although this might sound great in practice, any adaptation will be generally very slow due to statistical limitations and paucity of data. Fast adaptation can produce unstable internal parameters, have little statistical significance and be detrimental to performance.

6.10.5 *Model transparency*

Systematic models are usually intuitive and readily comprehensible. They are often very simple to the point of being mathematically trivial. Importantly, other participants in the investment process including risk managers and even investors can understand the principles behind systematic strategies.

Most ML strategies are entirely opaque black boxes. This renders explanations for their rationale and behaviour difficult. Arguably the least black box ML technique is the simplest kNN and the blackest box are like deep neural networks.

6.11 The Future of Machine Learning for Investing

Both systematic trading and ML techniques allow us to apply statistical rigour and remove emotion from trading decisions. ML techniques have the benefit that they can discover new trading rules and data associations. However, their principal pitfall, due to the limited data available in financial markets, is over-fitting. Systematic and ML strategies are equally vulnerable to regime changes and structural breaks in markets. The ostensible learning benefits of ML often prove too slow to evolve to changing regimes. Essentially, computers suffer from a lack of imagination and comprehension and cannot assign meaning to news flow and changing fundamental conditions that are sometimes trivial for humans.

ML is arguably better suited to data treatment and analysis prior to forming data features. For example, ML processes are well established in conjunction with *natural language processing* (NLP) to read articles, earnings, news and social media and categorise and calculate various metrics such as sentiment scores. Neural nets have proved very adept in analysing company reports and extracting useful information. This type of process can allow textual analysis of thousands of documents and saves human time and removes subjectivity. Unlike market prices, the data set is virtually unlimited which is perfect for ML approaches. The text variables produced by ML can then be mapped onto time series and used as signal inputs to systematic or discretionary trading systems. In our previous kNN L/S equity example, the feature of news sentiment scores was actually calculated from many years of news articles using neural nets. We discuss this NLP process in more detail in Chapter 8.

Increasingly, developments in ML are focused on the role of causality between events. It is hoped that this might provide a breakthrough for ML based investing. In a typical regression analysis, it is difficult to separate cause from effect. This can lead to some nonsensical but high correlations. An often-quoted example is that of David Leinweber's study of Bangladeshi butter being 75% correlated to S&P 500 index equity prices (1981–1993) and increasing to 99% if sheep populations were included. Without human common-sense, machines can mine some very high and irrelevant correlations between unrelated variables. If causality is better reflected in time series ML approaches, more relevant data associations can be derived from data.

The typical approach to measuring causal linkages in data is Granger causality (Appx. E.5) but other approaches exist. By considering the influence of time lagged variables, we can determine if an event was a precursor to a current event and has statistical validity to be an explanatory cause. However, it remains to be seen if this improves the quality of the ML in market prediction and can mitigate the endemic over-fitting problem. Already, much lagged data is used in the form of integrated variables and ML features such as momentum and this already has an implicit causality. Also, in finance many events are so close to be almost simultaneous, thus the cause is close to the event. Careful data timestamping is required. If company news is suddenly announced, the movement of the equity is virtually instantaneous. Sometimes the news is leaked and the equity starts moving before you see the headline. The cause and the effect are mixed or indecipherable. Known anomalies that would be more amenable to "discovery" by causality analysis are for example, the rally effect of equities after Fed meetings, economic data releases and company reporting. The Fed effect and many others are due to traders de-risking before a "scary" event and an effective option premium is "paid" due the skew involved — generally the Fed pleases but sometimes there is a nasty downside. Thus, there is a feasible explanation for such cause and effect. If causal ML discovers an anomaly, a valid rationale must exist before an investment strategy can be implemented — and this still requires human understanding and insight.

Chapter 7

ESG Investing

7.1 The Ethics of Don Draper

If you are worrying about "plastic-bergs" in the Pacific Ocean but everything in the supermarket is wrapped in convenient and apparently "deadly" plastic, then you are not alone. Perhaps you are wondering, as you drag out your blue recycling bin, why nobody addressed this and many other glaringly obvious environmental issues years ago? Although you might feel like joining Extinction Rebellion, arguably a more powerful route to change is how we collectively invest our cash.

It turns out that public awareness of the environmental concerns facing the planet is a relatively new phenomenon and only a few decades old. Back in the 1960s it was not even questionable to have the biggest gas guzzling car possible or as Don Draper in the series *Mad Men*, throw your picnic rubbish over the park. Only in the early 1980s did the UK decide it was unreasonable to dump radioactive nuclear waste in the sea just off the English coast.

Although they did not manage to resolve the existential plastic bag problem, groups like Greenpeace and Friends of the Earth became major early influencers of public opinion. They educated the public and highlighted the need for more environmentally aware policies. The environmental agenda has moved slowly but surely, addressing and publicising a range of important topics from holes in the ozone layer to logging in amazon rainforests and more recently, global warming and climate change.

Social concerns were gradually added to the environmental factors as the unrelenting progress of globalisation led to offshoring of manufacturing. Western consumers, despite enjoying cheaper clothes, sneakers and zillions of plastic toys, realised that having them made by child labour under terrible working conditions whilst polluting third world countries was simply unethical by modern standards.

In response to this evolution of higher ethical standards, the finance industry has been struggling to catch up. Believing for many years that ethical or responsible investing was a fad or fashion amongst a few hippie, fringe types or eco-warriors, they chose to ignore it. The reason for the intransigence of fund managers was the painful realisation that many of their current practices, honed over decades, would have to be modified. Instead of looking at how much profit a company made and various other financial metrics before investing, they would instead have to interrogate companies on a range of subjective issues like how they made a profit and whether it was aligned with ethical considerations. Much of this new information was previously not disclosed by major corporations and the extra new focus would lead to some awkward conversations with CEOs and company directors. Some major companies would become "un-investable" unless they too changed.

The fund management companies now realise the writing on the wall and are changing their products and services to align themselves with the evolving mainstream customers' views on a range of environmental and social issues. Behemoth money managers such as Blackrock, Fidelity etc. have re-orientated their entire business models to address responsible investing. This is the biggest ideological revolution in how and why money is invested, arguably since the advent of the first publicly traded stocks and it is here to stay. In the new paradigm, pure profits and monetary shareholder value are not the only performance criteria for a company investment.

There is rising interest for *environmental, social and governance* (ESG) related investments from both retail and institutional investors. ESG investments are finally migrating out the niche area they once occupied and into the mainstream. To accommodate this trend, many fund managers have simply relabelled existing equity and bond funds and slightly modified their investment criteria. The relabelling of existing equity funds is what many cynics would call "greenwashing", but at least it is a starting point for most asset managers who are dipping their toes in the ESG water. Outside the long-only space and in the world of hedge funds, ESG investing remains a minor consideration as the investor base's primary concerns are uncorrelated returns or alpha. The most forward looking ESG focused hedge fund investors are arguably in Scandinavia and a minority of family offices but the ESG alternatives wave is gradually growing.

7.2 An Unsustainable Forest of Sustainability Jargon

However, for the uninitiated investor, environmentally and socially responsible investing has become jargon orientated and confusing. As if investing literature is not difficult enough, the fund management industry has come up with a whole new range of expressions and acronyms. Responsible or ethical investing sounds reasonable but what are SRI, ESG or impact investing?

The early funds addressing ethical or responsible investing used a simple "exclusion" methodology. If a company was in what was viewed as a "sinner" sector, such as traditionally firearms, alcohol or tobacco, it was removed from the portfolio. Added progressively to the list of exclusions were casinos, weapons, fossil fuels, coal mining etc. This sector-based "negative'" screening process became labelled sustainable or *socially responsible investing* (SRI).

Although this approach had huge clarity for investors and was a first stab at the problem of responsible investing, it was perhaps overly simplistic and quickly limited the universe of investable companies. Another shortcoming was that companies that lay outside these specific sectors but exhibited irresponsible and unethical behaviour could not be automatically excluded.

A more nuanced approach called ESG investing was developed, where equities would be individually screened on the basis of detailed environmental, social and governance scores. This modernised style of ethical investing provides a more holistic and scientific method for investment allocation but the E, S and G perhaps needs a bit more clarification.

Whereas ESG investing might include companies that are positive or neutral from an ESG perspective, another more extreme form of ESG investing is so called "impact" investing. An ideal impact portfolio only includes companies that are highly ESG positive and have beneficial impact for the World. Typical examples of such companies might include water treatment, healthcare, electric cars and renewable energies like wind farms, solar etc. Impact portfolios are thus much more positively focused than generic ESG portfolios and consequently some fund managers find the pool of available companies too constrained.

7.3 What are the E, S and G?

E is for environmental. Obviously, we are all aware of climate change and pollution but environmental impact of companies and the factors considered are much more wide ranging. It will include measurements of carbon footprint, water usage, waste management, pollution, environmental litigation and moves towards clean energy (Table 7.1). For example, chemical companies polluting rivers, mining companies with toxic tail-offs and packaging companies with non-recyclable products would all be penalised. Companies with high levels of environmental disclosure and improving practices would be promoted. Even oil companies that are divesting themselves of fossil fuels, building sustainable energy portfolios and transitioning to a low-carbon future could be considered in certain ESG portfolios.

S is for social. High street retailers making Christmas cards in foreign gulags, smartphone manufacturers using rare earth metals mined by children and on-line distributors with bad labour practices in their warehouses are all high-profile media examples of violations of socially acceptable practices. However, S encompasses many minor considerations that are not newspaper headline worthy but nonetheless important, such as human rights, workers' rights, controversial products, employee turnover, business facilities and health and safety practices. Positive practices such as

Table 7.1:   Example ESG considerations.

E Environmental	S Social	G Governance
• Carbon footprint • Water usage • Waste management • Pollution • Litigation • Clean energy • Land use • Conservation	• Human rights • Workers rights • Controversial products • Employee turnover • UN GC signatory • Facilities • Health and safely	• Board independence • Remuneration • Independent directors • Combined CEO/Chair role • Business ethics • Corporate culture • Transparency

personnel diversity, maternity rights and charitable donations would result in higher social rankings.

G is for governance. Governance is a bit less clear for most investors but is arguably the most important factor for future share price performance. Governance concerns how a company is run and controlled and includes corporate culture, board independence, renumeration policy, role of independent directors and business ethics. Bad governance can lead to business destroying decisions and massive lawsuits. For example, banks that have allowed money laundering and sanctions busting, German car manufacturers that fixed emissions tests with the complicity of senior management or raiding the company's pension scheme to pay extra-large dividends or bonuses. Companies that are well managed, transparent and with clear policies and business plans achieve higher Governance scores.

7.4 Arctic Drilling but No Beers Please, Especially at the Casino

A cursory overview of most long equity ESG funds, particularly in the US, reveals large-cap and tech-laden portfolios and often includes most of the FANGS (Facebook, Amazon, Netflix and Google) equities. The inclusion of so much tech is a big contributor to the much lauded recent out-performance of most ESG funds. However, most investors would be somewhat disappointed with the composition of these portfolios and would be expecting equities that are good for the planet or provide some societal benefits. If you were expecting wind-farms, solar panels, electric cars and socially respectable employers, then think again. Instead, you'll probably end up with companies that dominate the competition, sell your private data and have battery farms of employees stacking things in boxes for the minimum wage. But on close inspection you have even worse. For example, you have oil companies that are pretending to turn green, aerospace companies that develop smart bomb components to drop on tribal minorities and mining companies that are polluting vast regions but act within self-determined guidelines. The list of aberrations is extensive. Bizarrely, many of the latter are preferred over companies that run casinos or fabricate tasty beer and liquors that many people enjoy. Apparently, while casinos and cognac are excluded (since they are gambling and alcohol sectors), drilling for oil in the arctic circle is fine provided you have an eco-friendly logo.

How did we end up with such a state of affairs you might ask? Well, the problem is that ESG criteria are highly subjective and open to different interpretations. Many of the World's public investable companies have both good and bad points. Determining what is relevant for the ESG case requires analysis, judgement and some human bias. Carbon emissions for a cement manufacturer or most power companies are, although not desirable, not optional since we still need to build and power our houses. Maybe it is illogical to divest from these sectors completely but instead allow other ESG criteria to influence one's decision, such as speed to introduce renewables, equitable personnel policies, ethical governance decisions etc.

7.5 The Minefield of ESG Ratings

Unfortunately, most investment managers lack the time and expertise to drill down into a company's ESG fundamentals. Instead, they want a 3rd party "rubber stamp" on their fund's ESG credentials and easily justify to any investor the choice they have made in selecting particular equities or bonds. This has led to a rise of 3rd party ESG ratings providers which assign ratings to companies in a similar fashion to the well-known credit ratings agencies. Although originally fragmented, the ESG ratings providers have now consolidated into a handful of major brands, each with software and data products sold as subscription packages.

7.5.1 *Back to the future with the agencies*

Historically, I have a pretty dim view of ratings becoming institutionalised and investor behaviour being controlled by an "oligarchy" of ratings agencies. This is because I spent a large fraction of my career arbitraging agency credit ratings. Investors bought high yielding bonds through instruments called collateralised debt obligations (CDOs) that were specifically designed to obtain artificially inflated ratings. The agencies were not exactly non-partisan in these projects and were paid handsomely to authorise and approve these financial products. Eventually, as you know, things went greedily off the rails when US subprime mortgages (remember those NINJA — no income, no job, no assets … no problem loans) were crazily allowed exclusively as collateral. Despite the agencies involvement in the credit crisis (2008), their influence remains (almost) as great as ever but scepticism still runs high amongst the old guard of credit traders and investors.

Consequently, we should be vigilant over any ESG rating agencies and their future influence and control over the ESG funds sector. Recently I studied the ESG ratings of three major providers and I concluded that fortunately, for the moment, it seems there is little to worry about. In my view, near total confusion and chaos reigns over ESG ratings and it remains predominately a "brown field" site. Importantly, there is a lack of general consensus and methodology in ESG ratings. Whereas for credit ratings, well established metrics such as leverage, debt/EBITDA, cash-flow etc. are used and have been finely honed over the years, there exists no such metrics for ESG. For example, what is more relevant? Gross or net carbon dioxide emissions (an environmental factor) or the diversity of the board (a governance factor)? There is a high level of subjectivity and this is magnified by the problem of reducing a multidimensional space of potential ESG variables into one simplified overall ESG rating or ranking factor. One of the ratings providers boasts around 1200 possible ESG variables per company (although most are sparsely populated at present). Distilling this amount of information into a rating that is relevant and meaningful to a particular company and allows comparisons with other companies, is probably near impossible on any rational basis.

7.5.2 *Weak correlations*

This lack of consensus is evidenced in the correlation between ratings. For the STOXX 600, which is the equity index comprising 600 of Europe's leading companies, we find a correlation between ratings of less than 30%. This means they are weakly correlated with many disagreements of opinion between agencies. This result is corroborated by recent academic publications that ratings between agencies are weakly correlated but pure governance ratings have incredibly almost zero correlation. Since, as we shall discuss, governance has the biggest impact of the ESG factors on equity performance, this lack of agreement is remarkable.

7.5.3 *The disclosure bias*

In addition, we observe strange contradictions since the ESG ratings are mainly based on ESG disclosure of companies. Unfortunately, most of the published disclosure is produced or controlled by the companies themselves. The rating agencies often take little or no account of how fundamentally bad a company performs on ESG issues but just the amount of disclosure and how the ESG risks are managed (in theory). Thus, a mining company with a high level of ESG disclosure and flashy public relations can rank close to 100 and an internet company who believes they have no ESG exposure worth noting and thus no disclosure, can rank at a lowly 10. There was an interesting 2020 court case between ESG ratings provider ISS and a German image processing company Isra Vision which was rated D- on the basis of lack of disclosure and was (correctly in my view) granted an injunction against ISS. This reliance on disclosure is clearly an absurd state of affairs and at least one agency has taken steps to try and remedy this by recently revising their rating methodology. This is timely since the more one delves into the details and the vague, unscientific and poorly documented methodologies used, the more one can cast doubt over the validity of many ratings.

7.5.4 *Manageable versus unmanageable risks*

An increasing trend in ratings methodologies has been the use of the concept of manageable versus unmanageable ESG "risks". It adopts a pragmatic view that in any given industry sector there are inherent risks that cannot be managed away through new business processes and better corporate management. Thus, an airline company may try to manage environmental risks by purchasing a newer fleet or purchasing carbon offsets, but fundamentally the aviation sector is a highly polluting one. Based on current aircraft technology there will always exist a large component of unmanageable risk. Essentially, all airlines have bad "E" but it's how they improve it that counts. Similar analysis can be sensibly applied to any sector. For example, power hungry, cloud computing companies can mitigate carbon emissions and pollution through renewable energy sources and situate themselves in cooler locations like Iceland, but they will still remain resource intensive and have unmanageable risk in the production of their semi-conductors and construction of facilities. This analysis in my view is a step forward if the results are used wisely by ratings firms. However, a dichotomy quickly presents itself, which can readily confuse investors. If we rank companies based on how well they manage ESG risks rather than the overall ESG risk we are simply building a portfolio of the highest rated companies in each sector. Many investors do not wish to buy any airline since they view the sector as polluting and not aligned with their ESG views. A ratings approach based on the notion of managed and unmanageable risks needs to be clearly articulated to investors.

7.5.5 *Responsible managers and curious investors*

Investment managers should be ready to question ESG ratings and how they are derived. If they are only using one 3rd party ratings provider, they should delve into the methodology used rather than simply employing them as a rubber stamp. Engagement with ESG ratings agencies will eventually provide rankings that are more meaningful and aligned with investor expectations. Equally, the investors themselves should question how ratings are used in the investment process. Are they looking for a passive ESG portfolio that is screened merely on the basis of rating or are they looking for portfolios that have "impact" and are genuinely compatible with their individual beliefs and ethics?

7.6 ESG Investment Strategies

Having a methodology to establish ESG scores or ratings is a major step-forward but how can we use them to build portfolios and apply to the existing investment process? From simple rating-based approaches, we can expand to include both discretionary and systematic ESG based techniques.

7.6.1 *Ratings based investing*

Obviously, one could either ignore ESG rating inconsistencies or embrace the diversity of opinion and build your own proprietary ESG rating methodology. However, starting from raw ESG data is difficult and requires dedicated internal resources.

Instead, building a composite rating system based on several different ESG rating sources, including other alternative ESG data and adding a sprinkling of common sense, is an efficient and practical alternative. The final goal is obviously how ESG will be used in the investment process. If it is purely based on hard exclusions by "outlawed" sectors (e.g. oil/gas, coal, weapons …) then no ESG ratings are usually required. A "soft-exclusion" method would require industry sector diversification and then allocations based on these composite ratings.

7.6.2 *Discretionary versus systematic ESG*

ESG can be included as an investment signal within a systematic process but this requires extensive historical datasets for analysis and backtesting and this data is often lacking or of bad quality. The nature of ESG investing arguably requires employing human discretion. Often the context of a particular company is important and cannot be encompassed in a simple rating. Although passive ESG indices have started to appear, for example FTSE4Good and the S&P ESG Index, these are essentially rules based and the new, subjective domain of ESG is perhaps best handled by active managers. Active managers can analyse and review the ESG information and ratings from different providers and embed their own level of ethics into the process. This viewpoint was also supported in a 2020 article by Goldman Sachs.

Now, it used to be thought that ESG investing sacrificed performance but academic studies have shown that this is not the case. This was well illustrated by the out-performance of many ESG funds in the recent coronavirus stock-market sell-off, although arguably this could be due to over-weighting of tech. Higher rated ESG companies are found in numerous studies to have a lower cost of capital, deliver higher shareholder value and surprise markets less (Table 7.2). The latter consideration is important since although a company's ESG profile usually changes very slowly, sudden, unexpected ESG events (like a corporate scandal or chemical leak) can have a profound short-term impact on share prices. ESG criteria

Table 7.2:   Major ESG investment themes from academic research.

Higher Quality	Risk Reduction	Governance
ESG companies have a lower cost of capital, deliver higher shareholder value and surprise markets less (quality stocks).	ESG criteria in stock selection can reduce equity portfolio risk and lower volatility increasing long term risk-adjusted returns.	Of the three ESG dimensions, Corporate Governance appears most relevant to positive alpha. Better governance reduces event risk.

Materiality	Emerging Market	Forward Looking
The type of ESG criteria changes significantly across industry sectors and consideration can enhance returns.	Emerging market stocks are most impacted by ESG factors possibly due to higher dispersion in EM ESG scores.	ESG strategies, such as momentum, at a corporate or industry level that focus on ESG improvements increase alpha.

in stock selection is found to reduce equity portfolio risk and lower volatility, thus improving long-term performance.

Other academic research findings are also interesting. For example, emerging market stocks are most impacted by ESG factors due to higher volatility, large dispersion in ESG scores and often laxer regulations. Also, "forward looking" ESG strategies, such as ESG trends, that focus on improvements in company ESG factors, can increase portfolio performance. Studies show that companies with higher ESG momentum outperform, particularly when governance factors are considered. Thus, companies that were badly ESG ranked but are improving could also be considered for inclusion in portfolios. However, in my experience the highest alpha is derived from the inconsistencies between ratings combined with ESG event-driven signals (e.g., VW emissions scandal, Danske bank money laundering, …) which are better served by news-feed analysis than slower moving 3rd party ESG ratings.

7.7 Does ESG Investing Work?

So the big question really is: does ESG investing actually work? Other than making investors feel virtuous, does directing investment towards higher rated or improving ESG companies actually improve global ESG metrics? Ideally, rather than a few forward-looking companies adopting ESG principles and receiving investment flows, the goal of ESG investors should be to improve the aggregate real world ESG impact of entire industrial sectors. It is however early days, and true statistical evidence for any measurable improvements so far are scant. Despite anecdotal reports, the jury is still out.

Perhaps the highest profile impact of ESG investing is the recent ESG investor legal cases and shareholder actions against the oil majors. 9th June 2021 was a bell weather day for investor moves against fossil fuel. Shell was ordered by a Dutch court to accelerate moves to carbon net zero, slash emissions and speed the move towards renewables. At the same time Chevron shareholders voted a proposal to reduce pollution from its customers and ExxonMobil had two board members ousted by investors. It remains to be seen how any fossil fuel company can actually move to net zero in 20 years or so and still meaningfully exist but investors are now forcing their hand.

The advertised conviction of financial institutions and asset managers to ESG investing is also being tested. Just signing up to the UN PRI

(Principles of Responsible Investment) seems no longer sufficient to appease ESG investors and the general public. There is no place to hide from a wavering commitment to ESG. In 2021 the heat increased further. J.P. Morgan's windows in the city were smashed-in by Extinction Rebellion in response to a report by Rainforest Action Network that the bank was the largest lender to corporate polluters. DWS, the asset management arm of Deutsche bank, faced serious probes by the German and US authorities that it misrepresented the ESG credentials of numerous funds. Even the former Blackrock sustainability chief openly claimed that the firm's ESG initiative was nothing more than "PR spin". Increasingly, a manager's true ESG credentials must be fact and not fiction.

A major issue with measuring the success of ESG investing is benchmarking and quantifying the true long-term nature of improvements. Being virtuous and fashionable does not necessarily equate with what is logically and scientifically the best route. Take for example electric vehicles (EVs), a favourite of ESG funds. Now, we might subjectively rate a company like Tesla low on corporate governance (G) but it probably took someone like Elon Musk to shake the major auto incumbents into realising that EVs could be sexier and more practical than old fashioned milkfloats. Today the EV game has been sold to governments (over hydrogen) as the solution to inner-city pollution and reaching carbon neutral (assuming renewable energy). However, unless great care is taken, from EVs many more environmental problems will unexpectedly spout. It is estimated that to replace all the UK-based carbon-burning vehicles, it will require two times the world's annual cobalt production, the entire world's production of neodymium, three quarters of the world's lithium production and half of the world's copper production. The energy use for mining all these materials and the 3rd world pollution caused is colossal. Sadly, currently less than 5% of Li batteries are recycled. The carbon footprint of an EV becomes potentially much larger than building a traditional internal combustion engine. The best option if you are virtuous and want to promote "E" is to probably run that 10-year-old, VW Golf you own for another ten years while using public transport a bit more. Unfortunately, that is just not trendy and not a viable long-term solution. However, before we all junk our old smelly diesels, more ESG pressure needs to be placed on the EV makers to have a full EV lifecycle developed with extensive recycling and powered by renewables.

For most people, the environmental "E" is the most important factor of the E, S and G. Arguably, the environment is a global macro problem and cannot be dealt with on the micro scale of individual companies and their CEOs. This year (2021) the UN has declared three environmental planetary crises — climate change, loss of biodiversity and planetary waste. Unfortunately, our excessive global consumption of stuff is fed by a linear economic model of resource extraction, creation of things and discarding of waste products. It is difficult to see fundamental business models changing if companies are left to their own devices. ESG investing pressure and market forces will probably on their own be insufficient. Indeed, government regulation and leadership are most likely required to provide an international level playing field for companies to collectively improve ESG aligned processes and remain competitive. The notorious hole in the ozone layer was successfully solved by the Montreal Protocol (1989) which banned chlorofluorocarbons (CFCs). It set a precedent for showing that international rule backed by science can work in resolving global issues. The Stockholm Convention (2002) on chemical pollutants and the Paris Agreement (2015) on climate change will hopefully induce similar successes.

In addition to these international agreements that will drive ESG investment and innovation, to reduce "greenwashing", governments are now proposing and implementing legislation to provide reporting standardisation. For example, the EU is putting tighter measures on banks and rating agencies to ensure sustainability risks in accounting and financial reporting are correctly represented and assessed. Similar moves are afoot in the US and UK. Although this is primarily directed at green financing and the rapidly expanding green bond issuance, it paves the way for more transparent reporting of corporates. In March 2021, a major development was the introduction of the EU's Sustainable Finance Disclosure Regulation (SFDR) which ensures asset managers must present their ESG claims according to a new regulatory framework. Adverse impact statements, which must address up to 64 ESG indicators during the investment due-diligence process, must be provided. Importantly, articles 6 and 8 of the regulation concern the transparency of the promotion and marketing of ESG funds. A recent US Securities and Exchange Commission (SEC) comment (2021) sums up the ambient mood amongst regulators:

"There's a high risk that some money managers are promoting their funds as so-called environmental, social and governance products when the reality is quite different".

Just sticking ESG on a fund's label to increase sales is no longer a viable option. Already from 2018–2020, over \$2tr of assets have had their optimistic ESG labels removed. Hopefully in a decade, with these regulatory changes combined with consistent ESG ratings and company disclosure, the "brown field" site of ESG investing will be transformed.

Chapter 8

Towards Quantamental

8.1 Nowcasting

The essence of data driven approaches to investment is to determine the current state of affairs. Although you might think that our primary goal should be predicting the outlook of the economy or the performance of various companies, the major issue is we do not know accurately the present. The present state of the economy is actually unknown since all the major macro-economic variables are based on the past and are generally lagged due to the time taken to acquire country wide data, then statistically amalgamate, verify and publish the results. An entire bureaucratic process exists before you even receive an estimated GDP print and let alone the final revised value. The same retarded state exists for corporates. Corporate results are published long after they are internally audited and the underlying sales made. Having better current estimates for economic data and corporate results, can provide more profitable strategies and allow better future predictions.

For example, for many macro strategies, economic forecasts are required. Traditionally this relied on officially published statistics like US GDP, unemployment, housing data etc. However, by the time these statistics were released they were already out of date. The lag on some statistics could be several months. Estimating even the current level of economic activity required linear extrapolation or complex trend fitting.

In recent years there has been a move towards using surveys, which although noisier than official data, are more up to date. For accuracy, large baskets of surveys are averaged together to remove noise. For example, the Chicago Fed National Activity Indicator (CFNAI) is published monthly (and with a 1-month lag) and is based on 85 real activity indicators related to production, output, the labour market, real expenditures and income and business conditions. The more co-incident Goldman Sachs Current Activity Indicator (CAI) contains around 60 real activity indicators (levels and changes) with the largest weights given to surveys such as ISM, Philadelphia Fed Index, Conf. Board Consumer Confidence etc. The CAI uses no data smoothing but relies on diversification for smoothing.

The use of more current data to estimate current variables/conditions is called *nowcasting*. It has become widely employed by many financial institutions and hedge funds. However, in the era of the internet and big data, fund managers can supplement nowcasting with a range of highly up-to-date alternative data. The COVID-19 pandemic has introduced, through mobile phone analysis, the concept of footfall in restaurants, commuter activity, office occupancy and much more. Predicting the "now" of the economy and corporates is becoming more accurate than ever before. Combining up-to-date knowledge of the "now" from alternative data with historical data allows us to predict the future with more confidence.

8.2 Alternative Data

Virtually every day I am besieged by emails from data providers proposing various alternative datasets. This trend started about a decade ago but rapidly accelerated from 2015. By now there must be literally over 1000 datasets available for investors to potentially include in their investment process. Apparently, there are at least 400 data providers. Late to the party, Bloomberg fortunately now offers alternative datasets including 3rd party data through its platform. The alternative data market is growing fast and by some estimates will continue to grow by 20% per annum for the foreseeable future. According to a survey from alternativedata.org (2019), spending by asset managers on alt data is expected to rise from $200m in 2016 to over $2bn in 2020. Several major data vendor brands and data consolidators have already arrived on the scene and these include Quandl, Ravenpack, Neudata, Orbital Insight, Foursquare, Thinknum, Dataminr and Eagle Alpha.

Precisely defining alternative data is somewhat tricky since a large amount of non-market data such as economic numbers, commodities inventories, corporate results and satellite data existed well before the "alternative" designation even existed. Much of this data was already incorporated into investment strategies. For example, macro strategies used GDP and employment numbers and metals inventories are used in systematic futures. However, the difference now is the shear amount of data from many sources and the availability of computing resources to fully exploit and combine the data for investment purposes. A watershed moment was the infamous Twitter paper *Twitter Mood predicts the Stock Market* by Johan Bollen (2011) which demonstrated, albeit in a somewhat unrealistic way, that it might be possible to predict and trade financial markets using social media data. Several years later, it is well established that news, social media, blogs and other webdata can be employed to develop successful trading strategies if employed in the correct manner. Since around 2015, examples of hedge funds using alternative data have become more widely publicised by the media. These range from macro firms tracking millions of products online to predict inflation across dozens of countries to using geolocation, mobile app data and credit card transactions to predict burger chain sales.

8.3 Types of Alternative Data

There are already many different types of alternative data. By alternative data we can loosely encompass in our definition all non-market data such as price and volume data. We can generically group them by their original source — from individuals, companies and sensors plus more traditional economic data and let's not forget the brokers (Table 8.1). Data can be obtained in a raw form from a source via web scraping, feeds, sensors or be licensed from 3rd parties. Web scraping, where web pages are browsed and the relevant text extracted is an obvious source of data and essentially free. Apparently, web scraping is the most popular form of alternative data source, being employed by over 40% of funds. It requires clever algorithms to isolate the relevant data. Although you might like to try it yourself, you can save yourself the time since some vendors specialise in this scraped data.

8.3.1 *From individuals*

As individuals addicted to our mobile phones and the web, our behaviour can now be monitored and analysed to a historically unprecedented

Table 8.1:   Alternative data types and sources.

Individuals	Companies	Sensors	Economy	Brokers
• Social media	• Company news	• Satellite	• GDP	• Reports
• Crowdsourcing	• Accounts/	imagery	• Inflation CPI	• Earnings
• Online search	filings	• Geolocation	• Consumer	estimates
• Mobile apps	• Innovation	• POS data	spending	• Transcripts
• Transactions	(patents)	• CCTV	• Manufacturing	• Short interest
• Retail footfall	• ESG data	• Drones	• Unemployment	• Analyst ratings
• Surveys	• Receipts	• Internet of	• Trade flows	• Fund flows
• Demographics	• Supply chain	things	• Investment	• Models

extent. Although our immediate providers (Apple, Amazon, Netflix etc.) might be able to use our recent purchases to recommend the next movie to watch, book to buy, where we are looking for a house or have driven our car to, in theory our privacy is protected when the data is sold in an aggregated form to 3rd parties. Perhaps as Edward Snowden pointed out, all our personal electronic interactions and information is available to the intelligence agencies, but in the commercial world, regulations such as GDPR prevail. However, hedge funds are generally not interested in individual behaviour but our collective behaviour. For example, most Googled terms, trending social media topics, footfall near restaurants, negative product reviews, responses on news sites, employee company reviews etc. There are exceptions to following the individual. For example, hedge funds notoriously scanned market moving Trump tweets and if you are trading bitcoin in 2020–2021, you should probably scan Elon Musk's too. However, social media data is generally more useful for gauging aggregate public opinion and estimating brand virality.

An interesting aspect of using data from individuals is through crowdsourcing. In crowdsourcing, individuals contribute their prediction of a future event such as company earnings and through polling processes, the odds of the event can be used as an estimator. Although this ostensibly relies on the dubious "wisdom of crowds effect", modern technology allows refinement of the approach such as giving individuals with the best track record of prediction a higher weighting in the final estimator. As an alternative to broker analyst predictions of corporate earnings, the company Estimize provides crowdsourced earnings forecasts which apparently increases alpha in large-cap stock selection.

8.3.2 *From companies*

These days, companies spew out an electronic "exhaust" of data that they have accumulated from their day-to-day activities. As more and more companies transact electronically and via the internet, more data is being accumulated. You thought the cashier was being nice when she asked for your email address to send an electronic receipt? All consumer information is collated, tracked and sold on to 3rd parties (including hedge funds) hopefully in a suitable anonymised way. All credit card data, email receipts, sales data, website activity and ad clicks are usable to provide a nowcasting of company performance.

Company news flow and social media activity supplements the numerous official company statements, accounts and filings that are now offered in machine readable form. Company news and events are now widely available in curated format where they have been tagged and even pre-analysed by sentiment algorithms (Fig. 8.1). Arguably, corporate news (since it incorporates old fashioned newsprint that has been electronically archived) provides the longest alternative datasets.

In equity factor models, I often find myself in discussions that company innovation should be considered as a model factor. If a company is innovating and performing successful R&D, although it immediately only produces intangible assets, the research could later yield more profitable products, cashflow and earnings. Alternative data allows a measure of this innovation through not only patent filings but also news, H1B visa applications (for researchers) and awarding of research grants and funding.

A growing development since 2018, to meet investor concerns, has been the development of ESG datasets. The data (questionably relevant to an ESG assessment of a company) is far wider ranging than for a traditional purely financial analysis. Data might range from carbon emissions and water usage to employment policies and staff diversity. Although, most of this data is slow moving and based on company disclosure, the news flow regarding unexpected ESG events can have a big influence on the equity price.

8.3.3 *From sensors*

Sensing technology can provide useful alternative data sources. Some sources like satellite imagery have a long history, from use by commodity traders to predict crop yields, counting cars in parking lots of retailers such as Walmart, watching tanker routes to predict oil prices and

Corporate Events (positive or negative sentiment)

Merger, buyback, results, spin-out, sale …
> *Agilent to Buy Dako for $2.2 Billion // Lowe's Adds $5 Billion to Stock Buyback Program // Home Depot Profit Tops Estimates on Cost Cuts // J&J Kicks Off $5 Billion Clinical Diagnostics Unit Sale*

ESG Events (mostly negative sentiment)

Environment — leaks, emissions, pollution …
> *Kinder Morgan Shuts Natgas Pipelines After Fire in Texas // Monsanto Fined for Not Reporting Idaho Chemical Releases*

Social — strikes, workers rights, racism …
> *Lowe's Settles U.S. Claims It Fired Workers on Medical Leave // Intel to Cut 12,000 Jobs as It Confronts Decline in PCs*

Governance — fraud, key resignations, legal cases …
> *Dell Settles S.E.C. Accounting Suit for $100 Million // After a Data Breach, Visa Removes a Service Provider // Lowe's to Pay New Yorkers $1.1 Million for Deceptive Sales Practices // Abbott Agrees to Pay $12 Million Fine in China Price Fixing Probe*

Innovation (mostly positive sentiment)

New products, technology (mostly positive sentiment)
> *Abbott Gets F.D.A. Approval for Neck Stent with a Filter // Google Aims to Speed the Online Checkout Line etc*

Figure 8.1:   Example corporate news events classified with NLP.

monitoring construction sites for Chinese PMI. The list of applications is highly imaginative. Other techniques such phone geolocation, POS data, CCTV, drone data and the internet of things are newer or have required image storage and data analysis techniques to catch up. Although newer mobile phone data allows creation of novel foot traffic and consumer activity indices, it also allows a high granularity of data such as analysis of specific malls, restaurants and retail outlets. This data can improve prediction of corporate performance and earnings and supplement nowcasting.

8.3.4 *From the economy*

Various traditional organisations from central banks to government and international bodies produce economic data including GDP growth, inflation, consumer spending, trade flows, commodity data etc. Mainly this data is lagged, traditional fundamental data but also includes many up-to-date surveys and polls. Other useful data can be provided by exchanges and related organisations such as commodity inventories (e.g., metals and crude oil) and producer hedging activity.

8.3.5 *From brokers*

Broker ratings of companies are important and have been used for many years in trading strategies. One of the most famous is the TOPPs strategy of Marshal Wace, for which analogies have been created by many funds. Brokers can provide short interest for equities and earnings expectations. Also, broker reports on individual companies and sectors along with transcripts of interviews with key personnel and experts can be incorporated as alternative data.

8.4 Integrating Alternative Data into the Investment Process

In 2018 I moderated a panel "Leveraging Alternative Data Sets to Generate New Sources of Alpha" with representatives from Goldman Sachs, JP Morgan and State Street. It was an interesting occasion to review the development of the alternative data market and how alternative data can be used in practice. Although there is much hype in introducing alternative data, actually integrating successfully into the investment process poses many issues that must be carefully considered. We came up with a long list of issues that included: data selection, onboarding, structuring of data, coverage, alpha determination, integration issues, privacy, uniqueness, crowding/capacity, legal and privacy considerations and last but not least, the cost of acquiring the data (Fig. 8.2).

8.4.1 *Selection and onboarding of datasets*

The first problem with alternative data is the sheer abundance of different types and huge variation of quality. How does one filter the higher quality datasets from the hundreds available? Data brokers and 3rd party providers are inherently biased. They all claim their datasets are "high alpha", unique and priced correctly. Frankly, there are very few who employ research teams and write white papers that help clients recognise the value in their touted datasets. The heavy lifting on justifying a sale is actually left to the client. The preliminary analysis of the dataset is extremely time consuming and requires highly trained data scientists to distinguish potential alpha from junk.

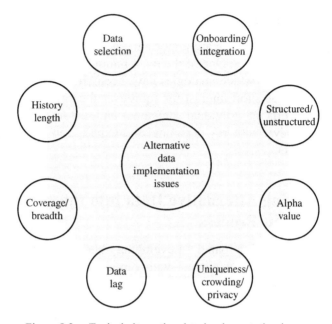

Figure 8.2:   Typical alternative data implementation issues.

A primary uncertainty will be how relevant the data is to the problem. Does the data represent a first or second order relationship with the market we are concerned with? For example, if we are running a macro commodity strategy, are we really interested in NLP analysis of specific, unrelated company reports or crowdsourced earnings data?

Once a decision has been made to explore a new dataset, a period of due diligence is required. Before a formal license agreement is signed, a trial period is usually provided, subject to a non-disclosure agreement (NDA).

The preliminary analysis of the data will include format of data, quality, frequency, coverage and history. Thus, points of exploration might include: is the data noisy, incomplete or have missing periods? Can the data be mapped as a time series and if so, for what frequency and time period? A difficult aspect to determine is if there exists potential or any evidence of bias in the data.

8.4.2 *Structured versus unstructured data*

Many datasets are based around raw unstructured data. Much time can be wasted assigning metatags, attaching market tickers and building time

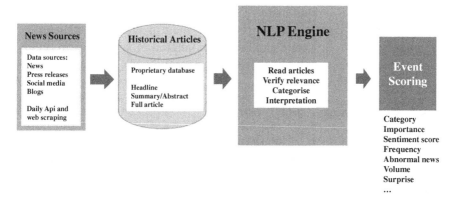

Figure 8.3:   Using an NLP data pipeline to provide corporate event scoring.

series that can be easily manipulated. Structured data has much of the tedious data manipulation already performed and some datasets have even been curated to allow ease of use.

For example, news or social media data may be provided in a raw form. Starting from scratch is hard work and requires building an NLP analysis to determine the corporate entities involved, the nature of the article and a scoring of the relevance or importance (Fig. 8.3). Often a textual analysis to extract a sentiment may be required. Having done this programming myself on the APIs of major news sources, I can attest that although it is good fun, it is time consuming and the need to maintain the meta tagging in a later production or trading environment is rather tedious. Some 3rd party providers such as Ravenpack, can provide structured, well-categorised news data that removes some of the pain and maintenance. One can instead focus on using the data and building algorithms.

Some providers go even further and provide trading signals that they have concocted from various alternative data sources to which they have access. These providers are not regulated investment advisors but are software firms with no market experience and importantly, no liability if things don't perform as expected. Caveat emptor applies. Somehow, I find buying an off-the-shelf strategy which purportedly "works" is slightly bad form. If it worked that well then surely the provider should be managing money themselves? It is also problematic since if you are managing other people's money, you should be involved in the signal design and control the research process within your own policies. A different level of scientific rigor is required if you are the manager who directly takes the flak when it goes wrong rather than researchers from the "sell side" who just tweak their model and publish a refitted analysis. One thing I have noticed in inspecting 3rd party signals is that often their methodology changes or is "improved" through time and makes validation of what was originally in-sample and out-of-sample difficult to control.

8.4.3 *Data coverage and history*

Unfortunately for those of us who live in Europe, most alternative data is currently US centric. Most datasets cover US companies and in particular, large tech companies and retailers that generate large amounts of data emissions. There are only so many times you want to see data on Amazon, Apple, Walmart, Costco etc. The chance of achieving an edge on trading these names through the addition of another alternative dataset is minimal. Hopefully data coverage will improve in the future.

The frequency of the data is important, as is the actual collection date. To provide a decent nowcasting we require data collection and publication to be as close as possible to any trade date. Lagging data is usually of little value in trading. Establishing true synchronicity with the timestamp supplied by the vendor is imperative. Optimistic but erroneous alpha can be suggested if the timestamps are incorrect and precede the actual dates that you can obtain the data in live-trading.

The length of history of the dataset increases our statistical confidence in using the data for investing. For systematic trading we require lengthy datasets of 10–15 years and even longer for machine learning approaches. Often this is not available for many alternative datasets. News data might be 25+ years but much social media is less than ten years and for newer data like ESG more like five years. Most alternative data is by definition new, and has only seen one market regime which is the bullish period of QE since 2010. Building a credible systematic trading system that relies on newer alternative data sources is a major obstacle.

For this reason, most alternative datasets are arguably better suited to the Quantamental world where human discretion can be applied. A human can readily distinguish whether a data source is relevant and what it might predict. For example, after the coronavirus crash in March 2021, humans were much better placed to interpret the novel geolocation data provided by mobile phones that measures economic activity between lockdowns.

8.4.4 *Dataset alpha determination*

The most important question is what datasets actually provide alpha? Data vendors say they all do but then again, they are financially motivated to be enthusiastic about every dataset. Sometimes I even receive emails with the title "high alpha" and "will only be sold to 5 top clients" etc. Well perhaps this is the case. However, I have a friend who is known for being a pessimist (or arguably a realist) who has tested hundreds of datasets for systematic trading. He claims less than 10% have value and he only uses a handful of these. I myself have found that news, social media, analyst ratings, company reports, short interest and various earnings data all have potential alpha for systematic trading on close examination. Many of the others have too short a dataset to be statistically valid for systematic trading but have value in a discretionary context.

An alpha analysis might include performing a factor linear regression or applying as a momentum strategy versus market price. Both the raw, smoothed, normalised level (Z-score) and differential changes in the data should be considered. One of the issues is that it is all too easy to perform a factor style regression analysis, but alternative data can influence market prices in non-linear and more complex ways. A second issue is whether the alternative data is a predictor of prices, or if features in the data are co-incident and cannot ever provide a predictive signal. The causal linkage is important. In the terminology of the scientist and philosopher Hans Reichenbach, if the alternative data and the market data are simultaneous and share a causal "common cause" then the alternative data confers no additional information.

In L/S equity strategies we can easily accumulate many alternative datasets for each equity. Figure 8.4 shows representative raw data for news, social media and analyst and ESG ratings for Amadeus IT Group SA, which runs most of the global airline booking systems. The news and social media's daily data are shown as the article count signed by positive and negative sentiment of the articles. The analyst and ESG ratings are slower-moving and derived from several sources. The data can be normalised and then combined as systematic investment signals or as inputs into a machine learning algorithm as outlined in Chapter 6.

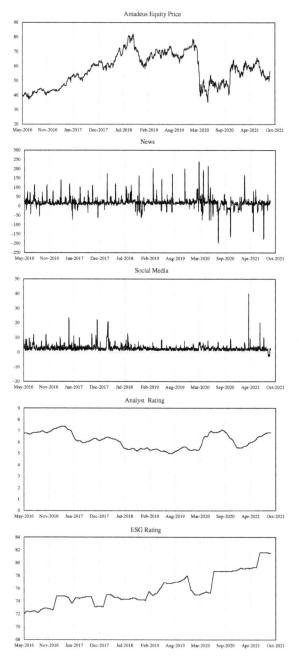

Figure 8.4:   Example of alternative data for Amadeus IT Group SA showing equity price, daily news and social media articles and analyst and ESG rating scores.

8.5 The Future is Quantamental

The scientific process places annoying but necessary constraints on scientific discovery. Repetition and measurement of observed phenomena is always required in an experimental enquiry. Numerous observations are a necessity to proving any theory or prior notions we may have, to a statistically convincing degree. In the domain of particle physics the threshold to discovering a new particle is very high and is often several standard deviations. In medicine, often due to small patient trial sizes, the threshold is unfortunately very low. In developing quantitative investment strategies, we face similar hurdles if we wish to retain any credible scientific rigour.

Alternative data is clearly the future of quantitative trading. It allows insights into companies and economies at a speed and resolution that have previously not been possible. It supplements nowcasting and improves the prediction of any trading strategies. However, all too often the data is messy, of poor quality and limited in coverage and history. To apply the scientific methodology to such data is often very difficult, particularly for AI and systematic trading systems.

AI has become fashionable with the advent of big data and machine learning techniques that can spot correlations across datasets. However, as we have discussed, the use of AI in predicting markets is constrained by its simplistic approach to causality and the one history nature of financial markets. The Achilles heel of AI systems is optimistic over-fitting and the subsequent disappointment in live trading.

Systematic investing combines human hypotheses and the empirical discovery of phenomena. The algorithms are simpler than AI based approaches and often far more intuitive and comprehensible. Often hand curated, they can in some sense be viewed as very "narrow" AI. However, since they are subjected to the scientific technique, they are again at the mercy of sufficient high quality, lengthy datasets. Systematic trading can readily integrate datasets such as news and analyst ratings that have existed for many different market regimes. However, flaky, short-term alternative data can become worse than useless and a noisy distraction of time and resources.

All too often in the hype of AI and computers, we fail to recognise that most of the vaunted achievements of AI such as Deep Blue beating Kasparov, Watson winning *Jeopardy!* and AlphaGo defeating Le Sedol at Go are in a very narrowly defined domain of AI. Watson had access to 200 million pages of knowledge to search. AlphaGo uses deep reinforcement learning, an ultimate pattern recognition machine that learnt from studying thousands of human players. The subsequent iteration AlphaGo Zero was even more impressive — from the basic rules it learnt by playing itself.

Recently, Ragnar Fjelland penned an article in *Nature* entitled *Why general artificial intelligence (AGI) will not be realized* and his thesis reposed on the earlier work of Hubert Drefus. Drefus's main arguments against AGI are that "computers are not in this world" and that humans acquire tacit knowledge and skills that are not easily learnt by machines or cannot be exactly encoded in algorithmic format. Narrow AI cannot be easily deployed across other disciplines. Indeed, when Watson was applied to medicine it apparently failed pretty miserably. Human skill is much underrated by computer enthusiasts. Being a skilled expert is accomplished by interacting with the external environment and world and being able to use insight and interpret causality between associated events. You cannot be a top surgeon or musician by reading any number of books. Humans possess comprehension and understanding. Computers in reality may never achieve the skill levels of humans in many domains and trading may arguably very well be one of them.

The major application of alternative data may be to enhance discretionary trading. When datasets are limited, humans can use their understanding of the world to extrapolate and draw meaning without recourse to a scientific process. The knowledge and skill of discretionary traders is often underestimated by those of the systematic mind set. Interpretation of sparse data is what discretionary traders have always been engaged in. Human intuition is derived from experience.

Seeking information and insights that are not widespread has always provided a discretionary edge. As an example, in the days of the film *Wall Street* (1987), Bud Fox might have tailed executives round town to ascertain that Sir Lawrence Wildman planned on purchasing Anacott Steel. In the era of alternative data, you can simply purchase corporate jet flight information and figure out mergers before the market. When Chevron bid $33bn for shale company Anadarko Petroleum Corporation, it was strange that on a Sunday evening, representatives of smaller rival Occidental were seen flying to Omaha Nebraska, the home of Warren Buffett. The next day it was announced that Buffett had agreed on a $10bn capital injection into Occidental so that it could bid $38bn for Anadarko. Several hedge funds apparently made money on the deal. It would be interesting to see if any computers could join the dots and figure that out. In my opinion, the future of fast-moving alternative data is in Quantamental investing — combining human discretion and the best quantitative, AI and data technologies.

Appendix A

Efficient Markets

A.1 Modern Portfolio Theory

Modern portfolio theory is based on the assumption that asset returns follow normal distributions. The joint return distribution of a portfolio of equities is given by the multivariate normal distribution $r \sim N(\mu, \Sigma)$ where μ is the expected return vector and Σ is the covariance matrix which is symmetric. For portfolio weights ω, the joint distribution of returns is

$$r_p \sim N(\omega' \mu, \omega' \Sigma \, \omega)$$

The minimum variance portfolio uses a Lagrangian method containing a budget constraint $\omega' i = 1$ and partial differentiation with respect to the weight vector

$$L(\omega, l) = \frac{1}{2} \omega' \sum \omega - l \, (\omega' i - 1)$$

This gives the minimum variance weight vector

$$\omega_{min} = \frac{\Sigma^{-1} i}{i' \Sigma^{-1} i}$$

If we wish to find the optimal mean-variance portfolio we must consider the vector of forecast returns, a risk-aversion parameter λ and maximise

$$\omega'\mu_e - \frac{\lambda}{2}\omega'\sum\omega$$

subject to $\omega'\mathbf{i} = 1$ giving the optimum weights

$$\omega_{opt} = \frac{\Sigma^{-1}\mathbf{i}}{\mathbf{i}'\Sigma^{-1}\mathbf{i}} + \frac{1}{\lambda}\frac{\left(\mathbf{i}'\Sigma^{-1}\mathbf{i}\right)\Sigma^{-1}\mu_e - \left(\mathbf{i}'\Sigma^{-1}\mu_e\right)\Sigma^{-1}\mathbf{i}}{\mathbf{i}'\Sigma^{-1}\mathbf{i}}$$

which is the minimum variance solution plus a term dependent on the risk aversion and the expected returns. Plotting the portfolio return versus the volatility gives the efficient frontier curve for different risk-aversion parameters.

A.2 Brownian Stock Prices

Stock prices are most frequently modelled as geometric Brownian processes. For each small discrete time period Δt, the change in stock price ΔS is related to an overall drift μ and a random change Δz

$$\frac{\Delta S(t)}{S(t)} = \mu\Delta t + \sigma\Delta z$$

Here σ is the volatility per unit time of the stock price $S(t)$ at time t. The random variable Δz is normally distributed with mean 0 and variance Δt. The expected return of $(\Delta S/S)$ over time period Δt is equal to

$$E[\Delta S/S] = \mu\Delta t$$

whilst the variance is

$$Var\left[\frac{\Delta S}{S}\right] = E\left[\left(\frac{\Delta S}{S}\right)^2\right] - \left(E\left[\frac{\Delta S}{S}\right]\right)^2 = \sigma^2\Delta t$$

Thus, the relative change in $S(t)$ is normally distributed

$$\frac{\Delta S(t)}{S(t)} \sim \phi(\mu\Delta t, \sigma^2\Delta t)$$

In continuous time the interval Δt approaches zero and the return of the stock price can be written as the differential change

$$\frac{dS(t)}{S(t)} = \mu\,dt + \sigma\,dz$$

A.3 Ito's Lemma

Ito's lemma is perhaps the most useful result from the field of *stochastic calculus* that is applied in option pricing. It can be used to evaluate the differential equation governing the evolution of option prices and allows derivation of the famous Black–Scholes option pricing equation. An Ito process for variable x (for example a stochastic equity price) has an equation is given by

$$dx = \alpha(x,\,t)dt + \beta(x,\,t)dz$$

where the random evolution of x depends on a drift α and a variance β both of which are functions of x and time t. Now consider a function $f(x,\,t)$, for example an option price, dependent on x and t. Ito's lemma shows that f follows the stochastic process

$$df = \left(\alpha\,\frac{\partial f}{\partial x} + \frac{\partial f}{\partial t} + \frac{1}{2}\,\beta^2\,\frac{\partial^2 f}{\partial x^2} \right)dt + \beta\,\frac{\partial f}{\partial x}\,dz$$

A.4 The Black–Scholes Differential Equation

The stock price follows an Ito process

$$dS = S\mu\,dt + S\sigma\,dz$$

and so, from Ito's lemma the price $f(S,t)$ of any single stock derivative, such as a call option, is determined by S and t

$$df = \left(\mu S\,\frac{\partial f}{\partial S} + \frac{\partial f}{\partial t} + \frac{1}{2}\,\sigma^2 S^2\,\frac{\partial^2 f}{\partial S^2} \right)dt + \sigma S\,\frac{\partial f}{\partial S}\,dz$$

Consider a portfolio of value Π where we have sold one option and bought $\partial f/\partial S$ shares. The value of the portfolio at any time is given by

$$\Pi = -f + \left(\frac{\partial f}{\partial S} \right)S$$

The instantaneous change in value of the portfolio in time interval dt is given as

$$d\Pi = -df + \left(\frac{\partial f}{\partial S}\right) dS$$

Substituting for df from Ito's lemma we have the result

$$d\Pi = \left(-\frac{\partial f}{\partial t} - \frac{1}{2}\sigma^2 S^2 \frac{\partial^2 f}{\partial S^2}\right) dt$$

which is independent of dz. The portfolio is thus hedged against price movements and instantaneously riskless over the period dt. Obviously, for a hedged portfolio in an efficient market, the investor in the portfolio cannot earn more than the risk-free rate r. Thus, we can set the riskless portfolio return to be r. This gives

$$d\Pi = r\Pi dt$$

$$= \left(\frac{\partial f}{\partial t} + \frac{1}{2}\sigma^2 S^2 \frac{\partial^2 f}{\partial S^2}\right) dt = r\left(f - S\frac{\partial f}{\partial S}\right) dt$$

Rearranging provides the well-known Black–Scholes differential equation

$$\frac{\partial f}{\partial t} + rS\frac{\partial f}{\partial S} + \frac{1}{2}\sigma^2 S^2 \frac{\partial^2 f}{\partial S^2} = rf$$

The Black–Scholes *partial differential equation* (PDE) allows evaluation of a wide range of derivatives which are dependent on the underlying variables S and t. Many solutions can be obtained depending on the boundary conditions applied to the two-dimensional PDE. For example, for a European call option of maturity T the boundary condition at time $t = T$ is simply the payoff

$$f(S(T),T) = \text{Max}(S(T)) - K,0)$$

The PDE can be solved using a variety of techniques including finite difference lattices and "trees". Generally, the boundary condition at the terminal payoff date is known and a solution is obtained as

$f(S(0),0)$, the option price today (at $t = 0$) for today's spot equity price $S(0)$.

A.5 The Black–Scholes Option Pricing Equation

The fundamental concept in options pricing is that in an "arbitrage free world" the option price is equal to the present value of the expectation of the option payoff. To calculate this expectation or expected value we must calculate a probability weighted payoff which is equal to the equity probability multiplied by the payoff for all possible equity prices at the option maturity. In a risk neutral world, present value discounting will use the risk-free rate r.

For a simple derivation of the Black–Scholes equation, consider a call option with final payoff $\text{Max}(S(T)) - K,0)$ at maturity T. Figure A.1 shows a hypothetical probability distribution for the final stock price $\text{Pr}(S(T))$. The probability distribution is lognormal and is centered about the forward price of the stock. Now for an option with, for example strike $K = 150\%$, the only non-zero payoffs are in the tail of the distribution (the shaded area). To calculate the probability weighted payoff, we must multiply the payoff $(S(T) - K)$ in this region by the probability. Effectively, this amounts to an integration over probability distribution $\text{Pr}(S(T))$ multiplied by the option payoff $\text{Max}(S(T) - K,0)$ to obtain the expected value. This expected value must then be discounted back to today using a discount

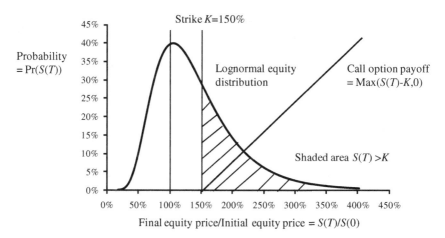

Figure A.1: Black–Scholes call option valuation.

factor $D(0,T)$ to give the present value of the expected payoff and the option value. Mathematically we can write this integral as

$$P_{Call}(0,T) = D(0,T)\int_K^\infty Pr(S(T))(S(T)-K)dS(T)$$

Since we know the stochastic process for S, we can perform this integration to arrive at the Black–Scholes call option price

$$P_{Call}(0,T) = S(0)N(d_1) - e^{-rT}KN(d_2)$$

where N is the cumulative normal distribution and

$$d_1 = \frac{\ln\left(S(0)/K\right)+\left(r+\sigma^2/2\right)T}{\sigma\sqrt{T}}$$
$$d_2 = d_1 - \sigma\sqrt{T}$$

The value of the put option can be derived in a similar way and results in

$$P_{Put}(0,T) = e^{-rT}KN(d_2) - S(0)N(-d_1)$$

The above equations can be easily modified to include equity dividends by replacing $S(0)$ with $S(T)e^{-qT}$ for a stock paying a continuous dividend q.

A.6 Ergodic Processes

In a dynamical system that is so-called *ergodic*, a given state of the system will eventually visit all the possible phase space points of the system. The average behaviour of the system can be deduced from the trajectory of a typical point in phase space. Thus, in an ergodic process every sequence or sizable sample is viewed as statistically representative of the whole process. It is a concept widely used in the physical sciences and in particular statistical thermodynamics for equilibrium systems. Whether it is applicable to finance is highly speculative.

A.7 The St. Petersburg Paradox

In the St. Petersburg game, a coin is flipped until it comes up heads for the first time. The player then wins 2^n where n is the number of coin flips. To play the game the player must pay an initial sum. How much must he pay? Based on mathematical expectations, similar to that used in option pricing theory, the sum paid should be infinity which is clearly absurd.

$$\text{Value} = \frac{1}{2} \cdot \$2 + \frac{1}{2^2} \cdot \$2^2 + \frac{1}{2^n} \cdot \$2^n + \cdots = \$\infty$$

This paradox arises from taking the probability weighted sum of coin flips which is an infinite sum giving infinite value. It illustrates the danger of integrating over low probability events that have large values in options pricing — for example, large OTM option payoffs.

A.8 Discount Factors, Zero Rates and Forward Rates

The discount factor for a period from time 0 to time t is given as

$$D(0,t) = \frac{1}{\left(1 + z_A(0,t)\right)^t}$$

where $z_A(0,t)$ is the annualised zero rate for maturity t. If $z(0,t)$ is the continuously compounded zero rate, we can write the discount factor as

$$D(0,t) = e^{-z(0,t)t}$$

The simply compounded forward rate at time t between T and $T + h$ is defined as

$$f(t,T,T+h) = \frac{1}{h}\left(\frac{D(t,T)}{D(t,T+h)} - 1\right)$$

A.9 The Hull–White Model

The widely used Hull–White model is probably the simplest one factor interest rate term-structure model that can be successfully applied to pricing a wide range of products. The high level of analytical tractability offered by the model allows many types of European structures to be evaluated as closed form solutions, which provides increased speed of computation. Structures with Bermudan and American exercise features can be priced with recombining trees and finite difference techniques.

The Hull–White model is an arbitrage free whole yield curve model. It provides an exact fit to today's observed term-structure and movements of the yield curve are modelled as approximately parallel shifts for low mean reversion parameters. The model is thus good for pricing products dependent on the level of floating rates or LIBOR but not really suitable for certain products where the payout is strongly dependent on changes in shape of the yield curve.

The Hull–White framework models the *spot rate r(t)* as a random normal process.

$$dr(t) = [\theta(t) - ar(t)]dt + \sigma dz(t)$$

The drift function $\theta(t)$ allows a fitting to the zero curve and the parameter a determines the *mean reversion* effect within the model to avoid rates being too high or too low. A simpler model with no mean reversion and $a = 0$ is known as the *Ho–Lee model*.

In a similar manner to the Black–Scholes PDE, it is possible to derive for the Hull–White model a PDE dependent on the variation of the spot rate

$$\frac{\partial V(r,t)}{\partial t} + \frac{1}{2}\sigma^2 \frac{\partial^2 V(r,t)}{\partial r^2} + (\theta(t) - ar)\frac{\partial V(r,t)}{\partial r} - rV(r,t) = 0$$

for which the solution for a discount bond at time t maturing at time T can be shown to be

$$D(r, t, T) = A(t,T)e^{-B(t,T)r(t)}$$

Thus, the discount factor is stochastic and depends on the level of the spot rate. Here $B(t, T)$ is

$$B(t,T) = \frac{1-e^{-a(T-t)}}{a}$$

and $A(t,T)$ is given by

$$\ln A(t,T) = \ln \frac{D(0,T)}{D(0,t)} + B(t,T) f(0,t) - \frac{1}{4a^3} \sigma^2 (e^{-aT} - e^{-at})^2 (e^{2at} - 1)$$

We can see that although the spot value r follows a normal process, the discount bond value has a lognormal process. A useful result that is used in the derivation of many closed forms is the stochastic value of a forward discount bond price at time t bought at a future time s and maturing at a later time $T (t < s < T)$. This is given by

$$D(t,s,T) = \frac{D(0,t,T)}{D(0,t,s)} e^{-\frac{1}{2}v^2(t,s,T) - v(t,s,T)Z}$$

where $Z \sim \phi(0,1)$ and $v(t,T,s)$ is the volatility of the discount bond.

$$v^2(t,s,T) = \sigma^2 \left(\frac{1-e^{-a(T-s)}}{a} \right)^2 \left[\frac{1-e^{-2a(s-t)}}{2a} \right]$$

This result is useful in establishing the closed forms for caps/floors, swaptions and more exotic derivatives.

A.10 Chooser Notes

To value a chooser option, we assume that investor is rational and will set the range to optimise his expected payout at the start of each period. This requires us to calculate the expected payout and maximise with respect to where the barrier is placed. This requires a calculation for each ith period, which involves a differential of the expected payout to determine the strike K_i of the form

$$\frac{\partial}{\partial K_i} E \left[D(0,t_i + h)h \left\{ \left(f(t_i,t_i,t_i + h) + q \right) \int_{t_i}^{t_i+h} \chi_{K_i < f(s,s,s+h) < K_i+U} ds \right\} \right]$$

This provides a solution for the *chooser accrual notelets* of the form

$$
\begin{aligned}
P_{\substack{\text{chooser} \\ \text{accrual} \\ \text{notelets}}} = D(0,t_i) \int_{-\infty}^{\infty} \int_{t_i}^{t_i+h} [N(d_2(K^*(Z),s)) - N(d_1(K^*(Z),s))] \, ds \, \frac{e^{-\frac{Z^2}{2}}}{\sqrt{2\pi}} \, dZ
\end{aligned}
$$

$$
-D(0,t_i+h)(1-hq) \int_{-\infty}^{\infty} \int_{t_i}^{t_i+h} [N(d_2(K^*(Z-v_3),s))
$$

$$
-N(d_1(K^*(Z-v_3),s))] \, ds \, \frac{e^{-Z^2/2}}{\sqrt{2\pi}} \, dZ
$$

with

$$
d_1(K(Z),s) = \frac{1}{v_2} \ln\left[\frac{D(0,s+h)(1+Kh)}{D(0,t)} \right] - \frac{(v_4^2 - v_5^2)}{2v_2} - v_2/2 + v_1 - \frac{v_4 - v_5}{v_2} Z
$$

$$
d_2(K(Z),s) = \frac{1}{v_2} \ln\left[\frac{D(0,s+h)(1+h(K+U))}{D(0,t)} \right] - \frac{(v_4^2 - v_5^2)}{2v_2} - v_2/2
$$

$$
+ v_1 \frac{(v_4 - v_5)}{v_2} Z
$$

and *K**, the optimised barrier level, is the solution for a particular *Z* to

$$
\int_{t_i}^{t_i+h} \frac{1}{v_1} \left[\frac{e^{-d_2^2(K(Z),s)/2}}{1+h(K(Z)+U)} - \frac{e^{-d_1^2(K(Z),s)/2}}{1+hK(Z)} \right] ds = 0
$$

with Hull–White discount bond volatility functions

$$
\begin{aligned}
v_1 &= v(t_i, s, t_i + h) & v_2 &= v(t_i, s, s + h) \\
v_3 &= v(0, t_i, t_i + h) & v_4 &= v(0, t_i, s + h) \\
v_5 &= v(0, t_i, s)
\end{aligned}
$$

A.11 Knock-in Reverse Convertibles

For a K_1 strike put with K_2 *knock-in* level the expected payoff can be written as

$$P_{KI \atop \text{put}} = E[D(0,T)\text{Max}(K_1 - S(T),0)\chi_{S(t)\leq K_2}]$$

Here we have used the indicator function $\chi = 1$ if $S(T) \leq K_2$ and zero otherwise, so the put with strike K_1 is activated if the barrier is triggered before maturity ($0 < t \leq T$). The closed form solution is given as a barrier option.

A.12 Equity Worst-of Options

The most common form of the worst-of option pays the worst performance in the basket and has no strike (strike set at zero) and is effectively the forward of the worst-of. The value of the option is thus

$$P_{\text{worst of}}(0,T) = E\left[D(0,T)\text{Min}\left(\frac{S_1(T)}{S_1(0)},\frac{S_2(T)}{S_2(0)},...,\frac{S_{N_B}(T)}{S_{N_B}(0)}\right)\right]$$

A.13 Pulsar Protected Notes

The Pulsar product can be decomposed into:

 (i) a zero-coupon bond redeeming 100% at maturity;
 (ii) a worst-of, knock-out binary paying $B = 200\%$ with a barrier at $K = 40\%$ of the initial stock price of each stock and
(iii) a worst-of, knock-in forward on the worst-of with a knock-in at 40% and forward strike at the initial stock price

$$R_{\text{Pulsar}} = 100\% + B\chi_{\left\{\left(\frac{S_i(t)}{S_i(0)}\right)_{\text{Min}} > K\right\}}$$

$$+ Min\left(\frac{S_1(T)}{S_1(0)},\frac{S_2(T)}{S_2(0)},...,\frac{S_{N_B}(T)}{S_{N_B}(0)}\right)\chi_{\left\{\left(\frac{S_i(t)}{S_i(0)}\right)_{\text{Min}} < K\right\}}$$

$$t_1 < t \leq T$$

Appendix B

Discretionary Adventures

B.1 The Gordon Growth Model

In the Gordon growth model, a company's stock price is the sum of all the future dividend payments present valued back to today. This can be written discretely as the infinite sum

$$P = \sum_{i=1}^{\infty} d_0 \frac{(1+g)^{t_i}}{(1+r)^{t_i}}$$

where d_0 is the current dividend, g the dividend growth rate and r the discounting rate. Evaluating the sum gives

$$P = \frac{d_0(1+g)}{r-g} = \frac{d_1}{r-g}$$

This can be neatly written as dividend yield plus growth is equal to the cost of equity or equity yield

$$\frac{d_1}{P} + g = r$$

B.2 A Brief Glossary of Corporate Events

B.2.1 *Corporate mergers*

Company A proposes to purchase company B. The deal can be financed in several ways as all cash (may require a bond/loan issue to finance), using equity or a combination of both.

B.2.2 *Spin-offs*

A company spins-off or sells an entity or subsidiary. This generates cash that can be used for deleveraging, special dividend etc.

B.2.3 *Private sale*

A company with a key shareholder or sponsor puts itself up for private sale. This could be to a new investor consortium or private equity group. It could result in a leveraging or equity issuance.

B.2.4 *Rights issue*

A company needing to raise capital can issue new shares in precedence to existing shareholders through a rights issue. If the company is in distress this may be at a measurable discount to the existing share price.

B.2.5 *Initial public offering*

An *initial public offering* (IPO) is a sale of shares to the public of a privately held company. This is a common exit strategy for private equity companies that wish to start to monetise their investment. Sometimes companies are taken private, restructured and re-IPOed. If you are a debt investor this is usually a positive event and gives much needed visibility to company performance through the share price.

B.2.6 *Company restructuring*

A badly performing company may restructure to reduce leverage and avoid breaching debt covenants. This could include cost reductions, asset sales, site closures etc. Some restructurings occur under bankruptcy protection afforded by Chapter 11 in the US.

B.2.7 *Balance sheet re-leveraging*

If a company has made progress de-leveraging its balance sheet it may be sub optimal and could be re-leveraged. This is particularly the case for privately held companies where special dividends can be paid (see below). More debt can be issued as loans or bonds.

B.2.8 *Balance sheet deleveraging*

Many companies that are too highly leveraged have a primary objective to deleverage if they have the free cashflow to allow it. Often these companies are "fallen angels" that have fallen from investment grade to junk and wish to regain their former investment grade status.

B.2.9 *LBOs and MBOs*

Leveraged buy outs (LBOs) and privately funded *management buy outs* (MBOs) take companies private by re-leveraging them through issuing debt to repurchase publicly held equity.

B.2.10 *Potential LBOs*

A rumored or attempted LBO is often sufficient to provide a significant company event. The news that a lowly leveraged company (often investment grade) is to be acquired, re-leveraged and burdened with large amounts of debt can cause equities to rise and credit spreads to widen.

B.2.11 *Share buybacks*

Companies with excess cash can indulge in share buybacks. Share buyback programs are generally supportive of company equity prices.

B.2.12 *Acquisitions*

A company can acquire new business subsidiaries or units. This can require leveraging and generating new synergies or be a prelude to building a bigger entity for say an IPO.

B.2.13 *Special dividend recap*

Private equity companies can revalue a company's debt/EBITDA either due to business growth, deleveraging or optimistic accounting and re-leverage to pay themselves a special dividend. Often new layers of subordinated debt are slotted in to finance the dividend.

B.2.14 *Distressed*

Distressed companies are either close to default or in drastic restructuring mode. Often their debt is very cheap and equity virtually worthless. The debt is volatile and trades close to the anticipated recovery value. The equity generally behaves as a deeply OTM option since on a debt for equity swap, it could trade to zero.

B.3 Present Valuing Cashflows

Consider an investment that pays fixed rate coupons C on dates t_i ($i = 1,2,\ldots,N$) until maturity T. The total present value is given by the sum of the coupons C multiplied by the individual discount factors from the times t_i when the future coupons are paid.

$$P_{\text{cashflow}}(0,T) = \sum_i^N C D(0,t_i)$$

This gives the present value of an *annuity* of rate C. Often it is useful to think of the value of an annuity where $C = 1$ bp or 0.01%, which is called the *PV01*. If we include a principal amount paid at maturity T we can price a fixed rate bond as:

$$P_{\text{bond}}(0,T) = \sum_i^N C D(0,t_i) + D(0,T)$$

where the *i*th discount factor is given as:

$$D(0,t_i) = \frac{1}{\left(1 + z(0,t_i)\right)^{t_i}}$$

B.4 Bond Yields

In general, whereas swap and derivative traders make use of zero rates and construct zero curves, bond traders prefer to work in terms of yields. The yield *y* can be interpreted as an effective discounting rate and for a given maturity of bond *T*, we can rewrite in annualised form the well-known yield equation for a bond:

$$P_{\text{bond}}(0,T) = \sum_{j}^{N} \frac{C}{\left(1+y\right)^{t_i}} + \frac{1}{\left(1+y\right)^{T}}$$

Here we have considered a coupon paid annually but coupons for a fixed rate bond are also usually paid on a semi-annual basis. If *h* is the *accrual period* corresponding to a coupon period for a bond of annualised coupon *C* the coupon paid at the end of the accrual period is given as *Ch*. In calculating actual interest accrued over a given period, several common *date conventions* are used to modify the accrual period and the most popular conventions for exactly calculating the interest paid over a given coupon period are Actual/Actual, 30/360 and Actual/360.

B.5 Floating Rate Notes

Floating rate notes (FRNs) are, to first order, immune to changes in interest rates. This commonsense fact can be a bit unexpected when you first encounter it. It is however easily mathematically proven. Consider a very basic FRN which pays a floating rate coupon *f* and no fixed spread at the end of each coupon period *h*. We shall assume that the reference or accrual period *h* is the same for all coupons. The floating rate used for the *i*th coupon period is usually fixed at the prevailing market rate at the beginning of each coupon period t_i. The floating rate thus corresponds to the forward rate between t_i and $t_i + h$ at time t_i. If we write the *i*th forward rate as $f_i = f(t_i, t_i, t_i + h)$ then we can write the FRN value as the present value of the sum of *N* expected floating rate coupons $f_i h$ plus principal:

$$P_{FRN}(0,T) = \sum_{i}^{N} D(0, t_i + h) f_i h + D(0,T)$$

By substituting from the definition of the forward rate

$$f\left(t_i, T, T+h\right) = \frac{1}{h}\left(\frac{D(t_i, T)}{D(t_i, T+h)} - 1\right)$$

we can show that the value of this FRN, which is exposed to no credit risk, is equal to par (100%). This is a very useful result in financial calculations and demonstrates what all FRN investors know — that the value of a FRN is insensitive to the level of or changes in interest rates since any changes in floating rates are cancelled by changes in discount factors.

B.6 Par Asset Swap

In a *par asset swap* the buyer purchases a fixed rate bond at an effective price of par (100%) and swaps it into a floating rate coupon. Importantly the market price of the underlying bond is probably not exactly par.

The *asset swap buyer* pays 100% and receives a bond plus a swap contract (Fig. B.1). Under the swap the buyer pays a fixed coupon c (plus principal) and receives a floating rate LIBOR plus spread s_{Par} from the *seller*. The value of the swap transaction for the buyer is

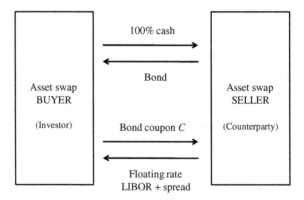

Figure B.1:   Par asset swap cash-flows.

$$V_{\text{par} \atop \text{ASW}}(0,T) = (P_{\text{bond}}(0,T) - 100\%) - c\sum_{j=1}^{M} D(0,t_j) l_j$$

$$+ \sum_{i=1}^{N} D(0,t_i) \left[f(0,t_i,t_i + h_i) + s_{\text{Par}}(0,T) \right] h_i$$

where $P_{\text{bond}}(0,T)$ is the market bond price for a bond of maturity T. Here the floating leg payments are received on dates t_i with daycount h_i and the fixed leg bond payments are made on dates t_j with daycount factor l_j. To balance the swap, we must set $V(0,T) = 0$ and $s_{\text{Par}}(0,T)$ is the *par asset swap level*. For a *market asset swap* the bond is swapped instead at the market value.

B.7 The Stochastic Default Model

A default occurs when the *firm value* $A(t)$ (or *enterprise value*) falls below the value of the company's debt B at maturity T so $A(T) < B$. The debt can be considered as zero coupon so no default can occur prior to T. In the simplest case the company firm value can be modelled by the process

$$\frac{dA(t)}{A(t)} = \mu_A dt + \sigma_A dz$$

The probability of default using Black–Scholes formulation is

$$Pr(A(T) < B) = N\left(\frac{\ln(B/A(0)) - \left(\mu_A - \sigma_A^2/2\right)T}{\sigma_A \sqrt{T}} \right)$$

We can consider the leverage ratio to be $L = B/A(0)$ and at maturity the value of the debt is given by

$$\text{Min}(A(T), B) = B - \text{Max}(B - A(T), 0)$$

which is equivalent to long a bond of value B and short a put on the company value A. The equity value $E(T)$ is given by a call on the firm value with strike B.

$$E(T) = \text{Max}(A(T) - B, 0)$$

The initial bond value is given by

$$B(0,T) = D(0,T)(e^{\mu T}A(0)N(-d_1) + BN(d_2))$$

and the equity value

$$E(0,T) = D(0,T)(e^{\mu T}A(0)N(d_1) - BN(d_2))$$

with

$$d_1 = \frac{\ln(A(0)/B) + \left(\mu_A + \sigma_A^2/2\right)T}{\sigma_A\sqrt{T}}, \quad d_2 = d_1 - \sigma_A\sqrt{T}$$

The effective credit spread s is

$$\begin{aligned}
s(0,T) &= -\frac{1}{T}\ln\left(\frac{B(0,T)}{D(0,T)B}\right) \\
&= -\frac{1}{T}\ln\left(\frac{e^{\mu T}A(0)N(-d_1)}{B} + N(d_2)\right)
\end{aligned}$$

The above model can be extended so that potential default occurs when the firm value A falls below a barrier at any time before the maturity date T (Fig. B.2). This is called the *first passage* or barrier model.

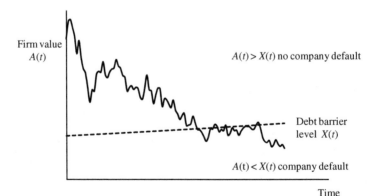

Figure B.2:   The stochastic firm value model.

JP Morgan published *CreditGrades*, a variant of the above model in 2002, for credit risk analysis which was widely adapted for capital structure and market spread analysis by many market participants. It was clearly demonstrated that such models are often leading indicator of ratings changes, credit deterioration and default. The major shortcoming of the previous stochastic models was that the default is represented by a diffusion process so cannot model well the level of short-term spreads and predicted short term default rates are too low. There cannot be a sudden default of a company in a diffusion-based model. The CreditGrades model addressed this problem by assuming the recovery rate follows a lognormal distribution so with an uncertain recovery rate the default barrier can be unexpectedly hit even for short maturities.

B.8 The Reduced Form Model

The *reduced form model* is widely used in credit derivatives trading and uses Poisson probability distributions to represent credit events. For a Poisson default process, the probability of default in time t to $t + dt$ (given no default has already occurred) is given by $\lambda(t)dt$. $\lambda(t)$ is known as the hazard rate or default intensity so considering this conditional probability we have

$$Pr[t < \tau \le t + dt | \tau > t] = \lambda(t)dt$$

where τ is the actual default time. From the definition of the Poisson distribution the survival probability $L(0,t)$ or the probability of no default occurring between 0 and time t (Fig. B.3) is given by

$$L(0,t) = Pr[\tau > t] = e^{-\int_0^t \lambda(u)du}$$

The probability of a default occurring between time t and $t + dt$ is thus given by the default probability density

$$Pr[t < \tau \le t + dt] = \lambda(t)e^{-\int_0^t \lambda(u)du} dt = L(0,t)\lambda(t)dt$$

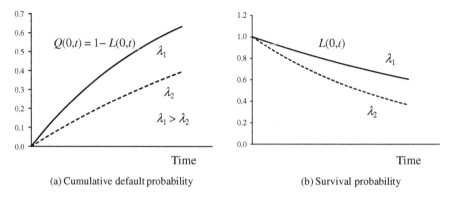

(a) Cumulative default probability   (b) Survival probability

Figure B.3:   The reduced form model: cumulative default and survival probabilities.

B.9 Credit Event Definitions

The major ISDA credit events are Bankruptcy, Failure to Pay, Restructuring, Repudiation/Moratorium, Obligation Acceleration and Obligation Default (Table B.1).

B.10 Pricing Credit Default Swaps

Using the reduced form model a valuation formula for a typical vanilla CDS can be derived. A *par recovery* framework is assumed where the bondholder on default is owed an amount equal to par plus accrued interest.

A CDS can be considered as (i) a premium flow, typically paid quarterly, that terminates on a credit event and (ii) a payment of (100%− recovery rate) on a credit event (Fig. B.4). If we consider a continuous time calculation, we can value the CDS of maturity T as the expectation of the value of the premium flows, which terminate at default time τ if $\tau < T$, minus the credit event payment which only occurs if default occurs before maturity so time $\tau < T$. The CDS value is given by the expectation

$$V_{CDS}(0,T) = E\left[q\int_0^T D(0,u)\chi_{\tau>u}du\right] - E\left[\int_0^T (1-R(u))D(0,u)\chi_{\tau=u}du\right]$$

If the recovery rate $R(u) = R$ is a constant we can simplify assuming that the default intensity and interest rates are non-stochastic. The effect

Table B.1: The six IDSA CDS credit events (simplified).

Credit Event	Description
Bankruptcy	Bankruptcy or insolvency of the reference entity. It is widely drafted so as to be triggered by a variety of events associated with bankruptcy or insolvency proceedings under English law and New York law, as well as analogous events under other insolvency laws.
Failure to Pay	Failure of the reference entity to make, when and where due, any payments under one or more obligations. Grace periods for payment and thresholds are taken into account.
Restructuring	Restructuring covers events as a result of which the terms, as agreed by the reference entity and the holders of the relevant obligation, governing the relevant obligation have become less favourable to the holders that they would otherwise have been. These events include a reduction in the principal amount or interest payable under the obligation, a postponement of payment, a change in ranking in priority of payment or any other composition of payment.
Repudiation/ Moratorium	The reference entity disaffirms, disclaims or otherwise challenges the validity of the relevant obligation. Usually applicable to sovereigns.
Obligation Acceleration	The relevant obligation becomes due and payable as a result of a default by the reference entity before the time when such obligation would otherwise have been due and payable.
Obligation Default	A relevant obligation becomes capable of being declared due and payable as a result of a default by the reference entity before the time when such obligation would otherwise have been capable of being so declared.

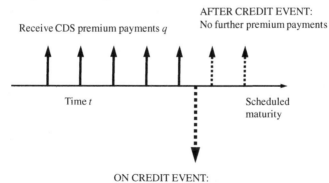

SELL protection using CDS

Receive CDS premium payments q

AFTER CREDIT EVENT:
No further premium payments

Time t

Scheduled maturity

ON CREDIT EVENT:
Cash settlement: pay $(1-R)$ to counterparty
and transaction terminates

Figure B.4: Pricing CDS credit contingent cash-flows.

of introducing these as stochastic processes can be shown to be very small. Also including correlation between rates and default intensity has negligible effect for reasonable correlation levels. This gives

$$V_{CDS}(0,T) = q\int_0^T D(0,u)L(0,u)du - \int_0^T (1-R)D(0,u)\lambda(u)L(0,u)du$$

which can easily be solved numerically but a quick closed form can be derived for $r(t) = r$ and $\lambda(t) = \lambda$.

$$V_{CDS}(0,T) = \frac{(1-e^{-(r+\lambda)T})}{(r+\lambda)}\{q - \lambda(1-R)\}$$

Now for a market value CDS, the swap value is zero and thus the fair value premium is

$$q(0,T) = q = \lambda(1-R)$$

B.11 Normal Copula Model for Correlated Default Times

The standard market model for introducing correlation in default processes is the *normal copula model* where default times are correlated. Consider a basket of M reference entities. Define $Q_i(t) = Pr(\tau_i \leq t)$ with $(i = 1,\ldots, M)$ as the cumulative probability of a credit event of the ith credit by time t, where

$$Q_i(t) = Pr(\tau_i \leq t) = 1 - e^{-\int_0^t \lambda_i(u)du} = 1 - L_i(0,t)$$

We can define a variable x_i such that $N(x_i) < Q_i(t)$ with inverse

$$x_i < N^{-1}(Q_i(t_i))$$

where N^{-1} is the *inverse cumulative normal distribution*. The joint distribution of x_i is *multivariate normal*. To simulate defaults by time t we must generate M correlated normal random variables x_i and if the condition $x_i < N^{-1}(Q_i(t_{ij}))$ is true then there has been a default of the ith credit in

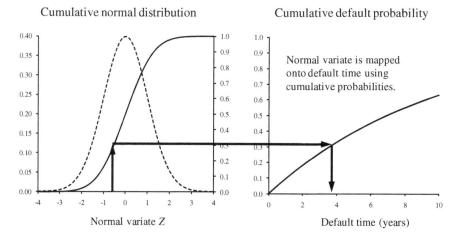

Figure B.5: The normal copula model: mapping a normal random variable to a default time.

the period (see Fig. B.5). This allows us to price baskets and via simulation, other correlated default products such as CDOs.

B.12 Credit Curve Trades

For a credit curve trade involving two CDS of different maturities, T_1 and T_2, we must consider the change in value ΔV of each CDS, which is the sum of the change in mark-to-market (MTM) plus the carry. The MTM is approximately the CS01 multiplied by the change in CDS premium. For the two CDS we have

$$\Delta V_1(t,T_1) = CS01(t,T_1)(q(t,T_1) - q(0,T_1)) + q(0,T_1)t$$
$$\Delta V_2(t,T_2) = CS01(t,T_2)(q(t,T_2) - q(0,T_2)) + q(0,T_2)t$$

If we sell protection with notional N_1 and buy protection on notional N_2 the profit is $PL(t)$

$$PL(t) = N_1 \Delta V_1(t,T_1) - N_2 \Delta V_2(t,T_2)$$

Additionally, if we assume for a duration hedged curve trade that the notionals are inversely proportional to the CS01 we have $N = N_1 CS01$ $(t,T_1) = N_2 CS01(t,T_2)$ so then

$$PL(t) = N(q(t,T_1) - q(0,T_1)) - (q(t,T_2) - q(0,T_2))$$
$$+ (N_1 q(0,T_1) - N_2 q(0,T_1))t$$

This can then be written as the change in spread of the curve trade plus a carry term

$$PL(t) = N(Spread(t) - Spread(0)) + Carry$$

and if $N_1 q(0,T_1) > N_2 q(0,T_1)$ then the trade is positive carry.

B.13 Sharpe Ratio

The Sharpe ratio is the most common measure of risk versus return and is defined as

$$SR = (r - r_f)/\sigma$$

where r is the strategy return, r_f the risk-free return and σ the volatility over the investment period.

B.14 Value-at-Risk

The Value-at-Risk (VaR) calculation is usually

$$\sigma^2_{Var} = \omega' \sum \omega$$

where ω is a vector containing all market weights and Σ a covariance matrix. The covariance $Cov(X,Y)$ between two data series X and Y is given by

$$Cov(X,Y) = E\big((X - \mu_X)(Y - \mu_Y)\big) = \rho_{XY}\,\sigma_X\,\sigma_Y$$

Appendix C

Systematic Profits

C.1 Generic Signal Methodology

Signals and indicators from systematic models provide predictions for trading. Signals can be discrete (e.g., −1 short, 0 flat, +1 long) or continuous where the size of signal provides a level of conviction for a particular trade. Thus, in some sense the size of a continuous signal should scale with the expected probability of the prediction.

A generic architecture for constructing signals is shown in Fig. C.1. Often, many signals from different strategies are combined to give a total signal for a market. This requires placing each signal on a similar footing using a process of normalisation. The assumption is usually made that signals, over a sufficiently long time period, are normally distributed with a mean and variance. Signals can then be normalised to the standard normal distribution $N(0,1)$ with mean 0 and variance 1. These normalised values are often called Z-scores.

Allocations to the different normalised signals can be made by introducing weighting factors. The combined Z-score is given by summing over the individual Z-scores from different strategies each multiplied by their respective weighting. Usually, weightings are assigned through their historical accuracy of market prediction and considerations such as trading cost and turnover.

Since correlations will exist between the individual Z-scores, the combined Z-score will have a standard deviation of different than 1 (generally lower) and it may also be that the combined mean has drifted from 0. The Z-score can be adjusted or renormalised back to $N(0,1)$.

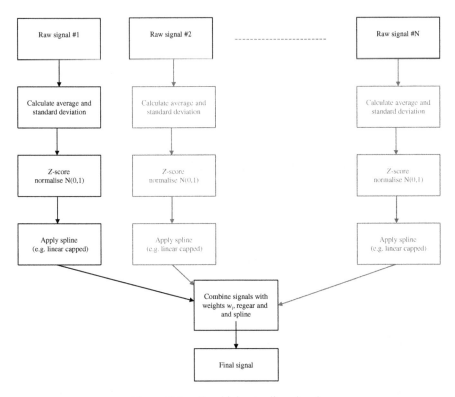

Figure C.1: Combining trading signals.

To prevent an infinite range of values, Z-scores are usually capped or have a response function or spline applied. The simplest response function is linear, with the Z-score held constant beyond certain values. For example, for "2-sigma" cap, if $Z < -2$ then $Z = -2$ or $Z > 2$ then $Z = 2$. Other types of response function exist that are continuous and gradually cap the signal or ramp the signal more quickly or slowly around $Z = 0$. The application and nature of trading will determine the best spline.

Lastly, signals need to be converted into real trading positions. For a single market this is often done in one of two ways — (i) directly with the allocated market notional multiplied by the splined Z-score or (ii) on a risk-adjusted basis to a target volatility. For risk-adjusted positions the notional traded is given by the response function acting on the signal Z-score multiplied by a volatility scaling factor of (target volatility/ market volatility). In this way more/less volatile market positions are reduced/increased in size to achieve the target volatility. The mathematical outline is shown below.

C.1.1 *Signal Z-scores*

A Z-score is a signal transformed to the "bell curve" distribution with mean 0 and half-width (or standard deviation) 1 and mathematically known as the standard normal distribution $Z \sim N(0,1)$.

If a random variable X is normally distributed $X \sim N(\mu, \sigma^2)$ with mean μ and variance σ^2 then the Z-score is given by $Z = (X - \mu)/\sigma$ which follows the standard normal distribution $Z \sim N(0,1)$.

C.1.2 *Combining signals*

Signal Z-scores can be linearly summed with weights w_i to give a combined Z-score

$$Z = \sum w_i Z_i$$

However, if the individual Z-scores are correlated a renormalisation process must be followed to make the combined Z-score truly standard normally distributed.

C.1.3 *Signal response functions*

A response function or spline is applied to the Z-score as a function $f(Z)$. The simplest linear response function capped at $\pm a$ is mathematical function

$$f(Z)_{\substack{\text{linear} \\ \text{capped}}} = \begin{cases} a & \text{if } Z > a \\ Z & \text{if } -a \leq Z \leq a \\ -a & \text{if } Z < -a \end{cases}$$

Figure C.2 shows examples of a linear capped response function, linear with a "deadspot" around zero and the exponential spline in Appx. C.4. A deadspot ensures that no trading position is taken unless the underlying signal is strong enough to trigger a response. The exponential response function reduces position size for large signals.

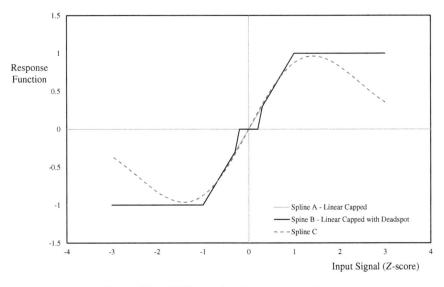

Figure C.2:   Different signal response functions.

C.1.4 *Position risk-scaling*

A position of notional N, market volatility σ, signal Z-score Z with response function R can be risk-scaled to a target volatility σ_T as

$$N(\sigma_T/\sigma)R(Z)$$

For futures contracts, the notional N is given by the market price multiplied by the number of contracts (lots) and the tick value

$$N = \text{Price} \times \text{Lots} \times \text{Tick Value}$$

C.2 Basic Time Series Manipulation

In computation it is often more efficient to use the Exponentially Weighted Moving Average (EWMA) than the Simple Moving Average (SMA).

C.2.1 *Simple moving average*

The SMA for an index or series y_t is calculated as

$$\hat{y}_t = \frac{1}{N}\sum_i^N y_{t-i}$$

C.2.2 *Exponentially weighted moving average*

The EWMA for an index or series y_t is calculated as

$$\hat{y}_t = \lambda y_t + (1-\lambda)\hat{y}_{t-1}$$

where λ is the smoothing parameter related to the exponential decay.

C.2.3 *Exponentially weighted volatility*

EWMA based volatilities can also be computed in a similar manner.

$$\hat{\sigma}_t^2 = \lambda(y_t - y_{t-1})^2 + (1-\lambda)\hat{\sigma}_{t-1}^2$$

C.3 Fundamental Signals

In systematic macro trading a variety of intermediate fundamental economic signals can be combined, which are adaptations of well documented academic fundamental economic indicators for example GDP (Gross Domestic Product), Unemployment, Output, Inflation etc.

C.3.1 *Output gap*

The output gap at time t is defined economically as the difference between the actual and potential output or $gap_t = y_t - y_t^T$ where gap_t is the output gap, y_t is output and y_t^T is the potential output. A positive number indicates excess demand and a negative number excess capacity.

C.3.2 *Phillips curve*

The original Phillips curve related inflation inversely to unemployment. Modern versions follow the generic form

$$\pi_t = \pi_e + a(y_t - y_t^T)$$

where π_e is the expected inflation and the current inflation π_t is proportional to the output gap or through Okun's law inversely to unemployment

$$\left(U_t - U_t^T\right) = -b(y_t - y_t^T)$$

C.3.3 *Taylor rule*

The Taylor rule is a linear equation that models the responsiveness of nominal interest rates to changes in inflation, output and other economic indicators. For example, if r_t is the base rate then

$$r_t = \pi_t + a_\pi\left(\pi_t - \pi_t^*\right) + a_y(y_t - y_t^T)$$

where π_t and π_t^* are the inflation and desired level of inflation and here y_t is the logarithm of GDP and y_t^T the log of potential output.

C.4 CTA Momentum Signal

A typical CTA time-series momentum signal is based on a weighted series of the difference of short- and long-term pairs of exponentially weighted moving averages (EWMAs). A generic recipe applicable to each asset class is as follows.

To span a range of momentum speeds, select K time scale pairs with different time scales for short S_k and long L_k EMWAs. For example, consider four pairs $S = \{8,16,32,64\}$ and $L = \{24,48,96,192\}$. The time scales represent decay factors in the EMWAs.

For each k, calculate the EMWA difference to give the raw momentum signal from the back-adjusted price series P.

$$MOM_k = EMWA(P, S, k) - EMWA(P, L, k)$$

Normalise with the effective volatility of the momentum signal measured over a long running window.

$$MOMNORM_k = \frac{MOM_k}{\sigma_{MOM_k}}$$

We can additionally first normalise with small window running volatility of the underlying price series to obtain stable normalisation of the momentum signal. Alternatively, since for slow momentum, often a history of momentum volatility is ill defined, a theoretical closed form can be used. The normalisation constant κ, is based on the EMWA decay times, multiplied by the underlying price volatility σ.

$$MOMNORM_k = \frac{MOM_k}{\kappa\sigma}$$

A suitable response function R is applied for each k to cap the signal. For example, using an exponential response function that is maximum at around $Z = \pm 1.5$ with a normalisation constant ($\gamma \sim 1.12$) (Fig. C.2).

$$MOMR_k = R(MOMNORM_k),$$

$$R(Z) = \gamma Z e^{-Z^2/4}$$

The final signal is then obtained by a normalised weighted sum of the individual signals with weights that sum to unity.

$$Signal_{MOM} = \sum_k^K \omega_k MOMR_k, \quad \sum_k^K \omega_k = 1$$

Thus, generally the signal is divided by volatility twice — once for signal normalisation and secondly for risk-scaling. The weights ω_k are fitted with consideration to the strategy market turnover and the implied trading costs.

C.4.1 *Momentum using kernels*

An alternative to using the crossing of EMWAs for momentum calculations is to use the a "kernel" approach. This allows a more flexible specification of momentum signals than applying moving averages. The momentum signal at time t is provided by the series sum of historical returns r_{t-i} with weights a_i and normalisation coefficient κ based on the volatility of the weighted returns σ_a.

$$MOMNORM_t = \frac{1}{\kappa(\sigma_a)}\sum_j^N a_j r_{t-j}$$

C.5 CTA Carry Signal

Where appropriate we can base the carry signal on the slope of the futures curve using the first few contracts, but the calculation varies somewhat with asset class. Often the raw carry signals are noisy and must be smoothed before constructing signals.

For equity index futures we compute the raw carry at time t as the relative difference of the futures for maturities T_1 and T_2. We can apply a seasonality adjustment which is the average spread of the raw carry and the 1-year moving average over the relevant month in the series Adj_t.

$$RawCarry_t = \frac{1}{(T_2-T_1)}\frac{F(t,T_1)-F(t,T_2)}{F(t,T_2)}$$

$$Carry_t = RawCarry_t - Adj_t$$

For commodity futures we can remove any annual seasonal effects by using the nearest future and the contract expiring one year later.

$$Carry_t = \frac{F(t,T_1)-F(t,T_1+1)}{F(t,T_1+1)}$$

Usually, currencies are traded as FX forwards and the carry can be computed from the 3M forward price $Fwd(t,t + 3M)$ and the spot price $Spot(t)$.

$$Carry_t = 4\left(\frac{Spot(t)}{Fwd(t,t+3M)}-1\right)$$

An alternative approach for currencies is to calculate the interest rate differential (IRD) using short rates in each currency.

For bond futures we can use the near minus far futures definition, similar to commodities above or build a definition using bond cash yields. For interest rate swaps the carry must be composed of the carry plus the "roll" down the swap curve for changing slope as the effective maturity changes. For a swap of maturity T_1 the carry is given by difference of the rate fixing $Fixing_t$ and the swap rate $S(t,T_1)$ divided by the modified duration $B(t,T_1)$. The roll considered is from maturity T_1 towards T_2 ($T_2 < T_1$) with rate $S(t,T_2)$.

$$Carry_t = \frac{S(t,T_1) - Fixing_t}{B(t,T_1)} + \frac{S(t,T_1) - S(t,T_2)}{(T_1 - T_2)}$$

Also, swap carry signals can be successfully built using the difference between two maturities, for example the 2 and 10 year swap rates.

C.6 CTA Value Signal

The value definition is more subjective and specific to each asset class. Some simple to implement definitions commonly used are described here.

For equity indices value is simply defined as the dividend yield.

$$Value_t = Dividend\ Yield\ (t)$$

For commodities we can use the current price $P(t)$ deflated using US CPI $CPI(t)$ divided by the deflated historical average price.

$$Value_t = \frac{P(t)/CPI(t)}{\langle P(t)/CPI(t) \rangle}$$

With FX we can employ a purchasing power parity argument for value between the FX rate $Spot_{C1/C2}$ of two currencies $C1$ and $C1$ with inflation CPI_{C1} and CPI_{C2}.

$$Value_t = PPP(t)$$
$$PPP(t) = \log(Spot_R(t)) - \langle \log(Spot_R(t)) \rangle$$
$$Spot_R(t) = Spot_{C1/C2}(t)CPI_{C1}(t)/CPI_{C2}(t)$$

With interest rate swaps we can consider the difference between the swap rate and the GDP or CPI.

$$Value_t = S(t,T_1) - GDP(t)$$

C.7 CTA Credit Trading

CTAs trade credit through index CDS such as the US CDX. To build a momentum signal in a similar manner to futures, we must build a back-adjusted time series of prices by stitching together CDS contracts of different maturities and including the carry and roll. Usually, the 5-year contract is the most liquid and is used. We have the daily change in the adjusted price ΔP as

$$\Delta P_{CDS} = -CS01 \cdot \Delta S + \frac{S}{d}$$

where the mark-to-market move is the $CS01$ times the spread change ΔS and the carry the contract spread S divided by the annual day count d. For a constant maturity contract with roll, we must include the slope of the credit curve between 3 and 5 years.

$$\Delta P_{CDS} = -CS01 \cdot \Delta S_5 + \frac{S_5}{d} + CS01 \cdot \left(\frac{S_5 - S_3}{2d} \right)$$

A similar approach can be used to building synthetic adjusted time series for bonds (using yields) and IRS, where the PV01 or duration is multiplied by the rate change and added to the carry and roll.

C.8 CTA Spread Trading

In a similar fashion, futures spread trading can be facilitated by constructing a back-adjusted time series where the daily returns are a function of the change of slope plus the change in curvature or convexity of the futures curve. If F_i is the ith maturity futures price we can write the back-adjusted return for the F_1 and F_4 spread as

$$\Delta P_{Spread} = (F_1 - F_4) + \frac{\left((F_1 - F_4) - (F_2 - F_5) \right)}{d}$$

where d is the days between maturities of F_1 and F_2. We can then remove seasonality effects and apply momentum or reversion signals to the spread price series as preferred.

C.9 Execution and Slippage

Slippage is the difference between the idealised asset price observed to generate the trading strategy and the actual price or "fill" achieved in the execution of the trading strategy. Slippage can be usefully defined in terms of a Shortfall measure. For buy orders, the shortfall is the average execution price minus the mid-quote at first order arrival time measured as a fraction of this first mid-quote. Sell orders have the sign reversed. This shortfall definition includes bid-ask spread and impact cost but excludes commissions etc.

Participation rate or "p-rate" is the order size divided by the market traded volume over a given time interval. Generally, the higher the p-rate of an order the higher the market impact and hence slippage. As discussed later, academic studies show market impact is a non-linear function of the p-rate and thus a low p-rate may provoke higher than expected slippage. For example, empirically for DOW futures YM, an order of size $1m provides around 0.5 bp slippage while $100m provides 2.2 bp. Thus 5.5x the slippage for 100x increase in order size is clearly non-linear.

Importantly, most academic models assume a "concave" function such as square-root functions for market impact models based on empirical observation. This means that even small orders with low p-rates can have larger than expected market impacts. For example, executing 1% of the daily volume can impact the price (on average) by $\sqrt{1\%} = 10\%$ of the daily volatility which is surprisingly large.

C.9.1 *Empirical market impact equation*

An academic consensus has formed around the main conclusions for market impact "meta-orders". Meta-orders are larger orders split into many "child" market orders that are gradually placed in the market order-book whilst the majority of the remaining order remains hidden.

In early studies, the market impact of orders was assumed to be linear with size but the majority of studies now show that the impact is a "concave" function and close to a square-root function of size multiplied by the market volatility. Some researchers would say that it is an exact square-root (a power of 0.5) and others would claim a range of 0.4–0.7, depending on the market traded. In my fund management experience, I have previously found around 0.4–0.5 for ES futures. The results are found to hold for a wide range of order size to total market volume and under standard market conditions.

The peak market impact of a meta-order of size Q is well described by the relationship

$$I(Q,T) \cong A\sigma_T \, (Q/V_T)^\gamma$$

where A is a numerical coefficient of order 1 ($A \sim 0.5$ for stocks), γ is an exponent in range 0.4–0.7, σ_T is the volatility and V_T is the market volume over the time T. For $\gamma = 0.5$ it is commonly known as the "square-root" law of market impact. The empirical relationship is found to hold over a huge range with Q/V_T in the range 10^{-5} to a few percent.

Appendix D

The Factor Game

D.1 Alpha and Beta

Generally, the beta coefficient of an investment in portfolio management theory is the risk arising from general market movements as opposed to idiosyncratic factors. A beta of 1 indicates an investment moves in line with the market. Thus, the daily return on an asset is

$$r_{i,t} = r_{f,t} + \alpha_i + \beta r_{m,t} + \varepsilon_{i,t}$$

and proportional to the market return $r_{m,t}$ with gradient beta β, a specific return α and an error term ε_t (the unexplained return or "noise"). The beta is related to the correlation between the investment and the market $\rho_{i,m}$ and the respective volatilities σ_i and σ_{im} as

$$\beta = \rho_{i,m} \, (\sigma_i / \sigma_m)$$

D.2 Capital Asset Pricing Model

In the *capital asset pricing model* (CAPM) the expected return of a security is proportional to its beta β multiplied by the excess return of the market above the risk-free rate $r_{f,t}$.

$$E[r_{i,t}] = r_{f,t} + \beta_{i,m} E[r_{m,t} - r_{f,t}]$$

242 Quantitative Hedge Funds: Discretionary, Systematic, AI, ESG and Quantamental

D.3 Arbitrage Pricing Theory

Arbitrage pricing theory (APT) is a generalisation of CAPM where any number of ad-hoc factors may be linearly related, in a mathematical superposition, to the expected return of an asset. The factors F_i each have their own beta $\beta_{i,j}$ with respect to the asset.

$$E[r_i] = r_f + \sum_j^K \beta_{i,j} E[F_j - r_f]$$

D.4 The Fama–French Three-Factor Model

The original Fama–French model extended the CAPM to three linear factors. The two additional factors are the returns on company size $r_{SMB,i}$ (Small market cap Minus Big) and the returns on value $r_{HML,i}$ (High book-to-market Minus Low).

$$r_{i,t} = r_{f,t} + \alpha_i + \beta_{m,i}\left(r_{m,t} - r_f\right) + \beta_{SMB,i} r_{SMB,i} + \beta_{HML,i} r_{HML,i} + \varepsilon_{i,t}$$

D.5 The Cahart Four-Factor Model

The Carhart four-factor model added momentum as the one month lagged 11 month returns $r_{UMD,i}$

$$r_{i,t} = r_{f,t} + \alpha_i + \beta_{m,i}\left(r_{m,t} - r_f\right) + \beta_{SMB,i} r_{SMB,i} + \beta_{HML,i} r_{HML,i} + \beta_{UMD,i} r_{UMD,i} + \varepsilon_{i,t}$$

D.6 A Quality Definition

For a quality factor many people adopt as the benchmark the definition proposed by AQR based on rewriting the Gordon growth model price-to-book value in the following way:

$$\frac{P}{B} = \frac{profitability \cdot payout\_ratio}{required\_return - growth}$$

The quality stocks are then chosen based on based on (i) higher profitability, (ii) higher growth and (iii) a lower required return.

D.7 Joel Greenblatt's "Magic Formula" Investing

The "Magic Formula" proposed by Joel Greenblatt is value investing with a dash of quality. The essential formula is as follows:

1. Minimum market cap of $50m with no financials and utilities.
2. Rank according to earnings yield and return-in-capital (ROC).

$$\text{Earnings yield} = \frac{\text{EBIT}}{\text{enterprise value}}$$

$$\text{ROC} = \frac{\text{EBIT}}{(\text{net fixed assets} + \text{working capital})}$$

3. Select 20–30 highest ranked companies and rebalance each year.

D.8 Implied Volatility Factors

Implied volatility surfaces can be used to create additional factors to the typical linear Fama–French–Cahart model. If the vol surface $\sigma(t, \tau, k)$ is a function of the expiration τ and the log moneyness $k = \log(K/S)$ various factors that can generate equity Sharpe ratios of 0.5–1.0 can be constructed. These include using skew

$$Skew(t, \tau, k) = \sigma(t, \tau, k) - \sigma(t, \tau, k = 0)$$

or the term structure of the skew and time series changes in implied volatility and skew can be used

$$\Delta Vol(t, T, \tau) = \sigma(T, \tau, k = 0) - \sigma(t, \tau, k = 0)$$

Also, *the volatility risk premium* (VRP) is a well-known bullish signal

$$\text{VRP} = \sigma_{\text{implied}}(t, \tau, k = 0) - \sigma_{\text{realised}}(T)$$

D.9 Statistical Arbitrage

In statistical arbitrage the price spread between different equities must be calculated to build a portfolio and determine entry and exit points for trades. The three basic methods for statistical arbitrage calculations are the distance, cointegration and copula methods.

D.9.1 *Distance method*

For each pair of equities, we compute the price spread and normalise using the mean and standard deviation of the spread to create a Z-score type signal. If the spread diverges by more than say 2 standard deviations, we open a long/short position and close when the spread approaches the mean spread.

$$Spread(t) = P_2(t) - P_1(t)$$

$$Signal_{DM}(t) = \frac{Spread(t) - \mu_{Spread}}{\sigma_{Spread}}$$

D.9.2 *Cointegration method*

The equity prices are considered cointegrated if there exists a cointegration coefficient β such that the linear combination $u(t)$ is a stationary time series.

$$u(t) = P_2(t) - \beta P_1(t)$$

The individual time series are considered $I(1)$ and their first difference form a stationary processes with mean reversion parameter α and stochastic process ξ

$$P_2(t) - P_2(t-1) = \alpha_2(P_2(t-1) - P_1(t-1)) + \xi_2(t)$$

$$P_1(t) - P_1(t-1) = \alpha_1(P_2(t-1) - P_1(t-1)) + \xi_1(t)$$

Thus, we assume that we buy one share of equity 2 and sell short β shares of equity 1. The effective spread is given as

$$Spread(t) = P_2(t) - \beta P_1(t)$$

The profit from the period t to $t+1$ is simply the change in spread

$$\Delta PL(t, t+1) = Spread(t+1) - Spread(t)$$

The normalised cointegration spread for deciding to enter and exit trades is based on the new spread definition

$$Signal_{Coint}(t) = \frac{Spread(t) - \mu_{Spread}}{\sigma_{Spread}}$$

D.9.3 *Copula method*

As with structured credit we can employ copula techniques to model the joint distribution and estimate the probability of one equity price moving higher or lower given the price of the other equity. Different probability distributions can be used from the Normal and Student-*t* to the Clayton and Gumbel, if the copula function is

$$C(u_1, u_2) = P(U_1 \le u_1, U_2 \le u_2)$$

If X_1 and X_2 are random price variables with probability functions $F_1(X_1)$ and $F_2(X_2)$. Mapping to uniform distributions U_1 and U_2 we set $U_1 = F_1(X_1)$ and $U_2 = F_2(X_2)$. The conditional distribution then is given by the derivative of the copula function

$$h_1\left(u_1|u_2\right) = P\left(U_1 \le u_1, U_2 = u_2\right) = \frac{\partial C(u_1, u_2)}{\partial u_2}$$

$$h_2\left(u_2|u_1\right) = P\left(U_2 \le u_2, U_1 = u_1\right) = \frac{\partial C(u_1, u_2)}{\partial u_1}$$

D.10 Principal Components Analysis

PCA is a statistical technique that assumes no underlying fundamental statistical model to fit the time series data. The data is fit as a linear combination of orthogonal factors with the largest factor chosen to represent the most important feature and explain the largest variance.

If X is an n dimensional random variable with covariance matrix Σ, the problem is to determine a new set of Y variables which are uncorrelated and whose variances decrease from first to last. Each Y_i is taken to be a linear combination of the X with constants a.

$$Y_j = a_{1j}X_1 + a_{2j}X_2 + \cdots + a_{nj}X_n = \boldsymbol{a}_j^T \mathbf{X}$$

The method becomes a familiar eigenvalue problem with

$$\mathbf{Y} = A^T \mathbf{X}$$

where A is an orthogonal ($n \times n$) matrix of eigenvectors and the covariance matrix of $\mathbf{Y}$ is a diagonal matrix

$$\Lambda = \lambda I = A^T \Sigma A$$

A useful result is that the eigenvalues represent the variances of the process

$$trace(\Lambda) = \sum_{i=1}^{n} \mathrm{Var}(Y_i) = \sum_{i=1}^{n} \lambda_i = \sum_{i=1}^{n} \mathrm{Var}(X_i)$$

Appendix E

AI Again

E.1 Machine Learning Basic Definitions

The ith instance of the vector x of all the feature values is $x^{(i)}$ and the desired output value for that instance is $y^{(i)}$. There are m instances. $\mathbf{X}$ is the matrix of all the feature values with one row per instance and the ith row is the transpose of $x^{(i)}$.

The prediction function h of the ML system or model acts on the feature vector and outputs a predicted value for that instance

$$\hat{y}^{(i)} = h(x^{(i)})$$

The prediction error for the instance is $\hat{y}^{(i)} - y^{(i)}$. The cost functions, like the *root mean square error* (RMSE), are performance measures calculated from the matrix of instances $\mathbf{X}$.

$$RMSE(\mathbf{X}, h) = \sqrt{\frac{1}{m} \sum_{i=1}^{m} \left(h(x^{(i)}) - y^{(i)} \right)^2}$$

E.2 Linear Regression Model

The linear model has parameters θ which act on the feature values x.

$$\hat{y} = \theta_0 + \theta_1 x_1 + \theta_2 x_2 + \cdots + \theta_n x_n$$
$$\hat{y} = h_\theta(x) = \theta^T \cdot x$$

The mean square error (MSE) cost function is given by

$$MSE(\mathbf{X}, h_\theta) = \frac{1}{m} \sum_{i=1}^{m} ((\boldsymbol{\theta}^T \cdot \mathbf{x}^{(i)}) - y^{(i)})^2$$

To minimise the cost function there exists the famous *normal equation* to estimate model parameters $\hat{\boldsymbol{\theta}}$

$$\hat{\boldsymbol{\theta}} = (\mathbf{X}^T \cdot \mathbf{X})^{-1} \cdot \mathbf{X}^T \cdot \mathbf{y}$$

For the simple case of linear regression we can use the closed form. However, for the general case we must employ instead numerical methods such as *batch gradient descent* where we seek to iteratively minimise the cost function by computing the partial derivatives to each of the parameters.

$$\nabla_\theta MSE(\mathbf{X}) = \begin{pmatrix} \dfrac{\partial MSE(\theta)}{\partial \theta_0} \\ \vdots \\ \dfrac{\partial MSE(\theta)}{\partial \theta_n} \end{pmatrix}$$

The parameters for the next step are given iteratively by using the learning rate η that defines the step size used.

$$\boldsymbol{\theta}^{k+1} = \boldsymbol{\theta}^k - \eta \nabla_\theta MSE(\boldsymbol{\theta})$$

E.3 The Perceptron

For an individual perceptron we have inputs x and associated weights w. The weighted sum of the inputs is given as $w^T x$ and the output the step function σ

$$h(x) = \sigma(\omega^T x)$$

The step function is typically a discrete Heaviside or smooth logistic or hyperbolic function. The logistic function allows smooth differentiation when using gradient descent parameter fitting and is given by

$$\sigma(z) = \frac{1}{(1+e^{-z})}$$

The iterative learning rule for updating weights increases the connection weights between the ith input neuron and the jth output neuron that could have contributed to the correct prediction.

$$w_{ij}^{k+1} = w_{ij}^{k} + \eta \, x_i(\hat{y}_j - y_j)$$

E.4 kNN Methodology

Training examples are vectors x_i in N-dimensional feature space. For each new input vector $\hat{x}$, a distance D is calculated from all the training examples. Common distance measures are Euclidean, Manhattan or Minkowski.

$$D_{Euclidean}(\hat{x}, x_i) = \sqrt{\sum_{j=1}^{N}(\hat{x}_j - x_{i,j})^2}$$

The regression output $\hat{y}$ is then the weighted sum of the training values y_i of the kNN of the input $\hat{x}$ being assigned in the feature space. Typically, weights can be $(1/K)$ and if required, include a distance weight $w(D)$ from object.

$$\hat{y} = \frac{1}{K} \sum_{j=1}^{K} w(D_j) y_j$$

E.5 Granger Causality

Granger causality is an empirical method for investigating the causality between two time series $x(t)$ and $y(t)$. If signal $y(t)$ "Granger causes" a signal $x(t)$ then the past, lagged values of $y(t)$ should help predict $x(t)$ better than the prior values of $x(t)$ alone. Thus, for the two hypotheses (no G-Causality and G-Causality) we can form two equations with lag coefficients α_i and β_i and test for statistical significance using an F-statistic.

$$x(t) = \sum_{i=1}^{\infty} \alpha_i \, x(t-i) + c_1 + u_1(t)$$

$$x(t) = \sum_{i=1}^{\infty} \alpha_i \, x(t-i) + \sum_{j=1}^{\infty} \beta_j \, y(t-j) + c_2 + u_2(t)$$

Further Reading

On Efficient Markets

Fama, E. F. (1965). The behaviour of stock market prices. *Journal of Business* 38(1): 34.

Fama, E. F. (1965). Random walks in stock market prices. *Financial Analysts Journal* 2: 55.

French, K. R. and Roll, R. (1986). Stock return variances: The arrival of information and the reaction of traders. *Journal of Financial Economics* 17: 5.

Kon, S. J. (1984). Models of stock returns — A comparison. *Journal of Finance* 39(1): 147.

Levy, R. (1967). Relative strength as a criterion for investment selection. *Journal of Finance* 22: 595.

Malkiel, B. G. (1973). *A Random Walk Down Wall Street*, Norton.

Richardson, M. and Smith, T. (1993). A test for multivariate normality in stock returns. *Journal of Business* 66(2): 295.

On Financial Derivatives

Bateson, R. D. (2011). *Financial Derivative Investments*, Imperial College Press.

Black, F. (1989). How we came up with the option pricing formula. *Journal of Portfolio Management* 15(2): 4.

Black, F. and Scholes, M. (1973). The pricing of options and corporate liabilities. *Journal of Political Economy* 81: 637.

Cox, J. C. and Ross, S. A. (1976). The valuation of options for alternative stochastic processes. *Journal of Financial Economics* 3: 145.

Dupire, B. (1996). Pricing with a smile. *Risk* 7: 18.

Haug, E. G. (1998). *The Complete Guide to Option Pricing Formulas*, McGraw Hill.

Kat, H. M. (1998). *Structured Equity Derivatives*, Wiley.

Merton, R. C. (1973). Theory of rational option pricing. *Bell Journal of Economics and Management* 4(1): 141.

Rubenstein, M. (1994). Implied binomial trees. *Journal of Finance* 49(3): 771.

Taleb, N. N. (1996). *Dynamic Hedging: Managing Vanilla and Exotic Options*, Wiley.

On Interest Rate Models

Brace, A., Gatarek, D. and Musiela, M. (1997). The market model of interest rate dynamics. *Mathematical Finance* 7(2): 127.

Heath, D., Jarrow, R. and Morton, A. (1992). Bond pricing and the term structure of interest rates: A new methodology. *Econometrica* 60(1): 77.

Ho, T. S. and Lee, S. B. (1986). Term structure movements and pricing interest rate contingent claims. *Journal of Finance* 41: 1011.

Hull, J. and White, A. (1990). Pricing interest rate derivative securities. *Review of Financial Studies* 4: 573.

Vasicek, O. (1977). An equilibrium characterisation of the term structure. *Journal of Financial Economics* 5: 177.

On Credit Derivatives

Duffie, D. and Singleton, K. (1999). Modeling term structures of defaultable bonds. *Review of Financial Studies* 12: 687.

Finger, C. C. (2000). A comparison of stochastic default rate models. *RiskMetrics Journal* 1: 49.

Hull, J. and White, A. (2006). Valuing credit derivatives using an implied copula approach. *Journal of Derivatives* 14: 8.

Li, D. X. (2000, March). On default correlation: A copula approach. *Journal of Fixed Income* 9(4): 43.

Merton, R. (1974). On the pricing of corporate debt: The risk structure of interest rates. *Journal of Finance* 29: 449.

Pan, G. (2001, November). Equity to credit pricing, *Risk*, pp. 99–102.

On Discretionary Management

Bubinski A. *et al*. (2007) *Surfing the LBO Wave*, The Credit Line (US), Goldman Sachs.

Capocci, D. (2013). *The Complete Guide to Hedge Funds and Hedge Fund Strategies*, Palgrave Macmillan.

Havad, M. and Mish, M. (2006). *When Lightning Strikes — Understanding Investment Grade Structures in an Event-driven Environment*, The Credit Catalyst, Barclays Capital.

Miller, S. and Barnias, S. (2005). *A Guide to the Loan Market*, Standard & Poors.

Stefanini, F. (2006). *Investment Strategies of Hedge Funds*, Wiley Finance.

On Systematic Investing

Asness, C. S. *et al.* (2013). Value and momentum everywhere. *The Journal of Finance* LXVIII(3): 929.

Bartsch, E. (2009). *Tailoring Rates for the Exit*, Morgan Stanley.

Baz, J. *et al.* (2015). *Dissecting Investment Strategies in the Cross Section and Time Series*. Available at SSRN: https://ssrn.com/abstract=2695101.

Bollerslev, T. *et al.* (2009). Expected stock returns and variance risk premia. *The Review of Financial Studies* 22.

Bouchard, J. P. *et al.* (2019). *Trades, Quotes and Prices*, Cambridge University Press.

Brooks, J. (2017). *A Half Century of Macro Momentum*, AQR.

de Brouwer, G. (1998). *Estimating Output Gaps*, Reserve Bank of Australia.

Carver, R. (2015). *Systematic Trading*, Harriman House.

Chan, E. P. (2013). *Algorithmic Trading*, Wiley.

Chincarini, L. B. (2008, Spring/Summer). Natural gas futures and spread position risk: Lessons from the collapse of Amaranth Advisors L.L.C. *Journal of Applied Finance*.

Dudley, B. (1999). *Revitalising the Taylor Rule*, Goldman Sachs.

Faufman, P. J. (2005). *New Trading Systems and Methods*, Wiley.

Harvey, C. R. *et al.* (2021). *Strategic Risk Management*, Wiley Finance.

Ilmanen, A. (2011). *Expected Returns*, Wiley Finance.

Kliesen, K. (2019). *Is the Fed Following a "Modernized" Version of the Taylor Rule? Part 2*, Federal Reserve Bank of St. Louis.

On Equity Factor Investing

Asness, C. S. *et al.* (2013). *Quality Minus Junk*. Available at SSRN: https://ssrn.com/abstract=2312432.

Avellaneda, M. and Lee, J. (2008). Statistical arbitrage in the U.S. equities market. *Political Methods: Quantitative Methods eJournal*.

Carhart, M. M. (1997). On persistence in mutual fund performance. *The Journal of Finance* 52: 57.

Chatfield, C. and Collins, A. J. (1995). *Introduction to Multivariate Analysis.* Chapman & Hall.

Chincarini, L. B. and Kim, D. (2006). *Quantitative Equity Portfolio Management.* McGraw Hill.

Fama, E. F. and French, K. R. (1993). Common risk factors in the returns on stocks and bonds. *Journal of Financial Economics* 33: 3.

Graham, B. (1973). *The Intelligent Investor*, HarperCollins.

Ghayur, K. *et al.* (2019). *Equity Smart Beta and Factor Investing for Practitioners.* Wiley.

Greenblatt, J. (2006). *The Little Book that Beats the Market*, Wiley.

Jegadeesh, N. (1990). Evidence of predictable behavior of security returns. *The Journal of Finance* 45(3): 881.

Kakshadze, Z. (2015). 101 Formulaic alphas. *Risk Management & Analysis in Financial, Institutions eJournal.*

Lehmann, B. N. (1990). Fads, martingales, and market efficiency. *The Quarterly Journal of Economics* 105(1): 1.

Markowitz, H. M. (1952). Portfolio selection. *The Journal of Finance* 1: 77.

Novy-Marx, R. (2013). The other side of value: The gross profitability premium. *Journal of Financial Economics* 108(1): 1.

Qian, E. E. *et al.* (2007). *Quantitative Equity Portfolio Management*, Chapman & Hall.

On Machine Learning

Banko, M. and Brill, E. (2001). *Scaling to Very Very Large Corpora for Natural Language Disambiguation*, Microsoft.

Bateson, R. (2018). *Machine Learning and Alternative Data in Long/Short Equity Portfolios.* Ravenpack, https://www.youtube.com/watch?v=JoZwWRBiqEc

Bird, S. (2009). *Natural Language Processing with Python.* O'Reilly.

Elson, J. *et al.* (2007). *Asirra: A CAPTCHA that Exploits Interest-Aligned Manual Image Categorization.* Microsoft.

Raschka, S. (2016). *Python Machine Learning*, Packt Publishing.

Smola, A. and Vishwanathan, S. V. N. (2008). *Introduction to Machine Learning.* Cambridge University Press.

Trippi, R. R. and Turban, E. (1992). *Neural Networks in Finance and Investing*, Probus.

Wolpert, D. H. and Macready, W. G. (1997). No free lunch theorems for optimization. *IEE Transactions on Evolutionary Computation* 1(1): 67.

On ESG Investing

Amel-Zadeh, A. and Serafeim, G. (2018). Why and how investors use ESG information: Evidence from a global survey. *Financial Analysts Journal* 74(3): 87.

Clarke, G. L. (2015). From the stockholder to the stakeholder: How sustainability can drive financial outperformance. Available at SSRN: https://ssrn.com/abstract=2508281.

Horter, S. (2015). *ESG in Equities*, Allianz.

Khan, M. *et al.* (2016). Corporate sustainability: First evidence on materiality. *The Accounting Review* 91(6): 1697.

Krosinsky, C. (2012). *Evolutions in Sustainable Investing*, Wiley Finance.

Messini, F. *et al.* (2020). *Sustainable Finance Disclosure Regulation — Is the Financial Industry Ready for the Big One?*, Deloitte.

On Quantamental Investing and Alternative Data

Bollen, J. *et al.* (2011). Twitter mood predicts the stock market. *Journal of Computer Science* 2(1): 1.

Cavallo, A. and Rigobon, R. (2016). The billion prices project: Using online prices for measurement and research. *Journal of Economic Perspectives* 30(2): 151.

Denev, A. and Amen, S. (2020). *The Book of Alternative Data*, Wiley.

Drogen, L. and Jah, V. (2013). *Generating abnormal returns using crowdsources earnings forecasts from estimize.* http://www.ssrn.com/abstract=2337709.

Fjelland, R. (2020). Why general artificial intelligence will not be realized. *Humanities and Social Sciences Communications* 7: 10. doi:10.1057/s41599-020-0494-4.

Hatzius, J. (2016). *Quantifying FOMC Surprises*, Goldman Sachs.

Hatzius, J. (2017). *Trackin' All Over the World*, Goldman Sachs.

Pandl, Z. (2015). *Keeping Current: Updating the CAI*, Goldman Sachs.

Russel, M. A. (2013). *Mining the Social Web*, O'Reilly.

Index

Printed in the United States
by Baker & Taylor Publisher Services